BOLLINGEN SERIES LXXIX

M. ESTHER HARDING

THE 'I' AND THE 'NOT-I'

A STUDY IN THE DEVELOPMENT

OF CONSCIOUSNESS

BOLLINGEN SERIES LXXIX

PRINCETON UNIVERSITY PRESS

CONTENTS

FOREWORD

THIS BOOK IS WRITTEN for the general reader who may not be acquainted with Professor Jung's own writings, many of which, intended for the specialist, are not easily comprehended by those who lack the technical knowledge which would enable them to appreciate the value and significance of Jung's researches. Such knowledge is particularly necessary for an understanding of the work that occupied so much of his time and thought during the last twenty years of his life.

I have tried to set forth here the basic ideas on which his psychology rests. Although I have not attempted to make an exhaustive résumé of his writings, since the material of these chapters was originally prepared for an intelligent group of men and women who were not very familiar with Jung's work, I hope that this relatively simple presentation may also meet the needs of a larger public.

The lectures were first given at a conference arranged by the Educational Center of St. Louis, Missouri. They were repeated under the auspices of the Education Department of the Diocese of San Francisco, California. In 1963 they formed the first series of lectures sponsored by the C. G. Jung Foundation for Analytical Psychology in New York.

My warm thanks go to all those who have helped to make the book a reality and especially to the editors for Bollingen Series, who have taken much work off my hands, not only in the preparation of the text but also in supplying the index and the details of the bibliography. I want to thank Mr. Henry Hoyer for his excellent work in executing the diagrams.

I should like particularly to thank Mr. Allen Dulles for his permission to cite some remarks he made in a television interview regarding Professor Jung's attitude to the Allied cause during the war years. Mr. Dulles, who was working in Switzerland for the Office of Strategic Services, was attached to the American Legation in Bern as Special Assistant to the Minister. In his letter giving me permission to quote him he says: "The reference to my comment on Jung in a television interview is, to all intents and purposes, accurate. . . . I did have several talks with Jung, which covered chiefly the psychological reactions of Hitler, Mussolini, and one or two others of the Nazi-Fascist leaders in the face of the events as they developed toward the close of World War II. . . . I was frequently in Zürich and often journeyed to Jung's house on the Lake. I greatly profited from my conversations with Jung during these days."

And, as always, my grateful thanks and affectionate memories go to Professor Jung, whose insights enable every sincere seeker after the truth to understand how his own unconscious assumptions and projections have distorted his view of the world and have influenced his inner thoughts and convictions. By following the way that Jung has marked out each of us can begin to fulfill the old command: "Know thyself."

M. E. H.

New York, May 1964

THE 'I' AND THE 'NOT-I'

I

INTRODUCTION

In the following pages I plan to explore the stages by which consciousness develops in the human being, so that, from being merely an integer in a continuum, he gradually becomes a person in his own right, a whole person, or, one might say, becomes the unique and complete individual he was intended to be.

This is an enormous assignment, for it involves not only the development of the personal part of the psyche that we call "I," together with that other part that contains the forgotten and repressed experiences, impulses, and memories constituting what Jung calls the *personal* part of the unconscious, but it further demands that this personal "I" be differentiated from the psychic elements of the *collective* unconscious, including both instinctive and spiritual experiences, that exert so profound and inescapable an influence upon us. Until this differentiation has taken place, we are and remain merely the puppets of unknown forces, having hardly any power of choice or of self-determination at all. But if, by the use of a suitable technique, we do become aware of them and of ourselves, and succeed in developing a working and satisfactory relation between ourselves and these forces, the whole psychic picture changes, and we become truly individuals with all the dignity of responsible human beings.

Through the long history of mankind, many techniques have been devised and used for this purpose, some with more and some with less success—some quite blindly, others with more insight. I refer, of course, to all those religious and cultural disciplines that aim at the initiation into secret wisdom, enlightenment, and participation in mysteries available only to those who have undergone the necessary experiences. This does not mean that they are necessarily *kept* secret, but that they *are* secret—they are inaccessible to us unless we have had the experiences that render us able to enter into them and to appreciate their meaning.

It is in this sense that Jung uses the term "process of individuation." For it is a process of psychic development that is accompanied by a progressive increase in consciousness—a development that is greatly helped and speeded up by a psychological analysis, not by a Freudian analysis, which is concerned only with the personal unconscious and the achievement of a workable adaptation to the external world and takes no account of those superior values of the psychic and spiritual world that are hidden from us in the darkness of the unknown hinterland, but by a Jungian analysis. The work of Jung was chiefly concerned with the contents of the collective unconscious, and any Jungian analysis that goes at all deeply into the psyche will activate the dynamic factors of the inner world. Jung has demonstrated that it is *only* by coming into direct relation to these superordinated values, in all their numinosity, that the individual can realize—make real—his true individuality, but this result cannot be achieved through a merely intellectual understanding. For the individuality consists not only of the personal ego, but of the personal ego plus the nonpersonal psychic factors, which together make up the totality of the *Self*. The process by which this is brought about corresponds to the religious experience of the "Journey of the Soul" in a most remarkable way. In my *Journey Into Self* I took a classical religious text of the journey, John Bunyan's *Pilgrim's Progress*, showing how closely it corresponds to the psychological experience of the process of individuation, and pointing out in what respects the Puritan point of view differs from the psychological one. Obviously then, from the psychological viewpoint, these disciplines have a very close connection. They are not identical, but they deal with the same material.

Before starting to discuss the development of consciousness it is necessary to decide how the term is to be used. We speak, for instance, of a person's being conscious as opposed to his being asleep or comatose. An animal, even an insect, can be conscious in this sense, but, given that a human being is awake, he yet may be unconscious in the psychological meaning of the word. He may perform many acts, even quite complicated ones, without being aware that he is doing so, while his memory of what he was doing at this time may be vague, or perhaps completely blank. A man may start out to the office one morning with something on his mind. He arrives in due course, but he has walked there in a state of complete unawareness. He has crossed streets, avoided cars and passers-by, possibly even greeted acquaintances, but so far as his awareness of the situation is concerned, he might as well have been sleepwalking. Such a man could hardly be said to have been conscious of what he was doing during that walk. Quite complicated acts can be performed in just such an absent state. It is even possible to read aloud accurately and with all the intonations the text requires and yet be utterly unaware of what it is one has read. The repetition of familiar words is all too often done quite automatically (one criticism leveled at the use of a set religious ritual is based on this fact), but a set form

5

of words is not a prerequisite for such absent-mindedness; an orator can be just as unconscious while making a seemingly impassioned speech.

There is another condition in which one can be unconscious of one's words and deeds. In the situation just described, the actions are unconscious because they do not have sufficient interest or energy value to hold the individual's attention. They are weak in psychic energy. But if there is an excess of energy or of emotional content arising from the unconscious, one is also prone to act unconsciously. In states of excitement, whether of anger, fear, erotic passion, or any other overwhelming emotion, one can do and say things, sometimes appropriate things and sometimes the reverse, without knowing what one has done. This, of course, can be disastrous, all the more because sometimes the unconscious speaks more truly than we know. Some of the amusing tales one hears about absent-minded people depend on this mechanism. For the unconscious can take over and substitute something of its own in place of the intended words, as in the case of the hostess who is reported to have sped the parting, and not too welcome, guest with the words, "Must you stay, can't you go?"

People in such conditions as these are not asleep, except metaphorically, but they can hardly be said to be conscious either. So that the first stage of consciousness depends on awareness of *what* you do or say. Even this is not enough, for unless you also know *who* it is that speaks and *what* the things said or done *mean*, your consciousness is not of a very high order. And so the word "consciousness," as used psychologically, implies *self-awareness*, awareness of who it is that acts, and also awareness of what it is that is done and its meaning. The girl who walked right into a tree and, when her companion protested, "But didn't you see the tree?" replied, "Yes, I saw it, but I didn't realize it," was certainly not conscious in the psychological meaning of the term.

Consciousness of this psychological kind, so far as we

know and can deduce from observation, is a purely human achievement. An animal acts skillfully and purposively, but apparently it does not *know*, is not aware, that it is itself that so acts. A television interviewer [1] once asked Jung when this kind of consciousness arose in man and what had brought it about. But Jung disavowed any knowledge of how or when this significant happening had occurred, saying, with characteristic humor, that it must have been millions of years ago and that he was not present at the event. Indeed we cannot possibly know the answer to such a question, and so it is useless to speculate about it. It is what Jung has called a "just-so story," a *fact* that we have to take into account but for which we can find no explanation. The biblical account that God breathed his spirit into man and so made him different from the animals, capable of consciousness, is a symbolic way of describing the event, but it still leaves us with an unfathomable mystery. Jung went on to say that we can observe *how* consciousness arises in a child, and this is important for educators, for obviously both the matter and the method of teaching should be, must be, different according to whether this kind of self-awareness has come into being or not.

Naturally it is possible to observe how consciousness arises in a child only from the outside, as it were. From our greater height of consciousness we can sometimes, if we are perceptive, actually see the birth of self-consciousness in a child. But we were none of us conscious of that important event when it was actually taking place in ourselves—in common parlance, we were too young. In psychological terms we had no standpoint of greater consciousness from which to view this transformation, nor do we have any memory of ourselves before it happened, nor of what it felt like to awake to the first glimmer of consciousness. I said "that important event," but it is really a series of events, a gradual development, whose

[1] Television interview by John Freeman, British Broadcasting Corporation, 1959. See F. Fordham, "Dr. Jung on Life and Death."

progress is by steps and which can sometimes be observed in a child and undoubtedly happened in ourselves in that period of prehistory that we call infancy, or rather in the period when the child changes from infancy to childhood.

However, this process still goes on in the most conscious and mature person right through life, and so we do have a criterion, a standpoint of actual experience from which we can view its early beginnings in a child. There is, too, another source of information on the subject, namely, the observation of primitive peoples, and of primitive individuals in our own society, and even of ourselves. For primitivity depends chiefly on the level of consciousness the individual has attained, not on his intelligence or education. There are many educated persons who have remained exceedingly unconscious of themselves and are therefore primitive beneath their cultured exterior.

A person who is unconscious of himself does not live life—life just happens to him. This condition may be reflected in his speech. I once knew a woman who never said that she *did* something, but always that "it happened." This gave a most curious impression that she just drifted through life without any conscious direction, and with practically no sense of responsibility towards her own life. In her the ego had been most inadequately formed, but this did not prevent her from having very strong reactions regarding her own comfort and her expectation of what was due her. Any frustration would be met by resentment, not by an effort to do something constructive about the difficulty. This is a very important point. Resentment always means that we are not willing to do something about the situation. We prefer to assume that it is someone else's business to take care of the difficulty or that "it ought to happen to us in a better way." We do not definitely say, even to ourselves, that "Life" ought to treat us as favored children; nonetheless, that is the implication. Resentment stems from the unconscious. It is based on an unconscious assumption of the way things *should* be, and when this expectation is not ful-filled, the individual is unable to react directly to the actual situation, because his assumption is not conscious to him. Even if he were made aware of what his expectation was in any given situation, he would probably have to repress the knowl-edge, because it would be too painful and embarrassing for him to recognize how inappropriate his unconscious demand was. And so instead of facing his own childishness the indi-vidual has a mood of resentment, voiced perhaps in such terms as "People ought not to do this to me."

Of course, such a condition is very infantile, very primi-tive, but an actual infant is even more unaware of itself and its own impulses than this. At first it is not even aware of its own body limits; there is no differentiation whatever between the "I" and the "Not-I." One can observe a three- or four-month-old infant playing with his fingers and toes as if he were discovering them and see his surprise that they move at his behest. Up to the age of four or five years he still regards cer-tain parts of his body as separate entities, especially those parts that have an instinctive function, such as defecation and urination and, to a certain extent, the functions of the mouth, eating and spitting, for instance. The penis, in particular, is frequently personified, regarded as a little man, a thumbling, it is often given a personal name, a habit that may persist, as a half joke, into adult life. In mythology and the ancient re-ligions the organs of the body are frequently personified as demigods, such as the Cabiri and Dactyls. These are personi-fications of the phallus and symbolize instinctive impulses and unorganized creative energy.

This state of half-awareness, so characteristic of the dawn of consciousness in the child, is also met with in folklore, myth, and fairy tale. Hunger, for instance, is frequently per-sonified as a wolf. With us the "wolf at the door" is merely a metaphorical way of speaking, but the phrase stems from an actual personification prevalent in more primitive times.[2] In *The Golden Bough,* Frazer [3] gives many examples of cases where children are forbidden to go to the corn fields about harvest time because the "wolf" may be there. In these cases the "wolf" is thought of as an actual animal who would literally kill the children.

The story of how human awareness emerged from animal-like unconsciousness is told by the Winnebago Indians in their myth of Trickster.[4] Trickster is a semihuman being who blunders through life doing all the things that are taboo in the tribe. The story of his doings is greeted with gales of laughter. (In much the same way we find the antics of the circus clown or the misadventures of a drunken man hugely amusing.) For to the Indians, Trickster represents "the way things are in nature," before the religious and social taboos arose to curb man's natural instincts. And the hilarity with which the stories are greeted clearly shows that the same attitudes are only just below the surface in the audience. Just so do risqué stories among more sophisticated people elicit a kind of amusement that betrays the unconscious condition of the listener.

Trickster had not yet discovered that his organs were a part of himself. The stories tell how he put his penis into a box and carried it about with him; how he detached his anus and sent it on errands into the lake and so on, and how he considered himself to be quite separate from his own instinctual acts. When the threshold of consciousness is lowered by the use of alcohol or other depressant drugs, a state of consciousness not unlike that of the Trickster stories is induced even in Western man, but it is not only in states of intoxication that we experience ourselves in this way. For we tend to dissociate

[2] Harding, *Psychic Energy,* p. 62. (For complete bibliographical citations, see the List of Works Cited. *Psychic Energy* is always cited in its 2nd edn., 1963.)

[3] Frazer, *The Golden Bough,* pp. 431 ff.

[4] See Paul Radin, *The Trickster.*

ourselves, our "I," from all compulsive or autonomous acts and emotions. Apparently it is someone else, not I myself, who does the unacceptable or unwilled thing. We say in excuse, "I didn't mean it; the angry words just jumped out." One woman I knew used to say that a frog jumped out of her mouth. Or we excuse ourselves for failing to keep some good resolution by protesting, "But I can't help it; I just have to eat—or smoke" and so on. This attitude of irresponsibility is even more obvious in regard to compulsive emotions, anger, passion of all sorts, positive as well as negative. We say, "Something got into me; I was beside myself." In each of these situations the individual has regressed to an infantile level of consciousness or perhaps has never really emerged from it.

To go back to the development of consciousness in the child: about the second year a child begins to talk and soon verbalizes everything he does. At first he speaks of himself in the third person, using the name everyone around him uses: "Baby do this, Baby do that," and so on. This verbalization is the precursor of thinking and of consciousness, for a child at this age not only *acts*, as the infant does, but he *knows* that he acts—or at least he knows that an action is taking place, although he does not know himself as a separate person. Then, usually sometime after his second birthday, an important change occurs in the child. He begins to speak of himself as "me" or "I." That is, he discovers that to himself he is no longer just like other objects or other people. He becomes self-aware, and so speaks of himself in the first person.

When an adult says "I," it is obvious that he does not always refer to the same entity within himself. There may be, indeed there *is* more than one "I" within us. For instance, the "I" that says, "I want—I am hungry or sleepy," is other than the "I" that exercises some control over this somatic "I." In another place I called this most primitive "I" the *autos*,[5] the

---

[5] Harding, *Psychic Energy*, p. 24 n.

Greek form for "self" that is found in such words as auto-erotic, autonomous, and so on, to distinguish it from the more developed "ego" that has gained some freedom from the instinctive demands of the body. The "I" that the child discovers in his third year refers chiefly to his bodily separation from others, his physical identity, and corresponds to the *autos*.

We do not remember the time when we first say "I"—we are too little. Before that it is as if nothing has happened at all; there is no criterion for judgment. We have been living in a time of "prehistory." We do not remember the time when we did not know ourselves as "I." In his memoirs Jung tells how he experienced the emergence of a new stage of consciousness when he was seven years old. He writes:

> In our garden there was an old wall, built of large blocks of stone. . . . In front of this wall was a slope in which was embedded a stone that jutted out—my stone. Often, when I was alone, I sat down on this stone, and then began an imaginary game that went something like this: "I am sitting on top of this stone and it is underneath." But the stone also could say "I" and think: "I am lying here on this slope and he is sitting on top of me." The question then arose: "Am I the one who is sitting on the stone, or am I the stone on which *he* is sitting?" This question always perplexed me, and I would stand up, wondering who was what now. The answer remained totally unclear, and my uncertainty was accompanied by a feeling of curious and fascinating darkness. But there was no doubt whatsoever that this stone stood in some secret relationship to me. I could sit on it for hours, fascinated by the puzzle it set me.[6]

And so the child Jung began to struggle with the problem of his own identity. "Is it the rock that is 'it' and I who am 'he'; or is the rock 'he' and I only 'it'?" He was beginning to differentiate the "I" from the "not-I" and to recognize the reality of the object and its autonomy.

By the time we reach adulthood, we are mostly aware that we are "I," but it takes only a slight depression of the level of

[6] Jung, *Memories, Dreams, Reflections*, p. 20 (English edn., p. 33).

consciousness for even this certainty to be disturbed. For the sense of the "I" at this stage has to do with the development of what Jung called the *persona*. When the delicate, gelatinous stuff of the immature psyche is met by the reality of the outer external world a hardening process takes place, which we speak of as adaptation; and around the natural psyche there forms a kind of skin, a mask, by means of which the sensitive individual can adjust itself to the requirements of the environment. The initial sense of "I-ness" is largely concerned with this persona "I." In its initial stages, in the child, it is quite precarious, and indeed it may even remain so into adult life. When something happens by which the individual "loses face" he feels himself to be depreciated, depotentiated, diminished. When we lose face we become little.

When we were tiny children my mother used to tell us stories before we went to bed. One of these was a nursery rhyme and had to do with loss of face, or loss of the persona. As I recall it, it went like this:

THE LITTLE OLD WOMAN

There was a little woman, as I've heard tell,
Who went to the market, her eggs for to sell.
She went to the market on a market day,
And fell fast asleep on the king's highway.

When by came a peddler, and his name was Stout.
He cut up her petticoats all round about.
He cut up her petticoats right up to her knees,
Till the poor little woman was fit for to freeze.

She began to shiver and she began to shake.
She began to quiver and she began to quake.
She began to wonder and she began to cry,
"Oh, Lawk-a-mercy-on-us, I'm afraid it isn't I!

"But if it be I, as I only hope it be,
I've a little dog at home and he'll know me;
And if it be I, he'll wag his little tail,
But if it be not I he will loudly bark and wail."

13

Home went the little woman all in the dark,
Up jumped the little dog and he began to bark.
He began to bark—and she began to cry,
"Oh, Lawk-a-mercy-on-us, now I *know* it isn't I."

At this point we, as small children, were so upset that my mother invented a less tragic ending to the story. Her additional verse was:

So the little woman went to fetch a light,
When up jumped the little dog and barked with delight.
He began to bark, and she began to cry,
"Oh, Lawk-a-mercy-on-us, now I know it is I."

The cutting of the petticoats not only made the woman cold, but by it she lost face. Her persona was seriously injured, with the result that she lost her sense of identity.

Then in her uncertainty as to her own identity, she turned instinctively to her dog for confirmation ("If it be I, as I only hope it be, I've a little dog at home, and he'll know me")—that is, she turned to her *instinctive* sense of "I"-ness to decide the point for her when her persona failed her. And I think it is probable that our disturbance as children at the ending of the tale depended on the fact that we had ourselves only just emerged from such a condition of insecurity about our own "selfness," and our delight when my mother amended the outcome was an expression of our reassurance that we would not lose our so recently won sense of identity either, even though we might lose our personas, and our sense of personal dignity, at least temporarily, through some misfortune. For the sense of being "I" is a very precious possession. If it is threatened, a child may go to pieces, or may fly into a tantrum, and an adult may sink into complete despair and possibly either commit suicide or go insane.

The first experience of "I"-ness is followed during life by many others, usually not so distinct and definite as the first one, though of course this differs in different individuals, and the whole development may take place in a series of quite

14

gradual steps, so that an individual may be unable to recall any definite turning point. But with others, another definitive moment may be experienced, usually around puberty, when the sense of "I"-ness becomes suddenly clearer. In the B.B.C. interview,[7] Jung tells of his own experience of "stepping out of a mist" at about eleven years of age, when he suddenly realized himself to be separate from his parents and capable of making a judgment about *them,* a thing he had never dreamed of doing before. After that he *knew* that he was *I,* an awareness, a consciousness much greater than that achieved in his former experience of being "I," when he speculated about the big rock.

It is not until this step in awareness has been taken that it can dawn on an individual that others, too, may have a similar sense of being "I." And indeed this state of consciousness is by no means always achieved by the average man. Many people go about most or all of their lives still under the impression that they are the only "I," they alone think, sense, experience, and particularly feel; all the others remain to them robots—a situation that results in a great deal of unconscious cruelty. To such people, I am the only "I"; virtually I am God, a state of unawareness that accounts for the extreme egotism so often met with in adolescents—and in many adults as well. But the awakening to consciousness of the real existence of others does not usually happen in one moment of enlightenment, like a conversion. More often it occurs in successive stages, at each of which it may seem as if one comes out of a mist, as Jung describes it, or it may seem that the sun comes out, or that a film has been removed from one's eyes.

[7] Freeman interview, 1959. See also Jung, *Memories, Dreams, Reflections,* pp. 24-25; 32-33 (English edn., pp. 37; 44).

II

THE "I" AND THE "NOT-I"

OF THE OUTER WORLD

THE DISTINCTION between what is "I" and what is "not-I" is not so easily made as most people assume. Everyone thinks that he has a clear and definite knowledge of what is himself and what is the object—the things, situations,[1] and persons, that make up the contents of the outer world. (See Appendix, Diagram II.) Indeed, this is a strongly held conviction. To be able to say, "I heard it with my own ears; I saw it with my own eyes," constitutes, for most people, sufficient proof of the reality of the object. We all think we see the world about us as it is in itself, and that we *see*, that is, observe, all of the environment that is within our purview. Actually this is far from being the case, as can be readily demonstrated by collecting an account of some happening, such as a motor accident, from several witnesses. Each witness feels absolutely sure that what he saw was true to the facts—the only trouble is

[1] The term "situation" is here used in a psychological sense. It might be defined as a dynamic relation between an object or objects and an experiencing subject.

16

that no two accounts agree in all particulars. The distortion of fact in the average person's observation of an occurrence is plain to see in the evidence given in any trial. Therefore we are compelled to admit that we see relatively little of the world about us. But we are far more accurate in regard to the physical world than we are in respect to the psychic world, the psychic reality, that surrounds us both within and without, for here the personal equation plays a dominant part. If we do not see the world as it is in itself, what kind of world do we see?

This question has been approached not only by psychologists but also by biologists who, in attempting to discover the nature of consciousness in animals, found themselves obliged to recognize that each creature sees only what concerns himself; for everything else he seems to be blind. To explain this situation Jakob von Uexküll, in his *Theoretical Biology*, suggested that each animal lives in a world of its own, an *Umwelt*, an enclosing world or, as I would say, "own world," which surrounds each creature and consists of only those objects in the outer world to which it responds. This idea of the *Umwelt* has been appropriated by the Existentialists, and they have added two other categories, the *Gegenwelt*, that is, the world of the society in which the individual lives, and the *Eigenwelt*, his personal world. But both Uexküll and the Existentialists regard the individual from the outside, as the behaviorists do, making judgments of his psychological condition from their own observations of the manner in which he acts. Here I propose to use the term in a more subjective fashion, that is, to try to explore how the world *looks* to the individual himself, what his own subjective experience of the inner and the outer reality actually is.

Uexküll discovered that a living organism responds only to stimuli that produce in it either an efferent or an afferent impulse; that is, it responds to stimuli that produce in it either an impulse to action or a sense impression. In other words, a living creature is responsive only to those stimuli that correspond to its own needs and capacities. To all other things it is indifferent, deaf and blind and unresponsive.

It follows that animals see only what, so to say, concerns them, or they see it and apperceive it only in its relation to themselves. To demonstrate this point, Uexküll described the world outlook of the wood tick. At a certain stage of its life cycle the wood tick needs the blood of a warm-blooded animal for reproduction. It climbs onto a twig or a blade of grass and goes into a dormant state until a warm-blooded animal passes its perch. Then the smell of the animal's sweat makes it let go its hold on the twig and drop onto the beast so that it can feast on its blood. Now there are many ticks and few warm-blooded animals in the jungle. Consequently the tick may have to wait a long time for its dinner. Uexküll gathered a number of ticks in the dormant state and kept them in his laboratory for varying lengths of time, where they remained entirely inactive until he put a drop of the acid which gives sweat its characteristic odor near them. They then promptly came to life and went through their whole cycle of movement. One tick was kept seventeen years, apparently dead—just a little brown mark on the twig—but on smelling sweat the inert creature came to life as if it had been born yesterday. It is obvious from this observation that the wood tick has a very limited *Umwelt*. The only thing that comes within its *Umwelt* at this stage of its development is the stimulus that sets off a mechanism by which it can get the necessary food to continue its life cycle.

In her book on East Africa, *Living Free*, Joy Adamson tells how the crocodiles would come when called by a particular sound but were oblivious to all other sounds, and this was true even of the baby "crocs," although they could not be considered deaf. Crocodiles are, of course, far more developed than the wood tick and the higher we go in the scale of development the more differentiated does the reaction to the outer world become. The *Umwelt* itself enlarges.

Uexküll in his book gave a diagram of a room, showing how it appeared from the point of view of a fly, a dog, and a man. To the fly every flat surface, including the ceiling, means "to walk"; [2] to the dog the ceiling is neutral, unobserved, while the floor means "to walk" and the chair means "to sit," while the music stool, which turns around, does not mean "to sit," but is only an obstacle. The bookcase, the piano, etc. are completely neutral—they are merely limitations of the external environment. To a man all these objects have a different significance; the floor is "to walk," the chair is "to sit," the table is "to sit *at*," the bookshelf is for books. For while man, too, is an animal, he has developed a much more differentiated consciousness of his surroundings than his brother animals, so that he sees not only what concerns himself but also, to some extent, what concerns his kind. For instance, if he is not musical, the piano may mean very little to him except as a convenient place on which to stack his books, but he knows it can produce sound as well. Here we have quite an interesting point: consciously he knows that if you strike the notes, you can produce sound, and some people think it is music—to him it is only noise. As it really affects him, his only reaction to it is as a place where he can put his books or his hat, for music does not enter his *Umwelt*, the enclosing world, the own world, that represents all of which this particular man is conscious.

All the same, man has a larger *Umwelt* than the other animals and has acquired a much wider knowledge of the world than they, including many things that can be demonstrated only with the aid of instruments, such as the microscope, that he

2 See Ruth Krauss, *A Hole Is To Dig: A First Book of First Definitions,* in which she demonstrates her educational method based on the observation that pre-school children understand by bodily action at an age when nouns have little meaning for them.

19

has himself devised for the purpose. As soon as a man has acquired any specialized knowledge his *Umwelt* enlarges to include a whole new category of facts, not only those that depend on instruments but also many others that result from closer and more conscious observation. If someone is interested in a particular subject, he is much more observant; it has entered his *Umwelt* in a way that it does not do to one who is not interested. For example, if a botanist and an ornithologist go for a walk together in the woods, the botanist will observe the plants, and he will see many more of them than the ornithologist, who is interested in identifying the many birds, while his friend possibly remains quite unaware of their presence.

Now while this work on the *Umwelt* was done to show the relation of the lower animals to the outer world, it applies to the human being in regard not only to his physical environment but also to the psychological environment in which he lives.[3] This is, of course, a much more complicated field of investigation, for while it is common knowledge that we see the world through our own spectacles—it is glorified for us when we are well and happy and the reverse when we are ill or depressed—yet the subjective experience of the human being cannot be checked by direct observation. Nor can we ever really convey our subjective experience to another even with the greatest effort. We can perhaps *describe* our inner experience, but how can we tell whether the image our words evoke in the listener tallies at all accurately with what we feel? In this we are indeed alone. And when we react to another human being directly, the chances of misunderstanding and misinterpretation are legion. For two unknowns are involved: my own reactions will be conditioned by my ability to differentiate my "I" from the objective "not-I," not only of the outer world but of the inner subjective world too;

[3] See Diagram II, in the Appendix, following p. 218.

and the other person's reactions will be similarly conditioned by his capacity to differentiate the "I" from the "not-I"; that is, his state of awareness or of consciousness will determine the appropriateness of his reaction. And so, whenever we enter the area of human relations, we are dealing with a very complicated field indeed. We are usually quite oblivious of how complicated and indeed problematical are our own everyday relations with persons in our environment. We think our daily intercourse is quite simple and aboveboard, but actually this is far from being the case.

In the preliminary examination of the *Umwelt* theory, as illustrated by the reactions of the wood tick, only one subject had to be considered in its relation to a static or given object. But when not only one but two living beings are concerned, one as object, the other as subject, the object, that is, the other person, does not remain static or passive in relation to the subject. For, first, he brings his own psychological elements into the situation, and these are mobile; and second, he reacts to the psychological factors brought to bear on him by the subject—the interaction is indeed continuous.

The way in which the "I" and the "not-I" get confused on the psychological plane can be made clearer by an example.

Suppose a husband and wife get into a disagreement. He says she made certain remarks that he felt to be insulting. She emphatically denies that she ever said any such things, but if she had said them, it was because he had done or said certain other most provocative things first.

A discussion started in this way can go on indefinitely, getting worse and worse at each round. Now it is probably quite impossible to determine any fixed point from which to unravel the tangle, because neither of the disputants is sufficiently conscious of his inner condition to be a reliable witness to the outer occurrence. They both simply see the external world through their own spectacles, which have undoubtedly caused a distortion of the external reality. And as they both suffer from the same disability they cannot, or rather should not, trust their own observation in such a situation but should be sufficiently open-minded to allow a doubt. This, however, is a state of grace that is not often met with.

Or, to take another common situation, someone enters a room where several people are already gathered. Some of them he knows and he immediately takes them into his realm of cognizance; others whom he does not know he may completely ignore, moving about and acting as if he did not see them—he may actually bump into them because he simply has not observed their physical presence. Or perhaps he responds politely to them when introduced, so that he recognizes them as physical objects, while still remaining closed to them psychologically, so that there is no possibility of communication. Psychologically they might as well not exist.

This sort of thing is not so uncommon as one might suppose—at times one is even guilty of just such lack of consideration oneself! On leaving the group, a person in such a condition of unconsciousness will promptly forget all about the people he has been introduced to, and, strange as it may seem, he will even forget he has ever met or perhaps talked with one of them for quite a long time. They do not really exist in his *Umwelt*. His reaction, if he has any at all, will be entirely subjective—a judgment based on the reaction set up in him by the contact, regardless of the reality of the person he was addressing. One might think that this kind of unconsciousness was limited to introverts, but extraverts, who are expected to be so well adapted to the external world, may be just as unconscious. It is not necessarily a question of type at all—it is a question of the degree of consciousness the individual has attained, not of his predominating attitude, whether introverted or extraverted.

As is well known, dreams portray the unconscious condition of the dreamer and contain a compensatory or complementary picture of the psychic situation. The following dreams give a very clear picture of the nature of a limited *Umwelt*; one is the dream of an introvert and the other the dream of an extravert.

In the first case, a young woman in her thirties dreamed that she was at a family dinner party, such as a Thanksgiving or Christmas gathering. But she noticed a very strange thing about the company, for they were all, with the exception of herself, enclosed in glass cases as though they were waxworks. She saw them eating and apparently talking, but no sound reached her at all, and neither did they seem to hear each other. She thought this was a very strange situation.

In the second case, a woman dreamed that she was traveling in a European-type railway carriage. She was alone in a special carriage, and there was a glass wall separating her from the corridor, up and down which people constantly passed, greeting each other and chatting animatedly, but she could not get to them, nor could she make them hear her. She felt isolated and alone, almost imprisoned.

Now, the first girl is deeply introverted. In consciousness she feels that everyone is able to talk and make contacts except herself. She feels shy and constrained even among a small group of friends. People like her and would like to draw her into the conversation, but she usually sits silent, not because she feels superior or bored—consciously she longs for companionship—but because she thinks the others are all clever and interesting and will find her dull or stupid. Yet in her dream she alone is alive—the others are all figures of wax. In other words, all the live-ness is within her; her reactions are all subjective and do not really concern the other people as realities—as they really are in themselves—for she sees them only through the distorting glasses of her own assumptions.

The other woman is of a very different type. She is extraverted and is apparently full of life and vivacity. At a social gathering she talks fluently and persistently, but her audience gradually melts away, and she finds herself alone. She cannot understand why they disregard and snub her, for she has made a real effort to interest and amuse them. At least this is her conscious reaction. But her dream says that actually she is imprisoned behind a glass wall, while the others are free. They exchange friendly greetings, but she cannot reach them. For while in conscious life she seems to be interested in other people, actually she is chiefly interested in having them interested in herself. And she feels baffled by their indifference and hurt by it. And so her dream shows her as isolated, all alone in her *special* compartment; it is the other people who are really alive.

In Thornton Wilder's play *Our Town,* when the girl, Emily, after having died, returns to life for one day, the realization she brings back with her is, "We never really look at each other." Even when people are "more to us," as we say, than the generality of our acquaintance, for most of us they exist only when we are actually with them. They flit in and out of our consciousness; they are only creatures in our dream, as the White Queen said to Alice. But then, you remember, to Alice it was the White Queen who was dreamlike and unreal! The Hindus speak of life as a dream partly for this reason. For example we expect to find someone we have been with exactly where he was both physically and psychologically when we last saw him. We are not really conscious of him as a living being, even though we may know where he has gone and his possible movements; still less are we aware of the subjective experiences he will be meeting—he does not really exist for us even as a matter of speculation. It is a case of out of sight, out of mind.

Of course human relationship, psychological relationship, is quite impossible under these circumstances. We cannot "know" the other person at all, for he barely exists for us, and, incidentally, we barely exist for him either. How can we reveal our real selves to one for whom we do not exist? We are lonely as stars in outer space. We cannot communicate. We are shut into our own most limited *Umwelt*.

In the two dreams I spoke of, the *Umwelt* was represented as a glass case or as a compartment shut in by a glass wall separating the individual from the surrounding world. This is a very apt image, for this *Umwelt*, this private world, is bounded by a transparent barrier separating one from the outside; like glass, it is also a reflecting surface on which one sees one's own image, while of course one thinks that what one sees is the outer world. Consequently one judges everyone else by one's own standard and from one's own standpoint. The universality of this condition is even reflected in the moral injunction to do unto others as you would that they should do unto you. For actually it is at least possible that the "other" would prefer something quite different from yourself. (I once heard a woman say, "I have learned to let people enjoy themselves *their own* way.")

Then, too, when enclosed in such an *Umwelt*, one is unduly dependent on the opinion of others—their approval and disapproval represent one's criterion of rightness and value. Thomas a Kempis' saying, "Thou art not the better for being praised, nor art thou the worse for being blamed," [4] has no meaning for such people. An attitude of this kind, attentive to the reactions one meets, could, of course, indicate a real concern for others and their situation, even though an exaggerated one, but in the case I am considering the individual is not concerned *at all* with the other as another human being, but is only concerned with the approval, or its reverse, he receives from him as it enhances or detracts from his own sense of personal value. It is as if he does not exist unless he is being actively approved by the environment. His sense of his own existence, his own being, is dependent on other people's opinions and reactions. His entire self is outside of him.

[4] *Imitation of Christ*, II.vi.2.

I once met a young man who had come to New York from a small Southern town, and I asked him how he liked the city. His reply was most illuminating. He said, "At home everyone knows me. The policeman on the corner, the bus conductor, everyone greets me and knows who I am. Here no one knows me. I feel as if I had lost my identity." Evidently his sense of selfhood depended on his identification with family and friends, his recognized place in the community. He had not differentiated the "I" from the "not-I," and so he was lost when he was no longer supported by the recognition of society that he existed.

Are we then imprisoned permanently in our limited *Umwelt?* Are we destined to live and die in unconsciousness of others? Do we just have to say "That is the kind of person I am"? There is a great tendency among educators to say just this, not about themselves but about the other—for the observer feels himself to be an exception! The statistical method of psychological evaluation lends itself to this kind of mechanistic judgment. But I do not agree with this, and neither did Jung. How then can a change be brought about?

It was pointed out above that the *Umwelt* is most limited in the lowest forms of animal life, and this condition was compared to that of the infant. As we go higher in the animal scale the *Umwelt* enlarges, and correspondingly in the normal infant his *Umwelt* also enlarges as he develops psychologically. This comes about as the result of pressures both from without and from within the psyche. For the impact of the environment forces on him a greater awareness of other people and their reactions to his behavior, while at the same time the natural tendency to development that obtains in the psychological as well as in the physical sphere presses for fulfillment, because the law of the living being is that it shall grow to its fullest stature.

But this kind of development does not always occur smoothly. Even where life has brought many experiences and many demands some people continue to live, as it were, in a mist, in a fairy tale, or to remain asleep like the Sleeping Beauty. In psychological terms they have never emerged from the collective unconscious.

Sometimes an individual who has always lived in a semi-unconscious state may "wake up" after a psychological shock, though of course such an experience can have the opposite effect, causing the individual to become numb, with the result that he drops down into self-absorbed nothingness. The death of the father or mother is particularly likely to present such a turning point. For to many persons the death of a parent is like a cataclysm that shatters their whole world, especially their psychological world, their *Umwelt,* and it is borne in upon the grown-up child that he can no longer be contained in the parent world. This can come as a surprise to one who has been separated from his parents for years and has thought of himself as entirely on his own. The experience usually comes to such a person as a sense that now there is no longer anyone behind him to take the ultimate responsibility. He is himself of the current, the extant generation. Such an experience can result from the death of the *personal* father. But it can also come about as the result of the death of a world-principle, of a religious order, of God. In his novel *The Thirteenth Apostle,* Eugene Vale describes what the death of the Father, that is, of the archetypal Father image, did for the so-called lost generation. He writes:

God having died at the hands of their elders, they had grown up in the twilight of the morning after the orgy of debunking. The revellers had passed away, leaving only the debris of spent passions, leaving the world as empty and silent as a mansion wherein the master had been slain. They had hoped to inherit freedom, and, instead, they inherited despair. In the first flush of revolt, they had considered themselves liberated; but soon it became apparent that people felt more oppressed, once the divine could no longer be used to oppress them. Contrary to all expectation, in the dawn of murder, the rebellious sons found themselves more inescapably in bondage, although the severe, demanding lord and father, at last overcome, lay murdered above and would not dominate any more. Suddenly, on their own, they saw that there was no one left in charge, nobody they could rely upon to keep the world running, for better or worse, fairly or unfairly, but at least under some sort of plan. . . . They had killed the belief that they were protected—they had murdered trust itself.[5]

When an individual finds himself in such a situation and realizes his own inadequacy, vis-à-vis life, he is likely to be thrown into despair. This is due, of course, to the very limited nature of his *Umwelt*. In such a case he may seek help from an analyst, and then it will gradually dawn on him that he has been living in far too personal a world and has never realized the need, the obligation, to develop a relation to the "not-I," whether this is represented in his case by other people or whether his need is really to develop a relation to the inner "not-I" of the spiritual and psychic world. And usually it is the latter that is the basic problem, especially for anyone of middle age or over. For, as Jung points out,[6] practically all his patients of over middle age have become neurotic because of a lack of relation to the inner not-personal values. And so some people find a way out of their prison through a religious experience of the inner values; others go to an analyst and in this way come into a relation with these same values through an exploration of the unconscious.

But there is another way in which imprisonment in the childish *Umwelt* may be ended and the individual be released into a larger world, namely, by the inclusion of another person. This, however, may not really open the prison door, for actually it only opens the door into another enclosure; the *Umwelt* has expanded to include another layer of the unconscious psyche. I refer, of course, to those situations where an individ-

---

[5] *The Thirteenth Apostle*, pp. 247-48.
[6] Jung, "The Stages of Life," pp. 387-403 *passim*.

ual finds himself compulsively involved with another individual. For if a man meets a woman, perhaps in some casual situation, instead of being indifferent to her, he may be seized by turbulent emotions. Such a woman is far from being non-existent to him; indeed her presence may engross the whole of his consciousness, blotting out every other object. All the other people in the group promptly disappear from his *Umwelt*. He finds himself arrested by something in her, something that absorbs his attention completely. Such a compulsive possession may be either positive or negative. In the first case, he has, in the common phrase, "fallen in love"; in the second, he may have an equally compulsive absorption of a negative quality. In either case he cannot get her out of his mind. She obsesses him and he walks about in a daze.

So here we have another aspect of the problem of the "I" and the "not-I." Is his sudden emotion really due to feeling for the woman herself—although he hardly knows her—or is it a sort of possession, a sudden uprush from the unconscious? How can a man in such a situation determine what part of his feeling is due to the reality of the other person and what part is due to the stirring within himself of some subjective factor which till that moment he was completely unconscious of, something that has only become visible, as it were, has only become operative within himself, as a result of some stimulus coming from her? In other words, does she symbolize to him something that like a match has set fire to materials lying ready in the unconscious? Unfortunately when a man is engulfed by such an experience, he is rarely in any condition to ask himself these questions. The flood of emotions seems so obviously to belong to the woman herself that he never suspects that much of his reaction may emanate from within himself, from his "I," while only a part corresponds to the reality of the woman, if indeed any of it does so. For love is notoriously blind. But so is hate!

When a reaction of this sort is so strong as to merit the

name of "falling in love," we know that a psychic element which we call the anima (or, in the case of a woman, the animus) has been evoked, or, as we say, has been constellated. A similar mechanism accounts for a strong negative reaction, especially if it persists, reverberates, "gets under the skin."

But quite apart from such major psychological happenings, there remain the countless situations in everyday life where our view of another person and our reactions to him are colored and distorted by a projection from within ourselves, so that we fail to differentiate between the "I" and the objective "not-I," and, in addition, we fail to differentiate between the "I," the conscious ego, and the rest of the psyche, which, because it is unconscious to us, is seen only in projection to the outer world.

For our awareness of the world around us is extraordinarily limited. We are all simply *unconscious* to an unbelievable degree. And not till we have undertaken a psychological analysis do we glimpse the extent of our unconsciousness. We simply take things for granted. On the objective concrete plane we assume naïvely that things are as they appear to our senses to be; and on the psychological plane our reactions are frequently based on assumptions rather than on the reality of the objective situation.

When an individual's attitudes and expectations are based on complete unawareness of others and their attitudes and expectations, he is of course entirely self-absorbed and remains so in spite of the many experiences that might be expected to arouse him from his dream. The "mind at leisure from itself" is far from his condition; any interest and concern he has in and for others will at bottom be motivated by his own autoerotism—a complete but unconscious autoerotism—which may go hand in hand with considerable conscious altruism. Indeed, it is by no means uncommon for an individual in this state of unconsciousness to devote himself to one of the do-good professions, for this gives him plenty of scope to put over onto others his own ideas of how things should be done, without getting himself involved in any direct human relationship of give and take with them. He is likely to avoid all close contacts, for any real relation might well challenge his self-absorption and the unconscious assumptions that rule in his personal *Umwelt*. The kind of emotion such a person experiences is really secondary. Pity, sympathy, patience, all those qualities that the social worker, the analyst, and even the priest are expected to have in superabundant measure, are secondary emotions. But, of course, they do not really touch us where we live. The emotions that touch us and that represent ourselves are I love, I like, I dislike, I hate, I want, I don't want, etc. But it is always I who experience the emotion—not I who have sympathy for somebody else who is experiencing it. And it makes all the difference in the world; one can remain completely unconscious of oneself while evidencing the most commendable sympathy and compassion.

An autistic state of consciousness is normal in the infant, and is also to be met with quite overtly in certain retarded children who remain completely self-absorbed, like infants. But it may also persist unrecognized into adult life. It came as a shock to most people to realize, as the result of Freud's researches, that what they had thought of as themselves, their conscious character, was only the surface layer of their true selves, while, underneath, the unconscious instincts remained quite untouched by education or conscious ideals. In spite of this general recognition the degree of autism prevailing in a large proportion of the population may be quite shocking, and certainly it faces us once again and more directly with the problem of what is the personal attitude or character, the conscious attitude of the ego, and what is the deeper, instinctive attitude or condition of the personality as a whole. For, as we have seen, the conscious ego may be altruistic while the real reactions of the individual remain purely instinctive and autoerotic.

The motivating power of the psyche operative at this level of development is pictured as a cold-blooded animal in the diagrams of the stages of consciousness, as taught in Tantric Buddhism. The dominant power at that stage is a creature half crocodile, half fish. Now, the consciousness of such a creature is entirely bounded by his own needs. He has no thought, no feeling for the animal he devours. He does not even get angry as a warm-blooded animal would, but merely reacts according to his "I want!" He has no compunction at grabbing his prey; he has no sense of regret or remorse, no shame or guilt at his cold-bloodedness. For he has no consciousness of any other psychological state. Food is present; he is hungry; he snaps it up. These are the boundaries of his *Umwelt*, and to him this is the law; there is nothing beyond it.

Such is the condition of the instinctive daemon that may rule in our own *Umwelt*. But of course such a shocking state of affairs remains entirely below the level of consciousness, conveniently covered by our acquired conventional good manners and our good opinion of ourselves. The denizens of the deep remain unconscious and show themselves only in moments when we feel threatened or are in the extremity of need. Then we may become beside ourselves, as we say, and act unconsciously, instinctively, hardly knowing what we do. But what then is our personal responsibility? Are we responsible for these acts, for these emotions, for these entirely unconscious impulses? These are questions that confront us not only with the problem of responsibility but, on a more subjective level, with the problems of sin and of guilt.

The crocodile neither has responsibility for its actions nor commits a sin by acting according to its nature. But when a human being acts through unconsciousness, is it sin or not? Here we come to one of the main differences between the Freudian and the Jungian schools. For the Freudians maintain that an individual is neurotic because he has repressed his natural impulses, that his sense of guilt has been imposed upon him by the superego, and that he is cured of his neurosis by the release of his repressions and especially by being freed from his guilt-feelings. And some, at least, among them encourage their patients to satisfy their aggressive and lustful impulses regardless of any other considerations. While Jung, on the contrary, teaches that while it is indeed necessary to become conscious of these natural drives within the psyche, it is also necessary to give heed to those other impulses that have led to the formulation of moral laws. For these too have arisen from within the psyche of man and still so arise in the modern individual. They are not merely imposed by society; they are inherent in the individual's own unconscious psyche. And they lie at the root of all religious and cultural teaching and especially of religious experience.

The state of consciousness we have been describing corresponds to the Hindu concept of *avidya* (unknowing), and it is the cause of much, very much, of asocial behavior and of unkindness. An individual who is not aware of the "other" as also a sentient being will behave towards him in an unfeeling way but, if he becomes aware of the other, it is quite likely that his attitude will change. *Unconsciousness* on the feeling side (that is, lack of development of the feeling function of the psyche) may be the cause of cruelty and callousness in a person who may nonetheless have a very kind heart. The problem then is: how can he become aware of the situation? While he is unconscious, is a man really guilty on account of acts of inconsideration and unkindness? We do not hold a small child guilty in similar circumstances, any more than we blame the fox for eating the goose. St. Paul said that the law came in that sin might abound,[7] meaning that awareness of moral law and the rights of others converted natural acts into crimes against the brother. This leads to the moral attitude that says, "It is wrong to *act* in such and such a way," but this moral rule can be heeded without any change in the inner attitude.

[7] Rom. 5: 20.

33

Unfortunately the principles on which children are educated and on which our social morality is founded are largely concerned with actions, while scant attention is given to the underlying feeling. As a result, natural instincts are not changed but only repressed. If, however, the offender can be made conscious of the other person, of *his* situation and *his* feelings, then he will, in most cases, experience a natural impulse towards a different attitude. The key word here is *if*. *If* he can be made conscious! This is the important factor that has a direct bearing on the education of children and also on our own attitude towards our own transgressions.

But how can this desirable change in self-awareness be brought about? First, one can observe oneself in relation to others, undertaking this as a definite task, not in order to assess one's thoughts and actions by any external standard, but in terms of: Where does the other fellow stand? What are his feelings, his interests?—and this may help. But usually an unconscious psychological condition is not really challenged until one explores the unconscious—and so the second step leads to a realization of *sin*. It is brought home to one, perhaps, that some catastrophe, some injury to another, is the result of one's own selfishness, one's own *unawareness* and self-absorption. So *sin* of this character falls under the head of transgression against one's neighbor. So long as one is unconscious, living in a circumscribed *Umwelt,* this kind of autoerotism is merely natural. But when one's callousness has been called to one's attention through the reaction of another person, or, when one realizes that some unfortunate happening was due to one's own unawareness, then one becomes aware of sin, and as a result one may possibly be more conscious in the future. This, however, is an infinitely slow process. Over and over again, one makes the same mistake; one has not differentiated the "I" from the "not-I," and so inevitably one acts in a blind and autoerotic way. But perhaps the recognition of one's unawareness of the other fellow begins to dawn on one nearer and nearer to the event. At first one sees it where it happened in the past, in childhood, perhaps, or one is "stabbed awake" by some gross misfortune that has resulted from one's carelessness. This is one reason why in analysis the patient is asked to recall significant experiences of childhood and youth, but as he becomes more aware, he may realize that last year's unfortunate occurrence, too, stemmed from a corresponding unconsciousness, and eventually there may come a red-letter day when he realizes with a shock that in this very moment he is disregarding the other person and concerning himself solely with himself and his own interest. When this happens, there is at last a chance that he may become aware, *really aware*, of the other person, and then he simply will not commit the sin against the brother. It is as if he comes out of a mist into the light, so that he actually sees his brother's situation as clearly as he sees his own. He has begun to differentiate the "I" from the "not-I."

III

"PARTICIPATION MYSTIQUE"

AND IDENTIFICATION

WITH THE FAMILY

IN THE LAST CHAPTER the theory of the *Umwelt*, the "own world" that surrounds each living being as with a glass wall, was discussed. We must now go back in our inquiry to the stage of psychological development before any real sense of "I" has dawned on the individual. The work of Uexküll was done on single or solitary creatures such as the wood tick. Man, however, as a social animal, resembles the social insects, such as ants and bees, in some of his psychological reactions. These creatures live not as single individuals but as a group— the social unit, not the individual insect is, so to say, the individual. Primitive man lives in a somewhat similar condition. He cannot survive entirely alone for very long; his strength lies in the group, the clan, the tribe. And this is also true of modern man. We could not long survive alone physically, nor can we develop psychologically alone, for psychological development requires both an outer and an inner environment. I say this advisedly in spite of the achievements of anchorites and holy men who devote themselves exclusively to the inner life. It is a point Jung has often emphasized, for psychologically we need a vis-à-vis, an I-Thou relationship in the outer world, and in the inner world as well.

But when we come to explore the nature of our relation to the outer and the inner worlds of the "not-I" more closely, we soon discover that these are not two clearly separated realms of experience. For subjective elements obtrude themselves between us, our perceiving I, and the outer object, so that the object is not seen as it is in itself, but only in a more or less distorted form, owing to our inner psychological condition. And in the far more obscure realm of the inner "not-I" the distortion is undoubtedly much greater. Yet just as we are convinced that what we see as the external object is as we see it and not otherwise, so is our conviction regarding the validity of our inner vision unshakable.

We do not fight a man to uphold a certainty, but only to force him to accept our belief, our conviction, of the truth. No one's life is endangered because he will not accept the fact that two plus two makes four—that is a truth that requires no champion. No, it is only for our beliefs—that is, for those things that are *not* provable—that we either kill or are willing to be killed. Fanaticism rests not on fact but on psychological projection. It is the correlate of doubt, not of certainty. This illusion is particularly apparent in the religious sphere, where every man is convinced that God is as he sees him and not otherwise—a conviction so strong, so invincible, that one would die for it, as many have actually done. For the conviction of the persecutor is just as strong as that of the martyr, and he feels himself compelled either to convince one who holds a different opinion or to eliminate him.

In the past, people have been persecuted for holding unpopular beliefs regarding even objective facts. Galileo may serve as an example. Today, we are more open-minded in this respect, for we pride ourselves on our scientific outlook. In many cases we are willing to put our observations to the test of experiment, so that the conviction that we see things as they actually are has been greatly strengthened during the nineteenth and twentieth centuries by the increase in our scientific knowledge. It is a well-known fact, however, that primitive people do not always share what we consider to be the rational and factual relation to objects and persons in the outer world. To them natural objects may seem to be endowed with attributes and powers that from our point of view are quite fantastic. A tree, for instance, or an animal, may be considered to have magic power, and it is put under strict taboos for this reason. Naturally such beliefs lead primitives to what seems to us to be quite irrational behavior.

The anthropologist Lévy-Bruhl [1] was the first to describe the psychological condition that lies behind such attitudes on the part of the primitive man. He named it *participation mystique*. Jung has used this same term to explain the psychological condition that still obtains to some extent among civilized people. [2]

Lévy-Bruhl pointed out that to primitive man certain persons and objects seem to have a peculiar power and value. He acts toward them *as if* they contained a part of himself, a part which he himself does not possess. It may be his thinking, or perhaps a part of his soul, sometimes even his life. He seems to be psychologically continuous with an object of this sort, as if part of himself were actually contained in it, and in consequence this object has a peculiar fascination for him. It is filled with mana—that invisible secret power that produces in a man awe, attraction, and dread and so exerts an unconditioned influence over him. To him such an object is *numinous,* to use the term introduced by Rudolf Otto. [3]

So *participation mystique* may be said to be a mysterious interchange or continuity between separate entities because

[1] *How Natives Think*, p. 129.
[2] See Diagram II.
[3] *The Idea of the Holy*, p. 7.

they are psychologically identified with one another. For the primitive man, like the very young child, has no definite boundaries to his psyche—everything that happens is both in himself and in the object; he feels with the animals, the trees, and so forth. It is a condition that modern individuals experience when they slip into the unconscious. It has been called the "oceanic feeling," and for many people it is a blissful experience, in which all responsibility is annulled. The primitive man's belief that the bear dance will inevitably bring the bear to the hunt depends on this unconscious identity, for the bear and the man are felt to be a continuum. And it must be admitted that sometimes the bear seems to feel it too, since reliable observers have stated that the bear *does* come when so called.

The primitive's identification with his tree may be so strong that if the tree is cut down the man himself may die. He may feel that his tree or snake or other mana-containing object has a superior wisdom and can tell him what to do in times of doubt. That is to say, his thinking *ability* has not been developed as a conscious function, but has remained as a potentiality in the unconscious and is only experienced in the projection to the tree or the snake, as the case may be. In certain aboriginal tribes in Australia, each individual possesses a churinga, a piece of wood or a stone, that is rather like a fetish or an amulet. This object is sacred to the particular man who owns it, and he has a peculiar relation to it. He keeps it in a secret place and tells no one about it. For him it contains mana, good power, and if he is ill or in any way distressed, he goes secretly to its hiding place, takes it out, and sits rubbing it for a long time. Gradually the good mana of the churinga passes into the man, while it absorbs his bad health. Then he replaces it in its hiding place and goes home. Meanwhile the good power of the churinga is building up again out of the earth, so that when he needs it its mana will be undiminished. There is something very right about this practice. For by contacting Mother Earth, nature in us can be restored. We are put once more into touch with our natural selves, and a state of both physical and psychological health is regained. Most people have experienced the healing effect of stretching out on the ground in the woods or by the sea when they are tired or depressed. It is as if in this way our connection with the source of life is re-established and we get back into a right relation with Nature.

In the West the ego, the intellect, and the will are considered to be of supreme importance almost to the exclusion of all other factors. We do not realize that we are not free from *participation mystique* and that many of our basic life assumptions depend on it and condition our *Umwelt*. With most people the *Umwelt* or enclosing world is, psychologically, very limited indeed. We are not, as a rule, at all clearly aware of the reality of the people and situations that surround us, and instead of making the enormous effort that is necessary if we are to be really related to the external world, we take the easy way and function, to a very great extent, on unconscious attitudes and a priori assumptions. We swim with the group we belong to and take on the coloring of all the others in it. We assert to ourselves, if not aloud, "This is the way things have always been done, and so this is the way they *ought* to be done in this case." To us, such things have a quality of "of courseness." But it is well to beware of those words "ought" and "of course." They usually stem from unconscious assumptions! The extent to which we are motivated and controlled by unconscious attitudes is unbelievable. We are quite unaware when we are taking a collective attitude, believing it to be individual. An individual who goes to live in a foreign country may get a little glimpse of his own unfreeness. He discovers that collective assumptions enter into the smallest details of daily life and influence his every reaction. His expectations and psychological attitudes are challenged at every point, from table manners to political opinions. He begins to realize that his attitude rarely rests on his own judgment of a particular situation but that in everything he is influenced by all sorts of overtones of meaning that may not be shared by his hosts.

This kind of collective identity makes for solidarity with the in-group. Conscience or, as Freud called it, the superego is made up to a very great extent of such assumptions. There is no doubt that psychologically they have a great value. Not only do they exert a restraining influence on the natural instincts and desirousness of the individual, but they also form the basis of a workable adaptation to the "not-I" of the community, that is, to the "not-I" of the outer world, as well as to the inner world of moral sanctions.

In any group of like background where the assumptions of good form and opinion are held in common, these often quite unconscious determinants of behavior make daily contact and interchange possible. For the members of the group generally understand what any individual means by his way of speaking and acting. But his words and actions may be disastrously misunderstood if he is in a strange group whose basic assumptions differ from his own.

Some of our assumptions have a general validity for the community as a whole, showing how we should conduct ourselves and also giving a criterion for judging the actions and words of other people. Without them we would be all at sea, not knowing what to expect or what was meant. Many travelers have found themselves in this situation, in remote and unexplored regions where at every turn they have been in danger of unintentionally violating some sacred custom.

Some of our assumptions *are* generally valid for the whole community and apply equally well to all, while others do not have general validity; for instance, those that stem from our own particular family background may not be applicable to other people. Every child takes his family customs and *mores* as universal, so long as he is contained within the home atmosphere. But they are likely to be challenged when he goes to school and later to college. The "old school tie" may then replace the home as a criterion of value. This may serve in his own country, but should he go abroad or find himself in a social group different from his own he is likely to meet with some surprises. When a person with unconscious assumptions marries, many of his "taken for granted" attitudes will come into question. This is one reason why boarding school, resident college, and exogamous marriage have a broadening effect on the individual.

Participation mystique, then, has to do with the projection of *unconscious* contents into the environment, into people or things or situations, where they are encountered as if they were properties of the object and are not recognized as having anything to do with the individual's own psyche, let alone really belonging to what should be his own contents. It is amazing to discover *what* may carry parts of the human psyche! It is as if the "should-be" contents of the psyche, having remained unconscious, are not recognized as part of one's self, but are found, discovered, in some object in the outer world. I recall an experience of my own. A visitor once offered to weed the garden for me. I rather casually accepted the offer, supposing that he knew weeds from seedlings, but my assumption proved to be quite off the mark for, when I went to look, I found he had made a clean sweep of every blade of greenness and had a nice tidy patch of earth for me. I was devastated. I managed to say the polite thing and then escaped to my room to deal with the totally inappropriate grief and rage that beset me. I had had no idea that these tiny seedlings represented anything more to me than plants. But obviously they symbolized something much more precious and important. A numinous value from the unconscious had betaken itself into the seedlings, and their destruction seemed to have threatened or destroyed the psychic value they embodied. I had a pretty bad time of it, until I could bring up to consciousness the inner value concerned and free myself from the quite disproportionate emotions my guest's unfortunate action had produced. But on further consideration, was it so unfortunate? If he had not blundered in this way, would I not have remained unconscious of this buried and unconscious value that his action forced me to pull up into consciousness from its earthy seed bed? As someone once remarked, "External reality has a way of not being so external after all." For the contents of the unconscious, both the personal unconscious and the collective unconscious, are encountered in the outside world.

It is these projected elements that form the basis of superstitions and of primitive religion, with its concept of mana, and of what used to be called "animism." They are also the cause of the numinous quality certain objects seem to possess. This psychological mechanism is not confined to primitives; it may function in ourselves just as well, as the incident of the seedlings clearly shows. For instance, certain objects have a peculiar relation to ourselves; a feeling of *my-ness* clings to them—my pipe, my chair are not merely objects, they have something of me in them. An author may be able to write only with HIS pen. While this feeling about an object is usually that of the owner alone, it can be experienced by others as well. The object has a kind of virtue—for instance, the sword of a dead hero carries something of the power of him who wielded it in life. One recalls the story of Elijah's cloak that fell upon Elisha,[4] carrying the implication that the mission and authority of the older man would now "fall" upon his successor. The value that is placed on relics of the saints is another example of the way in which mana is believed to cling to objects; after his death, the power of the owner still seems to be contained in some strange way in his possessions. With primitive man the identification of the unconscious value with the object may go even farther, so that, as I pointed out

4 II Kings 2: 12-14.

above, if his particular tree is cut down, the man himself may die. This belief is also the psychological background of many primitive burial rites and ceremonies where the personal belongings of the deceased have to be buried with him. Nobody else can touch them or use them, because they contain something of the personality of their former owner.

Even today people may have similar feelings. The loss of the special possession, for instance, is considered unlucky; and, however much we tell ourselves not to be superstitious, we may be obsessed with a sense of impending disaster. When a similar psychological projection affects a number of people simultaneously, we hear of portents. Jung's discussion of the "flying saucers" [5] gives a clear account of such a phenomenon. It is due to an unconscious identification of happenings occurring in the collective unconscious with an outer happening, and the phenomenon is closely related to synchronicity,[6] the term Jung used to denote a very strange phenomenon, namely, that outer happenings at times coincide in a *meaningful* way with an inner psychological condition. The important word here is *meaningful*. My colleague Dr. Bertine tells the story of such a happening in her consulting room. She owned a rather temperamental little dog that could not endure one of the patients, a very rational and intellectual woman. Whenever this patient arrived, the dog would snap around her ankles and threaten to bite her. So it was customary to exclude the dog from the consulting room when this particular patient was about to arrive. On the day in question, when the patient came in, she said that she had had a dream; she had dreamed that a little animal (she wasn't sure whether it was a cat or a dog) came to her and begged her (using actual words), "Please, won't you take care of my baby?" In the dream she stooped down, lifted the little animal into her lap, and said, "Yes, I'll take care of your baby." At that moment

[5] Jung, "Flying Saucers: A Modern Myth of Things Seen in the Skies."
[6] "Synchronicity: An Acausal Connecting Principle."

there came a great scratching at the door, and Dr. Bertine, not realizing what she was doing, got up and opened the door. In rushed the snappy little dog, jumped up in the patient's lap, and licked her face.

When such things happen to oneself, one has a feeling that it is in some way uncanny. For instance, the phenomenon of *déja vu* produces such an effect. Two women who were on a motor trip together spent the night at a motel. One of them dreamed that, as they were driving along the road, there was suddenly a terrific motor accident. On the next day they came to a place that seemed familiar to her, and at once she remembered her dream, which she had entirely forgotten until that moment. She turned to her friend and said, "Go slowly, there's a corner coming." Her friend said, "What are you talking about?"—but fortunately she pulled up, for a car swung around them from behind and smashed head-on into another car coming from the other direction.

Certain people have the experience of foreseeing coming events, and when their premonition comes true, they may feel personally involved in the event, perhaps with a feeling that in some mysterious way they were responsible for its having occurred, and consequently have a sense either of power or of guilt. Neither of these reactions is appropriate, for they have only foreseen, not participated in the happening. This is a common reaction with the insane, but it occurs, too, with normal people who are in close touch with the unconscious. Dunne gives many examples in his *An Experiment with Time*.

The predictions of apocalyptic visions, astrological prophecies, and suchlike are to be explained, from the psychological point of view, as due to projections of contents of the collective unconscious. Visions like these having a general nature and relating to future time are apparently concerned with movements taking place in the very remote layers of the collective unconscious that will be expressed in the historical development of the *Zeitgeist*. For the germs of man's spiritual development lie unseen and unrecognized in the collective unconscious, where they continue to grow until the time of their flowering arrives. These things are hidden from *our* eyes, but perhaps the seers may be able to glimpse them, if only in a glass darkly, so that the form in which they record their experiences is correspondingly dark.

These are the general effects of identification with the unconscious. We must now consider the more personal effects of this identification on the individual. When a large part of his psyche is projected, the individual is hardly separated at all from the environment. All that happens happens in him as well as outside, and he has very little sense of personal identity and no clear differentiation of the "I" from the "not-I" either of the inner world of the collective unconscious or of the external world represented by other people.

The sense of being a person will then be inadequate and dependent for its realization on others. And so, too, when someone is uncertain of himself, always needing the approval and support of others and being unduly depressed by their criticism, it means that he has no valid criterion of value from within himself. If he is disapproved of, he feels crushed; if he is not noticed, he ceases to exist; and if he is praised, he is in the seventh heaven of elation. He has little sense of his personal value, though he may give the appearance of being exceedingly egotistic, since he is always "fishing" for praise. He purrs and preens himself when it is given, literally basking in an atmosphere of approval, while he usually goes away by himself to hide his hurt if the desired notice is not forthcoming. His center of gravity is not in himself, but outside in other people. Now, of course, I do not mean to say that we ought not to take account of the judgment of our peers, but I do mean that if we do not have a valid judgment of our own actions, we should inquire whether we are not lacking in a true self, not able to differentiate between what is "I" and what "not-I."

In cases of this sort, the family, the clan, the tribe is the unit, while the individual, like the bee in the hive, is almost anonymous. He hardly exists as a separate entity. To the primitive tribesman, the individual life matters very little, either to the man himself or to the group, for the value of *being* is vested in the group alone. *It* is the individual, the operative and effective being whose life is of paramount importance. The individual man is merged in the group. He does not make any important decisions for himself. The council of the elders decides everything—when to sow the seed, when to go on the hunt, how to interpret big or important dreams, which are frequently taken as applying to the tribe as a whole. Consequently the individual has hardly any personal responsibility; his consciousness is practically identical with that of the group. Each man, in himself, is nothing, a mere integer, but he is also, or feels himself to be, a carrier of the tribal consciousness and importance, and this gives him a sense of dignity. This situation is illustrated in the ancient Hebrew idea of man's relation to God. For Jehovah was primarily interested in the tribe, not in the individual. It was what the chosen people did that mattered, while the individual man counted for very little.

Even among ourselves, far more conscious as we are than primitive man, the sense of "I" may be rather precarious, liable to be lost under certain circumstances. In any group where the group feeling is strong, as in certain secret societies, college fraternities, or political conventions, the sense of importance as a member of the group may be in marked contrast to the individual's sense of himself when alone. Especially in the case of adolescents who have broken away from home, but have not yet acquired an individual psychology, the support of a group may be very important indeed. Such groups may have a positive value, challenging and bringing out masculine traits of courage, co-operation, fair play, and so on; but, unfortunately, since the mechanism depends on the projection of unconscious parts of the psyche, a negative effect rather than a positive one can be uppermost, as in the gangs that today play such an important part in the life of under-privileged boys and girls in our large cities.

The answer to the problem of gangsterism is not to be found in terms of repression or of punishment, nor, I think, except in the case of adolescents, is it to be found in terms of group activities of a positive kind. Unless the destructive energies are first transformed in individuals, a group, however optimistic its organizers, will soon be subverted for destructive purposes. For, as Jung [7] has repeatedly pointed out, each individual must come to terms with the negative side of his own personality; otherwise this is inevitably projected onto the group. A group always represents what is common to its members, the common man in man, and never what is individual. For this reason, a crowd composed of decent citizens can become a mob that may even lynch a man on the mere suspicion that he is guilty of the crime for which vengeance is being sought.

The same mechanism can be seen at a social affair where there has been a good deal to drink. Individuals may then take part in antics, brawls, or even orgies, that they would never dream of countenancing when alone or cold sober. In group identification the elements of personality that are common to all the members of the group are the ones that emerge when conscious control is relaxed, and these are usually negative, the elements that have been repressed because of the moral and social requirements of the environment, the unadapted and negative factors that all men harbor in the background of the psyche.

In a group situation, if conscious control is reduced by alcohol or emotional excitement, it can happen that for the time being the usual collective mores are replaced by the sanc-

[7] "The Undiscovered Self," chaps. VI-VII.

tions of the group, so that people live out their instinctive impulses uninhibited by moral and social restraints.

Emergence from the condition of group identity comes about as the result of the gradual development of the individual, when a center of consciousness arises within him and he develops a sense of personal identity, which we call "I" or "me." This is the *autos,* and it is gradually superseded by the ego. Meanwhile, those elements that do not suit the requirements of the outer world are repressed into the personal unconscious—that part of the unconscious that Freud dealt with almost exclusively. These are the elements that are projected into a group situation, so that when a group of people get together, even though they may intend to form a positive organization of some sort, the negative qualities come up, as one can see at almost any committee meeting. People become more difficult, more unreasonable, more demanding, more egotistic, and those things that they ordinarily keep carefully under cover come out in any discussion where there is a difference of opinion.

The problem cannot be met by further repression and by saying, "You ought not to behave like this." This will not help. The solution to the problem of group identification is not to be found by a moralistic or punitive approach, but perhaps it can be found through the evocation or constellation of the helpful, life-giving archetypes of the collective unconscious, for these can lead the libido over into constructive channels.

After these general remarks on the phenomena of *participation mystique,* we must turn to consider in greater detail the part it plays in the development of consciousness in the individual. Before the "I," the *autos,* has been established as a center of individual awareness, the child has no personal consciousness but exists in a condition of identification with his surroundings. This state of affairs is to be seen particularly clearly in the infant's relation to the mother. He lives in complete *participation* with her, and she is related to him in a similar way though to a lesser degree. For at first the child is actually a part of her own body. Even after he leaves her womb, the infant is still entirely dependent on her and so partakes of both her physical and her psychological condition. After the child's physical dependence has been outgrown, this identity with the mother persists as a psychological reality. For in the unconscious the psyches of mother and child have no clear dividing lines. He is contained psychologically within her all-embracing protection until he has won his freedom and his psychological independence.

In considering the development of the individuality it is important to recognize the exceedingly close connection that exists between mother and child, for the condition of her psyche and especially of her unconscious has a profound effect upon him. If she is disturbed or anxious, and especially if she is in conflict, this will have an adverse effect on the child. For instance, if the parents are not happy together so that misunderstandings and mutual distrust or anger and hostility have developed between them, the child may begin to have night terrors or emotional upsets; an older child may fail in his schoolwork or show some other neurotic or emotional disturbance. He may not have heard anything of the situation but unconsciously he senses that something is amiss. He breathes the atmosphere and is poisoned by the wrong attitude in the parents' relationship to each other. The lack of harmony between the parents is especially liable to produce neurotic symptoms in the child if their conflict has been repressed, because then the difficulty in the parents' unconscious contaminates the unconscious of the child. For *au fond* there is no distinction between child and parent on the unconscious level; the psychological atmosphere is continuous, just as the physical atmosphere is. If the parents disregard the difficulties in their marriage, perhaps even avoiding any conscious acknowledgment of them, the child is particularly likely to be affected because of the unconscious *participation mystique* between him and them. But if the parents will bring the difficulty up to consciousness and face it squarely and seriously, the child is likely to be relieved of the burden, and the neurotic symptoms may stop. If, however, the problem between the parents is so serious that the home is in danger of being broken up, this will naturally cause a serious problem for the children, too. But they do not need to be burdened with the parents' conflict as well. As responsible adults, the parents should do all they can to carry it for themselves consciously, so as to safeguard the children as far as possible.

It is not only in the relation to the parents that *participation mystique* plays an important role in the psychological life of the individual. For, as we said above, man is a social animal and the first group of which he is a member is the family. Indeed, it has repeatedly been said that the family is the unit on which the nation or the state is founded. The very close relation that exists between the various members of a family is based in part on common experience and companionship but to a far greater degree on unconscious identification, that is, on *participation mystique.*

The identity with the family as a whole and with the various members individually naturally exerts a very considerable influence on each of the members. The psychological development of the children and their character traits depend to a considerable degree on factors within the family group that result from fate or, if you prefer to call it so, from chance. When we come to consider the interaction of the various members of a family on each other, we find ourselves in a mass of complications. At first glance it might seem that an individual's relation to his family would be a relatively simple subject to discuss. The facts are far different. The interrelations of a family group depend to a considerable extent on archetypal forms—forms that have been the subject of myths and fairy tales and legends all down the ages; and their psychological effects on the character and fate of the individual have been the subject of many novels and dramas and have also concerned psychologists of various schools. From this it is clear that relations within the family group are by no means simple, since they always contain both positive and negative elements and are the cause of all sorts of rivalries as well as of loyalties.

The positive elements contribute to making a united family, to the solidarity of the family group, and to love among its members; while, generally speaking, the negative elements have a reverse effect, leading to disagreements, quarreling, and a tendency of the members to separate, so that the family falls apart. But these results that appear on the surface, that is, that are conscious, are all compensated from the unconscious by their opposites. In an overaffectionate family, envy, rivalry, and disharmony may lie just below the surface, or they may make their appearance in recurrent outbreaks of a more or less violent nature. Correspondingly, where there is a negative relation in the conscious, giving rise to constant disagreement and bickering among the members, with feelings of conscious resistance, even of hate for each other, it is by no means uncommon to find that the children are quite incapable of leaving home, even though they have reached an age when it would be expected that they would go off on their own. It is a case of the necessity to cling to "my dearest enemy."

When we approach the problem of family relations, the first complication we meet depends on the fact that instinctive emotions have a dual character—one face is turned towards consciousness and the outer world; the other is unconscious and is usually hidden within the unconscious part of the psyche, from where it not only influences the total relationship but in addition is liable to burst forth in some untimely and unexpected fashion, if at any time the conscious control is lowered for a moment. This duality refers to "instinctive emotions"—love-hate, sadism-masochism, aggressiveness-submission, and so on. It does not apply to consciously worked-out relationships, where true love of the object has been developed.

It must not be thought that these considerations concern only the child psychologist. The whole psychological bent of the adult is profoundly influenced by childhood experiences; and, as the researches of depth psychology have shown, the character of the adult, his personality problems, and his neurotic difficulties may, and usually do, stem at least in part from the family situation in which he grew up. And these have to be explored and dealt with before he can go on to develop a true individuality of his own.

The second complication we are faced with in dealing with family relations depends on the fact that influences from both parties enter into the picture, not only on the conscious level but also from the unconscious. For instance, the relation of parent and child can and should be viewed from the point of view of the parent's relation to the child as well as from that of the child to the parent.

A third complication arises from the difference in sex of the individual members of the family. The mother's relation to her son is different from her relation to her daughter. And the son's relation to her is not the same as a daughter's. A corresponding difference affects the relation to the father.

A fourth complication depends on the size of the family. The relation of the parents to an only child is very different from that to one member of a large family. The relation to the eldest and the youngest brings in a special element. In western countries for many centuries the eldest has been the heir, but in certain African tribes the youngest holds this position. Fairy tales frequently emphasize the special value of the youngest: it is the youngest son who becomes the hero, the youngest daughter who is the most fair. But when we say that the first and the last have a special place, we are tacitly stating that the intermediate child or children also have a special place, namely that of *not* being either first or last, that is, they are *not* special. This position, too, leads to its special psychology—an expectation of being mediocre, of being overlooked, a feeling of inferiority and envy on the one hand, or of unusual freedom to be themselves on the other. Because they do not matter so much to the parents, their actions are not under such close scrutiny. In spite of the parents' care to be scrupulously impartial, they are freer from unconscious coercion.

Again, among the siblings, it is a matter of great significance whether there are many or few of them. The place each holds in the family also has its effects. To be one boy in a large family of girls, or one girl among many boys, naturally creates a special situation, both for the one who is single and for the group. And should one of the children die, perhaps as an infant, the psychology of those next in age is likely to be profoundly affected.

All these various family situations have archetypal backgrounds and should not be regarded as dependent only on the character of the particular persons concerned. This means that in seeking his freedom and in the whole process of becoming truly an individual, the young person will have to free himself not only from the members of his actual family but also from the unconscious bondage to them resulting from the projection of archetypal contents into the personal situation. It is only after this has been accomplished that any real psychological relationship can be established between members of the family or any real love be developed.

From the point of view of the child a final resolution of the problem dependent on *participation* with the family can only come through separation from the all-embracing mother-consciousness. The first step in this process is the discovery of himself as an independent "I," an *autos*, a happening that usually takes place about the third year. When he begins to call himself "I," experiencing his identity for the first time as separate from the persons and objects around him, he sees himself, as it were, from the inside, instead of only as one object among many. This is the birth of self-consciousness, and by it the first step has been taken in the lifelong task of discovering, on the psychological plane, what is "I" and what is "not-I."

At first glance it would not seem at all difficult to distinguish what is "I" and what is "not-I." We are all convinced not only that we know where our physical boundaries lie, but that we have the same insight as to our psychological boundaries. For instance, if there is anger in a situation, we are usually quite sure whose that anger is—ours or the other's—or if there is cheating, lack of integrity, we are in no uncertainty as to who is at fault. But are our observations any more reliable in this psychological realm than in regard to the details of an accident? Could it not be that we suffer in some degree from a psychological color blindness? These are sobering thoughts, and when we start to investigate our own reactions, taking into account the picture of them that the unconscious presents, we are likely to be in for some rather unpleasant surprises. For the problem of differentiating the "I" from the "not-I" on the psychological plane is far more difficult of solution than one would suppose at first glance. It will be accomplished only when the individual has succeeded in becoming whole, when all that truly belongs within him has been found and accepted as his own, and what does *not* belong legitimately to himself has been sorted out and relegated to its rightful place, either in the outer world, the physical world—including other people—or in the inner world, the metaphysical world, designated by the term "collective unconscious," and this is a lifelong task.

When we undergo a psychological analysis, we are continually amazed, and often chagrined, to discover how much of what we consider our own—our ideas, our attitudes to life, and the assumptions on which they rest, and especially our convictions, prejudices, and beliefs—is not really our own at all; and how much that should be recognized as our own we have disregarded or seen only in others, in the outer world, mirrored, as it were, in other people. This is perhaps the most disturbing discovery we make, quite early in a psychological analysis, when we first encounter the unconscious, and it is exceedingly upsetting. For much that we had thought of as our own, and to which we had given our conscious assent, proves to be illusory; while, on the other hand, we find that we have loved or hated in another person qualities of our own that are reflected in him, though he, of course, may also have his share of them.

When we undertake the task of sorting out what is "I" and what is "not-I" on this deeper level, we begin to realize how blind we have been, how amazingly unconscious, how naïve, how primitive! We have lived under a colossal error. As the ancient Coptic *Gospel of Truth* [8] puts it, we were deceived by Plane (Error) and, being lured by the illusory shapes she created, we left the Father, who had created us in our completeness, and went to live a partial life—one of error—with Plane, the illusion-maker. But when we come to knowledge (gnosis), i.e., to understanding, the error, the cause of envy and quarreling, is put away, and we return to our completeness which had remained with the Father. In other words, we become what we were intended to be from the beginning. In psychological terms we would say that our "wholeness" exists in latent and hidden form in the deepest layer of the unconscious, waiting till we have penetrated the darkness of error, or illusion, by conscious understanding, so that it can be revealed to us.

What steps, if any, can we take to release ourselves from this state of unconsciousness or, as the *Gospel of Truth* has it,

---

[8] *The Gospel of Truth: A Valentinian Meditation on the Gospel*, tr. from the Coptic with commentary by Kendrick Grobel, 17:20 ff. (pp. 46 ff.) ; 21:10-20 (pp. 70-72) ; 24:25 ff. (pp. 96-98) ; 25:2-3 (p. 98).

of error and illusion? If we observe ourselves and our reactions in everyday life, we begin to discover some of the places where parts of our own psyches are projected into other people. For instance, when we find ourselves the victims of an emotional reaction that is *out of proportion* to the situation, or where we have such a reaction in regard to some situation that is not really within the range of our concern but is strictly someone else's business, we should suspect that we are reacting to something of our own that we have not recognized as ours, something that is brought into view only in this external situation. Some situation reported in a newspaper, perhaps, or some imaginary happening in a play or novel, causes a personal emotion as if we were personally involved; or we find ourselves compelled to talk about another's faults, or his virtues, in season and out, or we gloat over the misfortunes of another—"It only serves him right"—or we make it our business to depreciate a colleague who has had an unexpected bit of good fortune—"Why did it come to him? He doesn't deserve it"—not realizing the envy concealed under the adverse judgment. Naturally, we do not like ourselves for doing these things or feeling in this way, but when it is a matter of the projection of unconscious contents, we may be unable to help it, for we are under an illusion. And to overcome illusions or attempt to do so by "prayer and fasting," or to repress them by an act of will, only pushes them down farther into the unconscious. These are errors produced by Plane, the illusion-producer. The *Gospel of Truth* speaks directly of envy and quarreling as the result of the error Plane produces. Yet, however much we may berate ourselves for our lack of charity and however much we may compensate our ill-feeling by a manner of kindness, still the ugly thoughts creep back when we are alone and off guard, or are confronted by what seems like evidence of the correctness of our suspicions. In cases like this, it is a very good rule to suspect that we are the victims of a psychological and unconscious projection. There is a tombstone near my childhood home in England which admonishes the passer-by: "The faults ye see in others take care to shun. If you'll only look at home there's enough to be done."

To become aware of our own unconscious contents challenges our identification with the mother-unconscious and produces a conflict not unlike the one the child faces when the time approaches for him to separate himself from his actual mother. The term "mother-unconscious" is used to denote the unknown matrix out of which life arises and in which we are all contained until we achieve separateness as individuals in our own right. For many children, especially those to whom the mother clings either consciously or unconsciously, it is a time of severe conflict. A patient of mine once asked me to see her little boy, who was having nightmares. He was a thin, nervous child of nine, and he told me that he had the same frightening dream over and over again. He would dream that he was in bed asleep and that he suddenly woke up to find a dark, uncanny figure standing at the head of the bed. Sometimes the figure just stood there, but sometimes it tried to drag the boy out of bed, and he awoke screaming in terror. Now the child was nine, prepubertal, and he was closely attached to his mother. So I asked him what he wanted to do when he was grown up, and we talked about how he would need to learn all sorts of things to get ready to be—I forget exactly what— an engineer, I think. And I pointed out that perhaps this man of the dream was not so dangerous after all; the figure might be a picture of himself, as it were, grown up, the man he was intended to be, who was coming to call him to take the first steps towards the achievement of his goal. Now, of course, I did not talk to him in quite these terms, and indeed he did much of the talking—the idea emerged from our conversation. The interesting thing is that the boy began to take more interest in his schoolwork and to show much greater independence at home. In short, he was started on that long journey by which in time he would become a man. The bad dreams stopped, for he was taking up his own responsibility and no longer needed a push from the unconscious.

To a child, the "man he is to become" seems like a threatening figure because the necessary development will mean the loss of childhood. Similar anxiety can be aroused in an adult by the premonition of a change that will inevitably demand the giving up of some adaptation that is familiar and seems desirable. This is a very common cause of neurosis in adults, and it is also one cause of the fear of death in the very ill or in the aged. But when we understand what this threatening figure that looms over us is, its uncanny and sinister menace is dissolved, and with our eyes open, we can face the conflict a radical change inevitably brings with it and so can summon some will, some inner determination to meet and accept our fate, no matter what. In Kazantzakis' novel *The Last Temptation of Christ*, Jesus is portrayed as constantly followed by a ghostly presence that represents his fate and causes him the greatest distress and anxiety until the time comes when he sees his fate clearly before him; then he learns to accept this figure and follow it, instead of being pursued by it. The same theme is developed in T. S. Eliot's play *The Family Reunion*, where Harry, the hero, is pursued by the Erinyes until he allows himself to become conscious of his own shadow, after which the roles are reversed. He follows the Fates and is no longer hounded by them.

In a similar way, if we will allow ourselves to become conscious of those things that really are our own, but that till now have manifested themselves only in projections, we too will be released from the sense of being forced, hounded, by something we cannot get hold of, something that may indeed seem like a ghost. In dreams and nightmares such an unconscious factor frequently appears as a ghost, for it represents a nonmaterial reality.

So far we have spoken of elements that really belong to the "I" being encountered as if in the "not-I." But when the "I" is not clearly differentiated from the "not-I," another source of "error" is at work; factors that do not belong to the "I" are claimed as mine, and the necessity arises to make a separation between what is mine and what is not. For instance, a child who has discovered himself as "I" usually claims possession of all the toys at hand, regardless of the rights of other children. An infant is not blamed for this, but a slightly larger child has to learn to make a distinction, and to recognize that others, too, have rights. In more subtle ways adults make similar claims, both consciously and, still more, unconsciously, because of identifications that enlarge the personality illegitimately. It may take a considerable increase in consciousness before we are able to make a valid distinction between "I" and "not-I," between *meum* and *tuum*.

For instance, most people identify themselves with their family. "My family is a superior one; its members are successful professionally, and so forth; therefore *I* am a superior person." "*We* came over on the 'Mayflower.' " Or perhaps the family lived on the wrong side of the railroad tracks and the children belonged to a lower social circle than their schoolmates or were members of a minority group. In each of these cases the child starts out in life with a bias of superiority or of inferiority; he expects either to be accepted, looked up to, and admired, or to experience the reverse. The reaction in the child may be one of acceptance of the situation or of resistance to it. For instance, the child of a wealthy family may feel inferior because he can never do or make anything that is as good as money can buy; or he may become a little snob, feeling himself to be superior to all the other children who in his view are only "common people"; while a child from a discriminated-against group may take the attitude of "I'll show them I am as good as they are," consequently becoming so hard and brash that he cannot be touched in any way, or he may be like Uriah Heep, cultivating an ingratiating manner calculated to avert the anticipated snub or the undeserved hostility.

Needless to say, children who start out in life with either complex are going to make very biased judgments about the people and the situations they meet in life. The boy who expects his boss to be a father to him, whether an indulgent or a tyrannical one, will encounter many difficulties that could have been avoided if he had been more conscious of himself. If he happens to be in a job where the boss fancies himself in the role of a father, such a boy will be favored, and the other employees will naturally resent it. Or if the boy has a chip on his shoulder, feeling certain he will be ignored or depreciated, he will probably so act as to bring on himself the very attitude he fears. For these things are reciprocal. One who cringes invites kicks; one who bullies attracts the weaklings; one who is really kind usually meets with friendliness. And so we bring our fate upon ourselves by our unconscious attitudes. In a sense, we can be said to create our own fate. For, as I have often pointed out, our outer fate is the reciprocal of the state of our inner being. Therefore it is no good to kick against one's fate—the only way to change it is to change oneself, through becoming more conscious of oneself, enlarging the scope of one's "I" to include the contents of the personal unconscious, separating oneself both from the "not-I" of the outer world and from the "not-I" of the inner world of the collective unconscious. In this way one clears up the entanglement with unconscious complexes and makes it possible to live in an environment that is "straight," not disturbed or distorted by the reflections and refractions of the glass wall of a too limited *Umwelt*.

The first step towards developing a larger and more satisfactory *Umwelt* requires an understanding of one's relation to one's mother and father and the other members of one's family. For it is in the family that the foundations are laid for the development of friendships in adult life. Identification, however, can be negative rather than positive, and in this case the interfamily relationships may sow the seeds of jealousy, rivalry, and hostility that will depend not on the new life situation but on the family complex that has biased the individual in his reactions to other people. And it is here too that the patterns for marriage and the management of one's home are laid down. Not without reason has it been said that the sins of the fathers descend to the sons. But fortunately the achievements of the fathers in the development of true maturity also descend to the children, a heritage of the greatest value.

For the characteristics of the relations developed within the family are carried over into the world beyond the family, as the commentary on the ancient Chinese "Book of Changes," the *I Ching*, points out: "The family is society in embryo; it is the native soil on which performance of moral duty is made easy through natural affection, so that within a small circle a basis of moral practice is created, and this is later widened to include human relationships in general." [9]

Unfortunately, not every family is as wholesome and as well organized as the ideal family depicted in the *I Ching*, and the bad influences encountered in a disturbed family are carried over into later life situations just as inevitably as the good ones described in the Chinese text. And when a child goes to school and later into life beyond the family circle, the patterns of behavior experienced in the family will influence the relationships he forms as an adult, not only in his conscious attitudes but unconsciously as well. If the family relations were founded on mutual trust, on affection and respect, he will create correspondingly good relations in his turn. But if, in his home, egotism, selfishness, hostility, and ungoverned passions ruled, the son or daughter will reproduce these bad things when he makes his own home. For when the son (or daughter) has not freed himself from the family, everyone he meets will seem like mother, father, brother, or sister—or at least he will react to people in the same way. On the other hand, people may be resented, feared, or ignored because they

[9] *I Ching* (Wilhelm and Baynes edn.), No. 37, p. 144.

62

do not fit these patterns. Reactions of this sort may be partly conscious, or there may be an entirely unconscious bias that profoundly influences the choice of friends and especially of the marriage partner. The man who is still quite unaware of himself will seek someone like the mother; the woman will choose a man for his fatherly manner—whether the parent was loved or hated. If there was a loving relationship to the parent, the marriage is likely to be satisfactory, at least until the individual begins to grow up, at which time it will become too narrow and constraining. But if the relation to the parent has been bad, the marriage will probably develop all the bad traits of the home all over again.

For an individual who has not become conscious of himself as a separate person but is still enclosed in the father-mother world has no ability to see others as they really *are*. His *Umwelt* contains only mothers, fathers, and siblings. In such a case a man will see all women as comfortable laps to sit in or as female governesses to be dreaded and avoided; while a woman may see all men as nothing but potential fathers. And when the object, the woman in the first case and the man in the second, clearly does not fit the assigned role or refuses to play that role, then she, or he, either is resented or simply fades out of the picture so far as the one enclosed in his *Umwelt* is concerned, leaving behind an unsatisfied hunger and possibly resentment or anger at the frustration unwittingly caused by the reality of the other person.

These are some of the effects of remaining unconscious— living psychologically within the father-mother world, that Jung [10] compared to the circle enclosed by the great world snake, who bites his own tail—the uroboros. This snake really represents the collective unconscious, the abyss or chaos in which all life begins. It is a world where everything merges into everything else, in which the child enclosed in the family

[10] *Aion*, p. 259; *Mysterium Coniunctionis*, p. 504 and *passim*. See also Neumann, *The Great Mother*, p. 18.

circle floats. This is, as it were, an enlargement of the idea of the *Umwelt*. Looked at from our own personal point of view, it seems as if *we* are the only "I," the master of our own little world, the center of that world; but looked at from another point of view, we are only minute animalcules swimming in the waters of the limitless ocean of the unconscious, not even born as yet onto the land of conscious reality.

But when at puberty the instincts seeking for independence and mating begin to stir, the young person starts to reach out, striving to get beyond the constrictions of the magic circle, because it no longer satisfies him as it used to do. This is the theme of all those legends that tell of the heroic task that awaits the young man. In somewhat different guise the girl must also fulfill her life task. The man must do battle—be it the slaying of the dragon, the search for the treasure hard to attain, or the rescue of the distressed damsel (that is, the anima). The forms are many, but the meaning is similar in all cases. The young man must win his spurs and find his *own* treasure; and the girl must submit to her feminine role as mother and nurturer of the coming generation.

The accomplishment of the heroic deed in which the dragon is finally overcome and slain is prepared for by a period of struggle in which many lesser fights have to be undertaken before the youth is ready to engage in the decisive battle. Unfortunately many people remain permanently in this stage. They struggle to be free, to grasp the advantages of freedom, but they lack the true heroic quality that is willing to put everything into the effort that is needed. Too often they want the best of both worlds and are unwilling to commit themselves to either. These are the ones that the analytical psychologist Erich Neumann has called the "strugglers." [11] They are the people who are always in rebellion against all restraint, moral or emotional, and against the old order, as

[11] *The Origins and History of Consciousness*, pp. 88, 96; and *The Great Mother*, p. 66.

well. But they are neither strong enough nor disciplined enough to undertake constructive reform. They still expect that the fathers whom they openly flout can and should change the order of the world to suit them. Or they continue to long for a mother's loving care but resent the form in which it is offered and refuse to make the response it demands. They are the malcontents, the lawbreakers, those who demand that society shall give them what they want.

Another common effect of this psychological situation is shown in the sexual adjustment the young person makes. In his struggle for independence, friendships or at least alliances are made with others of the same sex. These comradeships are very valuable in so far as they strengthen the masculine principle in the youth and correspondingly the feminine principle in girls. Such friendships frequently take on a sexual form, which may have a very positive value if real comradeship, a genuine friendship, is established. Then the sexual element is likely to be outgrown when its purpose has been fulfilled, leaving a friendship and understanding that may endure for a lifetime. From what I have seen of these homosexual relations, I am inclined to think that this is a more likely outcome with girls than with boys. It is more common for boys to persist in a homosexual phase, once it has been established on a physical basis, than it is for girls. This may be because in his relationship with his friend a boy finds an experience of eros—of love and relationship—that belongs with the feminine principle to which his masculinity gives him no access. The girl in contrast can develop a relation to this side of life directly through her own inherent femininity, so that when the block to her emotional development has been overcome through her love for her friend she can pass on to heterosexual friendships. But when a boy has remained immature on the emotional plane and has also failed to develop his own masculinity, he may indulge his growing sexual impulses in casual and promiscuous contacts that have no value

65

for the development of relatedness—the true eros. These are merely "monkey-play" that dissipates the natural instinctive libido whose purpose is to supply the motive power for the great enterprise of slaying the dragon and to enable the boy to make good his escape from the mother-father world, the enclosing world of the uroboros, which deadens all initiative and frustrates the development of consciousness. This sort of thing is much less common with girls, where promiscuous homosexual relations are relatively rare for two reasons, first, because sexuality without reproduction is so much less satisfying to her biologically than to the man, and second, because promiscuity inevitably precludes a personal relationship, an element that is very important to her because it is a part of the feminine principle.

Participation mystique plays a major part in family relationships and in the psychological development of the adult. It is an exceedingly unconscious state in which the "I" is identified with the "not-I" both within and without; and while it is characteristic of primitive man, infants, and the young among ourselves, it is by no means outgrown by large numbers of people, even though they may have reached adult years and made good in the world. For the cost of acquiring consciousness, in the sense in which it has been defined here, is very great, and not many people are willing to pay the price. In the following chapters we will consider the problems that have to be faced and the steps that must be taken if a person is to outgrow his limited *Umwelt* and become really a Self-conscious individual.

66

IV

PROJECTIONS TO PERSONS

OF THE SAME SEX:

THE SHADOW

UP TO THIS POINT we have been considering the way in which an individual whose consciousness is still very young and immature views the world. At first, a human being, like one of the lower animals, sees and is impressed only by objects and situations that directly affect himself. He is responsive only as his efferent or afferent capabilities are stimulated. Consequently his experience of the world is extremely limited, and his image of it is distorted for two reasons: first, because he excludes from consideration all those aspects that do *not* correspond directly to his own need, as he cannot help doing, since only those things that correspond to his need exist for him; and, second, because he expects a response valuable to himself in places and situations where it is not available. For the archetypal pattern within him leads to a definite expectation: an expectation of something favorable to him or the reverse. For instance, if an individual, upon being confronted with some danger or difficulty, is thrown into a panic instead of being able to form a just estimate of the extent of the threat, his unadapted or neurotic reaction is due to the activation of an archetypal situation. To him a molehill appears as big as a mountain, a three-foot drop seems to be a dangerous precipice, and so on. These are instances of the projection of archetypal situations into the external world. When the expectation is a positive one it may produce a similar distortion of reality. For instance, an infant will suck any rounded protuberance on his toy, expecting it to be a nipple, and he is frustrated and angry when no milk is forthcoming. In a similar way an adult may approach another human being with the expectation of being fed emotionally and may be correspondingly disappointed and even resentful when he finds that instead of bread he has been given a stone. That is, the archetypal image of mother has been projected into the situation and has been frustrated.

For, while each of us ventures forth into the great world beyond the family circle equipped with the potentiality of an individual character or personality, the environment in which our first steps toward consciousness have been taken has already impressed itself deeply on our psyche and conditions our reactions.

After a child has made the first important discovery that it is an "I," the sense of "I-ness," the center of consciousness, gradually shifts [1] from its elementary beginning as *autos* based on the instincts and their somatic correlates to the *ego*, the center of the conscious personality, whose development forms the focus of the life-energy, usually for at least the first half of the life-span and frequently for a much larger part.

The ego, in the sense in which the word is used in analytical psychology, represents the center of consciousness of the adult personality, the focal point of all we have known or experienced in life that has remained conscious to us. This focus of consciousness gradually becomes organized from its first nebu-

[1] For a further discussion, see Harding, *Psychic Energy*, pp. 23-24.

lous beginnings till at adolescence a recognizable and relatively stable personality emerges. The fluidity and plasticity characteristic of the child's psyche is replaced by a definite and structured conscious character, having at its disposal a certain amount of libido—psychic energy—that constitutes the will.

In the process of striving for a unified personality, however, the individual necessarily becomes aware of contradictory and disparate elements within himself. In order that a more or less consistent ego may be formed, the incompatible elements must be banished from conscious consideration; they must be denied, for, as Jung points out, the ego develops through having to make choices, that is, through inner conflict. But as the incompatible elements do not cease to exist when they are ignored, they are repressed by a deliberate act into the unconscious regions of the individual's psyche.

This whole process is very important for the maturing of the individual. By it he develops an ego-will with the ability to apply himself to a task even though this may be uncongenial; he learns to pursue a consciously chosen and accepted aim, a long-term project, regardless of the claims of the instinctive desires that would put present pleasure before future advantage.

The development of a consistent and disciplined ego may be said to be one of the chief criteria for a satisfactory life during the early and middle periods. But in the second half of life a new factor begins to be effective in the psyche and the center of consciousness then gradually shifts to a nonpersonal value within the psyche that takes precedence over the ego. It is this that Jung has called the Self. According to his definition the Self is the center of the total personality, including the relevant elements of the collective unconscious as well as those of consciousness.

The Self usually begins to be formed or begins to be apparent in an individual in later life. Actually, it is not correct to say that it is formed. It is present from the beginning, latent in the unconscious, or so it seems. Since we are considering very difficult and unknown aspects of human psychology, we cannot make such dogmatic statements as "the Self is formed." It may be that the Self is *found*, or recognized—the Self being equivalent to that element of the human being to which the *Gospel of Truth* refers when it speaks of our completeness as remaining in the Father.[2] It is as if, though we were formed originally as we "ought" to be, the Self we "ought" to be is not made manifest to us and is not brought into consciousness or into the reality of the individual human being except by the experiences of psychological development that can come about through our life on this earth.

When the child says "I," it begins for the first time to see itself as if from the inside—it recognizes its own subjectivity of which it had not been aware before. Our experience of *ourselves* is utterly different from our experience or knowledge of another. We *cannot* know how life is, seems, feels, to another, in spite of the fact that at times it seems to us that we do feel things from the point of view of someone else. We say, for instance, that we see eye to eye with another, only to find out later that this has been an illusion, for the other has had all sorts of ideas and associations connected with the subject under discussion or the happening we have been experiencing together—ideas and associations that we have not shared at all. When an individual falls in love, he is convinced that the thoughts and feelings of the loved one are completely known, even identical with his own. He and she seem to be "soul mates," known to each other as though they were identical twins. But this, too, is an illusion. Nonetheless it is held as an ideal of love to "do unto others as ye would that they should do unto you," a command based on the principle of identification that by no means always produces the expected result. For individuals are exceedingly different, and what

[2] *The Gospel of Truth,* 21: 9 (p. 70). Cf. 21: 18-25.

seems desirable to one may be quite the reverse to another. We *cannot* know how life is to another person; we are, every one of us, isolated in ourselves, "islands," forever alone. We may shrink from this realization, or we may glory in it, feeling ourselves to be different, stronger, more important than the others, who seem to us to be like mere automata. And so our "I" enlarges itself illegitimately.

Things that belong to *me*, that are *mine*, share something of myself; they are bigger, better, more important than similar possessions of other people, and indeed they may even seem sacred, taboo. One sometimes sees this attitude demonstrated in an amusing way. I remember seeing two boys playing together. When one of them picked up the bat belonging to the other, the owner snatched it away angrily, and proceeded to wipe the handle with his sweater sleeve, as if to wipe off some contamination from the other's touch. There was no such reaction about the things they owned in common. But the boy evidently felt the bat to be "his" in a particular way, so that it seemed as if his ego had been abused by the other's act. Certain possessions—particular books, a particular chair —must not be usurped by another. They are sacrosanct, that is, they are extensions of myself. My pen, my pipe, my car, my sword, my family are not like other people's; they are special with a specialness that is violated only at the risk either of arousing my ire or of causing me the most acute distress, as though something in myself had been attacked. This is the reason for either burying or burning the personal possessions of a dead man at his funeral. In ancient times this custom even went so far as to include the domestic animals and the wife or wives of the deceased. They were his possessions, and no one else might own them; their spirits must accompany him to the next world because they contained something of his spirit, and without them he would be diminished, a partial spirit only.

Earlier we considered this, as well as the identification of

the ego with the family which produces a fictitious enlargement of the "I," by giving a sense of superiority or its opposite, so that in the first case the individual is aggrandized,
in the second reduced or depleted, since identification can in-
flate the ego with either positive or negative elements. The
sense of superiority and the egotism that characterize some
people may stem in large measure from family identification,
as in other circumstances a corresponding sense of inferiority
and impotence may arise from a similar background.

Here the illusion of the individual in relation to himself
and to the outer world depends on his still unresolved identification with his family and the consequent projections he
makes to others. But there is another source of similar illusions that is just as important but is harder to recognize because its source is within the individual's own psyche. Here
the word "psyche" is used to denote the total personality, of
which part is conscious and a much larger part unconscious.
Such a term, of course, cannot be precisely defined or delim-
ited, but it is a useful concept which we really need in talking
about the development of consciousness.

When the "I," the *autos*, has been born, the child at first
expresses himself with all his needs, reactions, and desires
untrammeled by any thought of appropriateness or of consequences. But immediately he is subjected to a process of training—a training that has been imposed upon him before he
even had an "I" that could protest, a training whose object is
to teach him how to adapt to society, what is permissible or
not, what will produce love and acceptance and what will be
frowned upon or punished. At this very early stage in his development, a child begins to develop a *persona*, a mask of
good and adapted behavior. For instance, a mother says, "Now
you must be a good boy," meaning, "You must behave *like*
a good boy." For it is obvious that no one can become good
simply because he is told to do so; one's being is not to be
changed by admonition. When as children we had been

naughty, our nurse used to say, "Now you must sit on that chair until you say you are sorry." We were not in the least sorry and we knew it and refused to say we were. But the minutes stretched on interminably—we couldn't sit there all day, or so it seemed. So eventually we mumbled the required words and were released. But we knew we had lied, for we were not sorry at all. And so a child learns to repress, to thrust down into unconsciousness the unacceptable parts of his personality. As a result the personal part of the psyche becomes more or less clearly divided into three parts.[3] There is the "I," the ego, that represents what I call *myself;* then there is the *persona,* the mask that I wear to show to the world; and there is still another part that I know, or partly know, exists, but which I prefer to keep hidden because it is unacceptable to the world—this is called the *shadow,* and it is usually almost entirely forgotten—that is, it becomes unconscious to myself, although it may be quite obvious to others.

When the "I," the ego, comes into being and becomes the focus for consciousness, it is as if a light were lighted in the room of the psyche that had formerly been completely dark. As the light is small, it illuminates only a small part of the room. The rest is in shadow; its contents are invisible. But they are not nonexistent, and they may be perceived in projection.

The significance of the term projection as used in analytical psychology is not always understood correctly. The very word is misleading. In ordinary language, to project something means to throw it—this implies that the material projected is first known and possessed and is then discarded, thrown upon some external object. But in analytical psychology the term is used differently. True, when the concept of projection was first described, it was thought that the above definition would apply. Some trace of this idea still clings to the term as used by the Freudians, who are inclined to say

[3] See Diagram I.

that if you see negative qualities in another person, you are, so to say, unconsciously "paying him out" for some injury he has done, or you think he has done, to you. If you dream of injuring someone, it means that you have hate feelings towards that actual person, and if you dream that he injures you, it means that he is in some measure your actual enemy. However, if you take all the persons in the dream as parts of your own psyche, as Jung does, then such a dream would obviously have a very different meaning. It would refer to your attitude towards an unknown quality of *your own* that this individual represents in your dream. In other words, it is as if in your dream you have made use of this person's picture to enact a certain role, a role in your own inner drama, representing some factor of which you should be conscious, but of which you are unaware. So far, so good. But then the question must be asked, why did your dream choose this particular person to play this part? And here we encounter again the problem of the "I" and the "not-I," on a more subjective level. In actual life you probably feel that this person does possess the characteristics your dream emphasizes, and this may be so; but perhaps his negative quality is really slight, and you have to admit that the dream picture is definitely exaggerated. Or possibly, while the characteristics you object to are actually present, your reaction to them is stronger than the circumstances really warrant. When this is the case, whether you dream about this person or not, you must suspect that projection has entered into the situation: that his slight "evil" has served to act as a hook to catch something, perhaps not so slight, in yourself of which you were not aware. For the term projection, as used in analytical psychology, refers not to something that you have thrown on another but rather to that factor in yourself, of which you were entirely unconscious, that has been caught by something in the object and so has been made visible. Your psychic content becomes available to you because it has been mirrored in him.

When we have projected some unconscious element onto someone else, especially if it is a negative or unacceptable content, we always tend to try to deal with it *in* the other person. Those unacceptable contents that we have discarded in forming the ego personality have been repressed into the unconscious—into the personal unconscious—and, as they always have an emotional quality, an energy content, they act as if they were autonomous and so tend to be personified. For, as Jung points out, "Emotion is not an activity of the individual but something that happens to him." He continues, "Affects occur usually where the adaptation is weakest, and at the same time they reveal the reason for its weakness, namely a certain degree of inferiority and the existence of a lower level of personality." [4] Consequently these things are not recognized as our own shadow qualities but are projected to another person; we either blame him, criticize him, or revenge ourselves upon him for them. Or, if the material projected is not negative but positive, we admire him, love him, perhaps envy him, or possibly even hate him for having what we have not got.

But we cannot change anyone else; we can change only ourselves, and then usually only when the elements that are in need of reform have become conscious through their reflection in someone else. So long as they remain buried in the personal unconscious they are inaccessible to us and obviously cannot be altered. For the contents that have been discarded in forming the conscious ego personality are always repressed into the personal unconscious, and as they have an emotional quality and an energy content (witness our excitement over them when they are reflected in our neighbor) they act as if they were autonomous; they seem to have a personality of their own, a minor sort of personality. These things may become obvious to us when we have a discussion with ourselves, a conflict of attitudes or of duty. Then one voice within us says one thing, another answers it with objections, and so on. But more

[4] *Aion*, p. 9.

often we become aware of these contradictory things within us only when they are projected onto someone else, reflected in him as though in a mirror. It is as useless to try to deal with these shadow qualities in the projection as it would be to try to rub a smut off our nose by rubbing the image of the nose we see in the mirror.

As these things really belong to the unconscious part of the personality, they act as if they formed another person within us. This is what Jung calls the shadow. When this figure appears in dreams, as it frequently does, it will be of the same sex as the dreamer, since it really represents part of his personality. But because it is not recognized as belonging to himself it will be projected onto someone in the outer world. For we are blind to the unacceptable things in ourselves, and so they creep out into the external situation and are frequently focused on some particular individual in the environment. It is as if this person mirrors what lies behind our conscious "I." Or, at times, the projection of the shadow spreads out and contaminates our relation to many people.

The individual who carries the personification of my shadow will be of the same sex as myself, because the shadow is part of the personal psyche. A man's shadow is masculine and a woman's feminine. When it is projected to the outer world, it forms, as it were, a shadow personality that is likely to be encountered in some person in the environment who represents to the individual his own shadow qualities that he cannot see directly because they are unconscious to him. The carrier of these projections may even become his special enemy, perhaps a *bête noire*.

The repressed and instinctual elements that form the shadow originate in the personal experiences of the individual. Jung calls the part of the unconscious that contains them the personal unconscious.

Just as the conscious part of the psyche is focused in a center that we call "I" and that Jung discriminates as the *ego*, so the unconscious part of the personal psyche is focused and personified as a sort of *alter ego*, the shadow. We are all dimly aware of this alter ego residing somewhere inside us. It acts in us almost as if it were another being, an other self, that can carry on a conversation with us, taking part in a discussion or conflict when we are, as we say, of two minds about a problem, or it can initiate actions which we ourselves would not perform.

The shadow is quite close to us, almost in consciousness, and as it is part of the personality, it cannot be escaped but must always be somewhere in the immediate environment, either experienced as another, secondary self or projected to someone of the same sex close at hand. But the unconscious also contains elements and factors that have never been known to the individual—"archetypes," Jung called them— and that play an even more dominant part in his character than the repressed and forgotten ones that form the shadow. They are apparently universal, shared by all humanity, and for this reason Jung calls the part of the inner world from which they come the collective unconscious. Its contents are deeply unconscious and are frequently projected farther away than the forgotten factors that have once been conscious, often into distant lands. The archetype of the Wise Man, for example, is sometimes thought of as a remote or almost mythological figure living in inaccessible mountains. Contents which are beginning to stir but are in the still more remote depths of the unconscious may be projected even outside the world, and then we hear rumors of cataclysms in the sun, of strange rays which may some day impinge on the world, or even of flying saucers bearing visitants from outer space. But the shadow is part of the personality and only relatively unconscious—and we meet him everywhere.

If an individual is unaware of his shadow, being completely identified with his conscious personality, he will be entirely convinced of his own rectitude. The elements in his own nature which cannot be accommodated in this shining personality will be projected to someone in his immediate environment, a brother, son, friend, or, more often, a *bête noire,* the associate whom he particularly dislikes, whose faults he cannot avoid seeing and criticizing on every occasion, in season and out. And here we often see a very strange effect of unconsciousness. For the one on whom the shadow has fallen is unavoidably influenced in an unconscious way by the projection, and if the two people are closely connected, the recipient of the projection may be constrained to live the negative role projected upon him. We see this sometimes in a group where there is someone who is "completely right," who never, never raises his voice, never says an unkind thing about anybody. He seems to have no shadow, no natural human weakness. But then his shadow falls on the others in the group, and they are compelled to express his negative and all-too-human reactions. They find themselves making critical remarks that are really more incisive and destructive than would be warranted by their own feelings. For there is something peculiarly exasperating about someone who has no shadow. We find ourselves obliged to disagree with him whether we want to or not.

The compulsion to live another's shadow is most apt to occur within a family relationship, where the interaction of the members of the group is so profoundly influenced by unconscious factors. It can be the cause of neurosis or of delinquent behavior in the children of parents who have refused to accept the responsibility for their own shadows: the children have to live the shadow side.

The effects resulting from unconsciousness of the shadow are so numerous, so prevalent, and so far-reaching that I am at a loss where to begin to discuss them. In individual relationships projection of the shadow, or of parts of it, can produce misunderstandings, quarrels, endless bickerings. An attitude based on *unconscious* inferiorities may result in suspicion of everyone. For instance, a groceryman whom I once asked to review his bill immediately became defensive and even rude because he assumed that I was suspicious of him and was accusing him of shortchanging me, whereas the fact was that I thought he had shortchanged himself. But it took quite a bit of soothing talk to assure him of my good intentions. Unconscious inferiority may make us act in a domineering and demanding way in order to fend off the suspected or anticipated depreciation. Or we may project to others virtues they do not possess as a compensation for our own feelings of inferiority: this occurs when we are not living up to our real potential.

If we do not live up to our own potential, the positive qualities will be repressed into the shadow, and we will have what I have sometimes called a bright shadow instead of a dark one. When we project this bright shadow onto someone else, the person who carries the projection will seem to us to be "always right," able to do easily and well things that are difficult for us, and so on. We burden him with our expectations of his abilities instead of acquiring for ourselves the possibilities of achievement which are potentially present in us. A person who is content to take an inferior position, who prefers to have an easy job rather than to buckle down and develop himself and his work, and who then admires, and overadmires, someone else who does things well has projected his bright shadow onto his neighbor.

But the effects of unconsciousness of the shadow do not stop at the level of individual relationships. They spread out and take in whole groups of people, giving rise to class discrimination of all sorts. In the tragic relationship between Jews and Gentiles throughout the centuries, we can trace the projection of the shadow, not only in its personal form, but also in its archetypal aspect, which we shall consider in a later chapter. The Jew who suspects anti-Semitism where it does not exist and the Gentile who denies it in himself, and sees the unadapted behavior of the Jew as the sole cause of the difficulty between Gentile and Jew, are both unaware of the part their own personal shadows are playing in the situation. For in most cases there is a personal aspect in addition to the collective one, and when the personal shadow has been made conscious and has been accepted by both parties, the situation is relieved to an almost unbelievable degree. The two can then accept with tolerance their differences, whether these are personal or racial. But as long as the personal shadow is unconscious, the centuries-old wound will smart at the least touch, while the personal shadow will hide behind the collective problem. In this way the collective problem may be used to mask the personal one, and the individual will remain unconscious of his own shadow.

And so it becomes evident that the shadow poses a moral problem, and that to become conscious of it requires a moral effort. How can we, without undertaking a psychological analysis, become aware of our shadow? We have already noted that where we are unduly concerned with another person's shortcomings we should suspect a psychological involvement on our own part, and that we are projecting some part of our own unacceptable qualities to that person. Typical examples are the overvirtuous lady who concerns herself with "fallen girls" or the man who goes around with a chip on his shoulder, suspecting everyone else of lacking that particular virtue on which he prides himself.

There is another area in which we can observe the working of the shadow. When, for instance, we become aware that we have not produced the effect we intended, it may be that the shadow spoke louder than the ego. Perhaps, in talking to an acquaintance, we meant to be kind or sympathetic, only to find that he was hurt or offended by what we said, and still more by the way in which we said it, although we had thought our manner irreproachable. "It isn't what you said. It's the *way* you said it that hurt me so," is the complaint the shadow evokes. Now the *way* we said it comes from the unconscious.

We intend to say something that is rather neutral or pleasant, and we say it in such a way, or with such an intonation, that it produces the opposite effect from the one we intended. That is, our unconscious has spoken through us. This is the shadow. When someone complains, "It's the way you said it," look out for the shadow! You were not completely sincere in what you said—consciously you were sincere, but unconsciously someone else in you was contradicting what you said.

The shadow, too, takes a part in situations where we blunder over some task we would expect to be able to perform correctly. Here the one who acts, who does, is not the conscious ego but the shadow. We exclaim with considerable irritation, "How silly of me! Why, I *never* do that!" And the strange thing is we can go on exclaiming, "I never do that!" without ever stopping to take note of the frequency of these supposed exceptions to the invariable rule of our correct behavior. If we did pause to take stock, we would be in for a very unpleasant surprise and would probably suffer a severe shock to our self-esteem. But usually we prefer not to become conscious of these shadow contents, and then they fall upon someone in the environment where they become glaringly evident. This is a case of a projected shadow.

But what is the value of becoming aware of the shadow? Why should we take steps to unearth all this unpleasant stuff? What function does the shadow perform in the psyche? Since the shadow consists of all the elements of the natural personality that have been discarded and overcome as a result of training and in accordance with the demands of society, if we repress them, the conscious personality is obviously diminished. We have doubtless seen them at times and have prayed that we be not led into evil, but may walk in the good. But still the shadow persists, which is just as well, for if we could actually dispose of our shadow in this way, there would be nothing left but a well-disciplined ego, a robot, with its prescribed adaptation via the persona, and we would be able to function only in accordance with the rules and expectations of society.

But man is a natural living being, and the life spirit in him is maimed by such rigid restrictions if it is not entirely broken. It is essential for life that at some point the laws of society must be broken; the living spirit insists on transgressing the law. And here is the beginning of consciousness. So long as consciousness is nonexistent, to follow the natural way produces no conflict. An infant wets his diaper without any conflict, until the law of the nursery begins to be impressed on him, and even then for a long while this natural act causes no conflict or sense of guilt. It is only when a dawning awareness arises that the child feels fear or shame when scolded, and not until a good deal later does he begin to develop any inner sense of responsibility for self-control. I remember the child of a friend of mine, who was something under two. He would sit on the floor playing with his toys. One day he discovered that in the kitchen there was a whole row of little taps on the gas stove that were just within reach. Although he had been scolded a number of times for turning on the little taps, he could not refrain from playing with them. Finally his mother, feeling she must do something about this, slapped the child's hands and said, "No, no!" The child sat down on the floor once more with his toys and was quiet for a while. Suddenly a gleam came into his eyes, and he began to scramble up, but he paused and, touching the hand that had been slapped, exclaimed, "Oh, no! Oh, my, no! No, no, no!"

At some point in the child's life there is likely to be a more or less deliberate breach of the law, a transgression, perhaps committed without conscious intent, which is followed by a spontaneous sense of guilt. The child either runs to his mother and confesses (and the value of the happening may so easily be destroyed by her attitude), *or*, as with Adam and Eve, the child is obliged to take upon himself the guilt of his act, and so makes a most important step towards greater self-consciousness. This explains, perhaps, some part of the mystery of the presence of evil in God's world. For consciousness is not possible without freedom, and freedom involves the ability to deviate. But how do we know whether we are free to deviate if we always follow the law? And so we come back to the necessity of keeping the shadow in view, for to lose our shadow is a serious psychological mishap. As a result of the loss of the shadow, we lose at the same time our substance, our reality, and consequently are unable to make any impression on real objects which have substance.

We sometimes encounter this condition in everyday life. It is not unusual. Someone who has received praise for an achievement becomes inflated and temporarily loses his balance. He sees only the positive side of the experience; he thinks that all difficulties are going to melt away and that success will attend his every effort. He talks a little too much about his achievement, boasting more or less discreetly about it and about the triumphs that will follow. If he does not meet with immediate credence, he begins to exaggerate and to insist that "everything's coming my way." His friends become bored and indifferent and he finds himself ignored or isolated. He has lost his shadow and can no longer make any impression as a man of substance.

Even when the individual does not give himself away as obviously as this, his dreams may show what the situation is. In an actual case, a woman had had a success which she felt made everything "simply perfect," to use her own words; it was the fulfillment of all her hopes. Then she dreamed that she was in a large brilliantly lighted cave, a place of unalloyed joy and satisfaction. In the dream she was superbly happy, even exultant. But, as she looked around her, she became aware that she cast no shadow. At first this seemed merely strange to her, though perhaps a little uncanny, but she gradually became more and more worried at the unusual phenomenon and awakened in a state of great anxiety.

There is, too, a medieval legend of a man to whom the devil came and offered great wealth and his heart's desire. The man was much intrigued by the offer but, being of a cautious disposition, asked what price the devil wanted for his great gifts. The devil answered, "A mere nothing, something of no weight or substance, which can surely be of no value to you." "What can that be?" asked the man, and was told, "Only your shadow." Not realizing at all what he was giving up, the man agreed. He received the gift of wealth and went his way— minus his shadow. But then his troubles started, because nothing he did held any reality or substance, and when people began to notice that he cast no shadow they said he could not be a human being at all but must be a spirit having an evil intent, and they fled from him in fear. At last the man could stand his isolation no longer and went to look for the devil to demand his shadow back again. But the devil could not be found, for he cast the man's shadow round him like a cloak and became invisible. He always stood just in the man's shadow.

This legend, fantastic as it is, yet teaches a psychological truth. For if one does give away one's shadow in order to gain wealth or any other desirable good, that is, if one represses the shadow, allowing it to fall into the underworld of the unconscious, all the devilish evil of the nether darkness can find its way into one's life without arousing awareness or suspicion in oneself, though to others the diabolical effect one produces may be exceedingly obvious.

Diagram III shows that behind the archetypes of persons there exist in the unconscious more abstract "principles," the patterns or archetypes of good and evil, as well as of the other opposites—chaos and order, light and dark, and so on. The archetype of Evil itself (we may call it the devil, if we prefer) lies deep in the unconscious. If the shadow is not recognized, not taken care of, this evil can come through into the personal unconscious where it will contaminate the shadow.

Then the shadow, instead of being merely the repository of the natural impulses and reactions that are unacceptable to society, becomes a vehicle for all the evil from the unconscious that streams through it. When this evil is projected to someone in the environment, he seems to be the devil incarnate, and when the individual's ego becomes identified with such a shadow, he will himself embody this factor and become, as it were, a devil. This is the condition that has given rise to the idea of possession by the devil.

This threat is such a menace to the conscious personality that we go to all sorts of lengths to prevent ourselves from becoming aware of our own shadow, perhaps because we sense that this terrible evil lies latent in the background. We do not realize that our best defense against such an invasion is to accept what belongs to our own individuality, so developing a strong conscious attitude to set against the forces of the unconscious. Instead, we ignore the shadow within us, leaving the door open for a further invasion.

The successful businessman, for instance, who is known as a generous philanthropist may permit the most unscrupulous practices in his business, provided he does not have to become too closely aware of them. His subordinates can and indeed are expected to oppress the helpless or unfortunate, but *his* name must be kept out of the deal by which he enriches himself at their expense. There is a story about one of the elders of a Presbyterian church who was known as a very hard man. He indulged in every sort of sharp practice, always keeping just inside the law, and he certainly did not mind foreclosing mortgages on the widow and the orphan. As he got older and became aware that his life was coming to an end, he began to bethink himself about the future. It so happened that the church was planning to build a new vestry, and a request for contributions was made. The elder, to everyone's surprise, gave so generously to the fund that his gift paid for the whole of the new building. The other elders gave a supper to thank him for his generosity. One of his brother elders made a speech of thanks, at the end of which he said, "And now I would like to propose that we call the vestry 'Brother Mac-Farlane's Vestry,' or, better still, let's call it 'Brother Mac-Farlane's Fire Escape.' "

The woman who is, at least in her own eyes, all sweetness and light, generous and kind to everybody, may be a domestic tyrant in reality. The sweet, kind, affectionate mother, for instance, who ties her son or daughter to her may gradually suck all the life out of the child. Actually, although we subscribe to the general demand that people shall conform to the expected standards and maintain a suitable persona, if we see no shadow, no hint that there exists anything besides the commendable exterior, we begin to feel uncomfortable. And the more unconscious the individual is of his shadow, the greater is the likelihood that his motives will be suspected, for either he is not as good as he appears to be and is hiding his weaknesses with diabolical cunning or else he is not quite natural. He may even seem a little uncanny, or at least seem not to belong to this wicked world. One of the bitterest complaints one hears against the close companion is that he is always right—right, that is, in his own eyes. "Righteous" is perhaps a more appropriate word.

To be always right means to be not quite human and therefore to be terribly exasperating to the housemate or companion. Although we have a convention that everyone *ought* to be pure white—as if this were a condition perfectly easy to achieve—as a matter of fact, we are suspicious of anyone who does not show some flaw. If an individual persists in such an attitude, his natural psyche is inevitably split into two parts, and he is in danger of serious neurosis or even of a psychotic breakdown. This situation was shown in the book, *The Three Faces of Eve*. The girl, Eve White, was living the entirely immaculate side, which was utterly empty, sterile, and stereotyped, while her shadow side, Eve Black, was going about having a good time, flirting with everybody, buying expensive clothes, and so on.

It is, indeed, very necessary to be aware of our shadow for we cannot get rid of a part of the psyche by repressing it any more than we çan get rid of a part of the body by ignoring its existence. If we could really see our own shadow, it would be clear to us that in the depths of our own hearts we are not entirely the exemplary citizens we have always liked to believe ourselves. This is a very disturbing realization, and for the sake of the solidarity of society many people consider it necessary not to allow themselves to indulge in such subversive thoughts. And as it takes a great deal of moral courage to confront the shadow, it is far better, or so society itself believes, for us to throw a little dust in our own eyes in order to maintain our self-respect and good form. The dissenting voice of conscience can usually be silenced by some general form of self-depreciation such as by saying, "Well, of course I am not perfect. Who is?" And the Church provides the General Confession, but it is so very general that particular sins can slip by unnoticed. We are reminded of the man at the weekly prayer meeting whose prayer went something like this: "O Lord, I confess my sins. I have greatly sinned. I am the greatest of sinners, O Lord. I have been mean in my business dealings, for I am a great sinner; I have been angry without cause, for I am a great sinner," and much more to the same effect. Of course, everyone was greatly edified, and the man himself could not conceal his smug expression. But when his neighbor began to pray, saying, "Yes, O Lord, what Brother X has just said is quite true; he is mean and cussed," Brother X sprang to his feet, shouting, "How dare you say such a thing about me? There isn't a word of truth in it! You— slanderer!"

For when we say, "We have all gone astray," we are in perfectly good company and no one has the right to point his finger at anyone else. We have not lost face. But if we accept our particular and very personal sin against society's code, we shall find ourselves threatened with exclusion from the group, for to commit one's own particular sin means separation from society. To accept all that we are means that we are individual, different from everyone else, while our place in the continuity of the social order is assured us only when we accommodate ourselves to the general pattern.

The following true story is very illuminating. It illustrates Jung's remark that the real sin is never confessed—a statement that naturally has its exceptions, as Jung was fully aware. There were two brothers, the elder of whom was always favored by the parents, especially by the mother, who made excuses for him when he was surpassed by his younger brother on practically every score. However, the two boys were good friends, and the elder never showed any jealousy of his more successful brother. It was not till he was in his forties that he began to be aware of a feeling of guilt in relation to his brother. The idea that he was in some inexplicable way guilty bothered him constantly. He found himself brooding on it, especially at night, without being able to think what could be at the back of this vague feeling. Eventually, however, he remembered that some years ago he had done a commission for his brother and had carelessly pocketed the proceeds. Because only a trivial sum was involved, he had forgotten all about the incident. He realized that his brother would probably have said, "Oh, forget it," but the thought of his involuntary dishonesty would not leave him. At last he felt compelled to go to his brother and make a clean breast of the incident. As he had expected, his brother treated the whole matter as perfectly unimportant, but the man was not relieved. This is hardly to be wondered at, because he had not confessed his real sin—his jealousy of his brother's success. He still cherished, unknown to himself, the childish illusion that as the eldest he had a right to a similar or even greater success, without ever exerting himself to achieve it. His humiliation at his own failure produced the unconscious sense that his brother owed him something, that he had cheated him out of his inheritance, his birthright, as Jacob had cheated Esau,[5] and *quite unconsciously* he had taken steps to settle the debt in token, as it were, without his brother's knowledge, by pocketing the money for the commission. If he had had to confess to his brother his jealousy and resentment, he would have been touched to the quick; his self-esteem would have been completely broken up. Had he admitted his jealousy to himself he could hardly have gone on in his old easy-going way, and, moreover, he would have had to admit to himself that he had frittered away a good part of his life. These things would have been too devastating. His unconsciousness must be protected at all costs. But of course, if he should undertake to be analyzed, the unconscious would not spare him: his dreams would confront him with the truth about himself! And so the Episcopal Church provides a General Confession for public use and, very wisely perhaps, reserves the rite of the confessional for special cases.

The panic and demoralization that most people experience when they are faced by the realization of their own shadow is evidence enough that the psychic mechanism of the shadow and its projection are a necessary defense against the terror of the unknown. To most people the social order is still the all-powerful organization ordained by God himself. To accept one's sins against the conventional code is tantamount to being cast out of society, as Adam and Eve were cast out of Eden into a wilderness where they had only their own resourcefulness to rely on. This is a terrifying experience. One who has dared it finds himself with the necessity of facing life on his own responsibility, entirely unaided by society, that ancient order which has learned through the countless experiences of mankind how the problems and dangers of life may be managed. How can the individual face that experience

[5] Gen. 25 and 27.

alone without the support of the group and at the same time face the hate and suspicion that are always incurred by one who goes contrary to the general rule?

This is the cost of taking up the shadow, and one might say, "Why take it up? Better let sleeping dogs lie." But if one does not take it up and instead continues to project its contents to others, one may find oneself excluded from fellowship because of the negative projections one makes to one's neighbors. The suspicions then rest in one's own heart. One is convinced of the wickedness of the neighbor and suspects him of all the ill will and meanness one refuses to acknowledge in oneself; consequently one feels excluded by the group as if *they* hated or envied one, and does not realize this is due to the evil which one has failed to recognize within oneself.

For the shadow is really and actually a part of the personality. As long as it remains unconscious, the human being is not whole and in consequence suffers the pain of disintegration. Individuals vary very much in their ability to stand such unwholeness. Some go through life oblivious of their one-sidedness, while others are more sensitive to the demands of the repressed factors within them. To these the need to deal with their repressions becomes imperative. Some develop this need because of neurotic symptoms or emotional difficulties, while the urge to become whole takes possession of others either because the life that is possible within the conventional code is too narrow for them or because the need for wholeness has become a moral task which they cannot avoid.

This can happen, for instance, when life presents us with a situation for which we do not feel adequate. If the new task demands a bigger man than we are, obviously other parts of the psyche beyond the conscious ego will have to be called on to fill out the personality. This was the case with the hero of Conrad's story, "The Secret Sharer," which gives a very interesting picture of the confrontation with the shadow and its effect. The story concerns a young man, who had served only as first officer of a schooner and who was called upon to take over the command of a ship whose captain had died. The ship was strange to him, and he felt that the officers and crew, who were quite unknown to him, were suspicious of him both because he was a newcomer and because he was young and untried. On his first night on board while the ship was still in harbor, he decided to take the first watch himself, ostensibly in order to get acquainted with the ship, but really to confront himself with his new task. In the darkness a stranger, a naked man, swam to the side of the ship, and the young captain took him aboard. The man explained that he was an officer from a ship anchored on the other side of the headland, and that during a storm, when the ship was in great danger, he had killed a seaman who had shirked his duty. Now "they" were pursuing him as a murderer. The captain lent him a sleeping suit of his own and talked with him in whispers. (Conrad goes on: "The shadowy, dark head, like mine, seemed to nod imperceptibly above the ghostly grey of the sleeping suit. It was, in the night, as though I had been faced by my own reflection in the depths of a sombre and immense mirror." Conrad wrote this before the idea of the shadow had been formulated as a psychological principle!) The young captain hid his strange visitor in his cabin while he put his ship and incidentally himself to the ultimate test. But in the moment of greatest danger he found himself enraged at the slowness of one of the men and the sullen expression of the others. The mate, who should have been the first to support him, lost his nerve and wailed, "She's ashore already." The captain realized that he too could commit murder, but he controlled himself. Then and only then the shadow man slipped back into the ocean from which he had so mysteriously come, and we are given to understand that the strange tension that had hung over the whole ship and her untried captain dissolved, and they sailed home with a fair breeze. This story is well worth study. Conrad's deep insight into the unknown side of the human being has led him to portray the shadow unerringly, not only in its manifestations, but also in its meaning. For this young man lacked the self-confidence that could come only from self-knowledge, not merely of his capacities, but also of the potential violence of his own nature, which could and nearly did impel him to kill a man who refused orders in the moment of stress. That kind of self-confidence can be gained only through the knowledge of oneself that the experience of life alone can give.[6]

This young man confronted himself and in so doing recognized his shadow. As Jung says, with a little self-criticism this can be done fairly easily so far as the personal part of the shadow is concerned. The man in the story even went a little farther than this, for he glimpsed that behind his weakness lurked the shadow of a greater evil, the possibility of murder. But, having taken up his personal shadow, he was able to make a human contact with his shipmates. Without that confrontation he would have remained isolated and suspect. In such a case the world recedes farther and farther until the individual becomes enclosed in an iron cage, like the man in one of Christian's visions in *The Pilgrim's Progress.*[7] For not until the shadow has been recognized and to some extent assimilated can we begin to form real relationships with others. Only then can we really communicate with each other and begin to build a serviceable bridge between the island that is our self and the island that represents another human being.

This, Jung says,[8] is the effect of recognizing the shadow in so far as its nature is personal. But the shadow is not only personal; it is also an archetype, as we saw in the legend of the man who gave his shadow to the devil. And in "The Heart

[6] Jerome S. Bruner, in *On Knowing: Essays for the Left Hand,* p. 48, gives a similar interpretation of "The Secret Sharer," but his book did not come to my attention until after the above had been written.
[7] John Bunyan, *The Pilgrim's Progress;* for psychological interpretation, see Harding, *Journey into Self,* p. 123.
[8] *Aion,* p. 10.

of Darkness," the companion story to "The Secret Sharer," Conrad portrays this deeper and more sinister aspect of the shadow. Here the shadow becomes the devil, and the natural instincts, the old Adam in man, are replaced by Evil itself— evil for its own sake. As Jung writes, "It is quite within the bounds of possibility for a man to recognize the relative evil of his own nature, but it is a rare and shattering experience for him to gaze into the face of absolute evil." [9] This is the experience that Conrad describes in "The Heart of Darkness," and the horror, the uncanny horror, that this description not only produced on the characters of the story, but also produces on the reader, gives evidence that we are here confronted with something that reaches beyond the personal realm into the depths of the collective unconscious. The human spirit of Kurtz had been replaced by an alien spirit. In modern terms we would say that he was insane; in earlier days his condition would have been considered to be due to possession by a devil; and indeed in his own eyes he was apparently quite innocent.

Conrad wrote this story at the end of the nineteenth century and placed its scene in "darkest Africa." Was it a premonition of happenings in Europe in the second quarter of the twentieth? A review by Judge Musmanno of a book dealing with the trial of Adolf Eichmann is entitled "Man with Unspotted Conscience." [10] This man who, by his own admission, had sent millions of human beings to their death, treating them as "valuable biological material," felt himself to be entirely innocent of evil. In his own eyes his actions were justified because "there were no voices from outside to arouse his conscience." He had accepted the Nazi ideology as having absolute validity, being incapable of wrongdoing. He had given his shadow to the devil and in return he received wealth and honor in the society of his choice, but he no longer possessed

[9] Ibid.
[10] Michael A. Musmanno, in the *New York Times Book Review*, May 19, 1963, p. 1, reviewing Hannah Arendt, *Eichmann in Jerusalem*.

any inner criterion of right and wrong. And like Kurtz in Conrad's tale he became possessed by an evil spirit and lost all human semblance.

For when a man loses touch with his personal shadow and identifies himself with an ideology that claims absolute validity, whether it be a political, a religious, or a national authority that imposes the claim, he lays himself open to invasion by "absolute" forces from the unconscious and loses his human limits; and, as Jung points out,[11] this means the loss of his individuality, his Self. "The individual," Jung writes, "is so unconscious that he altogether fails to see his own potentialities for decision. Instead he is constantly and anxiously looking around for external rules and regulations which can guide him in his perplexity." He continues: "The individual who wishes to have an answer to the problem of evil . . . has need . . . of self-knowledge. . . . He must know relentlessly how much good he can do, and what crimes he is capable of [that is, he must be well acquainted with his own shadow] and must beware of regarding the one as real and the other as illusion. Both are elements within his nature, and both are bound to come to light in him, should he wish, as he ought, to live without self-deception or self-delusion." [12]

When the obligation to become whole is laid upon an individual, either because of some neurotic disturbance, because, like the young captain in "The Secret Sharer," he is obliged to face a situation that seems beyond his capabilities, or because of a religious experience, the first task he must undertake is to confront his shadow. There arises within him a great need to confess the sins of his personal shadow so that the excluded parts of his personality may be accepted as a part of his whole psyche. For the shadow is felt as a particular darkness, even a particular sin, because it is in opposition to the accepted standards not only of the ego but also of the

[11] *Memories, Dreams, Reflections*, p. 325 (English edn., p. 300).
[12] Ibid., p. 330 (pp. 304-5).

society in which the individual lives. But the fear of the unknown and the resistance against it may be so great, so deepseated, and so unconscious that the individual may be unable to recognize what the problem really is. Consequently he suffers from a vague sense of guilt or inadequacy that he may try to assuage by various forms of self-discipline, which only force him still further into the repressive mold of civilization.

Under these circumstances he will seek for any shortcoming, even an imaginary one, to account for his overwhelming sense of guilt, while the real sin is overlooked. The individual may use repentance for some obvious fault as a blind, not consciously of course, to safeguard him from the realization of the real sin, one that is often apparently quite trivial in its overt aspect—a childish sexual escapade, perhaps, of no importance at all from the adult point of view, or a lie told about stolen candy, or some other childhood sin—whose confession seems to have power to undermine the adult completely. As if he realized the abyss that confession would open up, even though he is actually unconscious of the whole affair, the individual going through such an experience may rationalize by fastening on any handy sin and trying to make it carry the burden of guilt he feels. In particular, perhaps, he accepts the onus for some unadapted *act* and so succeeds in blinding himself to the underlying motive, as did the man who was jealous of his brother. It is relatively easy to confess a sin compatible, as it were, with one's dignity or ego self-respect, while the real sin lurks unrecognized underneath. For it was not this particular childish sexual misdemeanor or petty theft that was the real crime against society. Rather it was the fact that one dared to act on one's own instinct instead of remaining obedient to authority, and this will remain as a sin on one's conscience until one has made good one's escape from the ruling of society and of the parents. It is the necessary sin!

After the eating of the fruit in the Garden of Eden, Adam and Eve became aware, we are told, that they had no clothes on. They were naked. But none of the other creatures had clothes on either. Why should this particular fact disturb them so badly? We are not told that even the Lord God was clothed. It was not their disobedience, but their nakedness, that made them hide when they heard the Lord God walking in the garden in the cool of the evening. They had never before been ashamed of their condition, but then they had not been aware of it. They had not eaten of the tree of the knowledge of good and evil and so were not self-aware.

The inner acceptance of our acts, our sins, whether they demand outward confession or not, frequently produces an unexpectedly favorable result. For to have committed childish sexual acts, or indeed other "unacceptable" acts not so childish, means that one has asserted oneself as an individual; one has stolen one's own individuality. I remember a patient in a transition stage like this who dreamed that she went into a public garden and stole a flower. She stole a rose—her name happened to be Rose—and she was carrying it along when she saw that one of the park guards was bearing down upon her from one side and a policeman from the other. She felt terribly afraid because of the theft she had committed. And then she thought, "No, the rose is my rose." She held it out in front of her like a banner and stalked down the road, and the guards all fell back and let her pass. She had stolen her own name, her own individuality. She had asserted herself as an individual. Such an act converts a puppet into a person. Instinctive stirrings and deviations from the accepted code are manifestations of human nature. Perhaps one discovers that others have had similar experiences and so instead of being an outcast, a black sheep, because of what seemed to be one's own particular wickedness, one finds that one is now, perhaps for the first time, truly one of the flock.

In dealing with children, one has to be careful not to overlook this aspect of sins against the established order. It is at least possible that the good child who suddenly becomes outrageously naughty is trying to assert himself, really to feel himself as a person. A too permissive atmosphere denies the child the opportunity to assert himself as much as a too repressive one does. Unless a child comes up against something, he cannot feel that he exists as a separate individual.

It is by no means always easy to discover where the real guilt lies. For it may not be a particular disobedience against the divine or the social ordinance, nor a particular injury to the neighbor, nor indeed a particular blunder of forgetfulness that is the real sin. It may be rather the power attitude underlying the overt act, the inveterate egotism that denies the very existence of others as persons. It is this that makes up the blackness of the shadow. In other words, when one is enclosed in one's own *Umwelt,* one is constantly sinning against the neighbor. One feels and acts as if one were the only *real* person, the others being merely wraiths. The darkness of the shadow falls on everyone else; the others seem to be the ones at fault. But when one accepts one's shadow, instead of feeling an absolute assurance that the other person is in the wrong, one may be able to recognize that the difficulty can have come from one's own unconsciousness.

In any human situation where one is really concerned to make a working relationship, it is most important to recognize the shadow. The evil that emanates from one's own psyche is in some measure under one's own control; at least one can do something about it; but the darkness that comes from the other person's unconscious is not accessible even to one's best-intentioned efforts. However, since it takes two to make a quarrel, it is possible that if one clears up one's own end of the difficulty, the other person may be able to accept his shadow, too.

But the shadow is not necessarily all dark. It carries, as well as the unacceptable factors, all those psychic elements that have not been selected to make the conscious adaptation. Most people contain potentialities that have been given no place in their lives. These undeveloped parts of the individuality possess a certain energy and seek, as it were, to be lived. They follow us wherever we go, diverting libido from our conscious life by their pleas for attention, even though we may remain deaf to their call. Although this self-mutilation is an almost essential condition of adaptation in the modern world, the unlived tendencies will tolerate repression only so long. Eventually they will give rise to irritability, depression, increasing fatigue, and so on, until they are given some attention, some outlet. These tendencies lying latent in the shadow will also be uncovered if we begin to pay attention to what the unconscious is saying.

For the shadow should really be a part of the whole personality. It has been split off from consciousness through the process of education and the development of the ego, but it should be restored to its rightful place in the psyche and so no longer be projected to someone else.

It is never an easy task to accept the inadequacy and inferiority the shadow represents. But if one has the courage to accept this other side of oneself, the outcome is not always what one had expected. It seems as if to accept one's shadow would put one inevitably in the wrong with the result that the external situation would be burdened with an evil that one had always kept carefully under repression. But this is not what happens. Strangely enough, when we take up the shadow side of our own personality, renouncing the silent claim to be entirely white, immaculately moral, the effect we produce on our environment undergoes an unexpected change. For, when we carry the burden of our own human weakness consciously, other people are relieved of it. As long as we remain unconscious, we cast a shadow dense in proportion to our conscious rectitude; but when we carry the shadow consciously, its blight no longer falls on others, and we begin to give the impression of being more complete and therefore wiser and better than the ordinary run of people.

Until a few years ago, there lived among the Navajo a wise man who had to go on all fours because of a congenital lameness. His people called him "He-who-walks-close-to-his-shadow," [13] a name that does indeed denote a wise man. If we would only walk close to our shadow, it would not cause so many difficulties in our daily life, nor would we remain at the mercy of collective opinion. Rather, we should achieve an inner criterion and individual standpoint from which to make a valid judgment of the rightness or wrongness of a situation and of our part in it. By the acceptance of the black substance which adheres to the shadow, we should have taken the first step in the individuation process and in the development of a true self-consciousness.

[13] I am indebted to Laura Adams Armer for this information.

V

PROJECTIONS TO PERSONS

OF THE OPPOSITE SEX:

ANIMA AND ANIMUS

THE LAST CHAPTER was concerned with the contents of the personal unconscious, those unfortunate episodes and unacceptable parts of the personality that we have repressed and conveniently forgotten, being urged, almost forced, to do this by the pressure exerted on us by training and the code of morals and behavior current in our environment. And since these things really are unconscious, that is, unknown to us, we cannot meet them directly, even by introspection, except under exceptional circumstances and then usually only in a very partial manner. But we do encounter them in our daily lives, projected to someone in the environment. These projections may become recognizable if, for instance, we meet with resistance and denial from the one we have loaded with our unwanted psychic contents. Granted that we have some insight into our own motives, we may begin to suspect their presence when we react to a situation with undue intensity, that is, when our emotions are aroused, especially our negative emotions. Finally, when we feel dissatisfied with ourselves for no apparent reason or have a vague sense of guilt and disquiet, it is well to look for projections of the shadow.

Whenever unconscious psychic contents are activated—that is, endowed with psychic energy and emotion—they tend to act autonomously, as if they were little personalities of their own; they become personified either as inner figures or as projections onto someone in the outer world. The shadow qualities which come from the personal unconscious are personified in an image of the same sex as the individual and will be projected onto someone who is also of the same sex. A man's shadow is male and will be projected onto a man—the brother, for instance, or some friend or companion. The woman's shadow, being feminine, will be projected onto a sister or some other woman.

The relation of an individual to someone of the *opposite* sex is a much more problematic area of psychological life than the relation between two people of the same sex. For just as we have a certain sense of knowing, of being able to *feel into* someone of the same sex as ourselves through the fact that we are in a sense alike, so we feel a strangeness, a definite unlikeness, when confronted with someone of the opposite sex. Yet in addition to this sense of strangeness, which might be expected to keep men and women apart, and indeed often does so, there is also an attraction between men and women, based in part on their difference. It is the pull of opposites towards each other, an attraction that is often so strong and unaccountable as to bespeak the intrusion of an unconscious element.

This unconscious element is what Jung has called the *anima* in the case of a man and the *animus* in the case of a woman.[1] He writes: "The source of projections [to the opposite sex] is no longer the shadow . . . but a contrasexual figure. Here we meet the animus of a woman and the anima of a man, two corresponding archetypes whose autonomy and unconsciousness explain the stubbornness of their projections"; and

[1] See Diagram IV.

he continues: "The anima and animus are much further away from consciousness [than the shadow] and in normal circumstances are seldom if ever realized." [2]

The attraction between persons of opposite sex is due not only to the mutual attraction of opposites. There is also the physical urge based on the instinct of sexuality which the Greeks called Eros, the great Binder or Uniter. But beyond this, it might seem impossible that there could be any hope of mutual understanding between a man and a woman were it not for the fact that within them both there exist elements of contrasexual character. In each of us there are both male and female genes, since we inherit elements from both parents, and these produce certain anatomical and physiological effects. The masculine characteristics become dominant in a male and the feminine in a female, while the contrasexual factors become recessive. In later life the contrasexual characteristics of a physical nature become more evident and on the psychological plane a similar condition prevails. During the early years of life, especially after puberty, the conscious personality shows the characteristics of maleness in a man and of femaleness in a woman, while the elements of a contrasexual nature recede to the background, that is, into the unconscious part of the psyche. It has been said that a man carries his female soul within him, while a woman conceals a man in her own depths. Since unconscious psychic elements tend to be personified, those contents of opposite sex to the individual's conscious personality appear in consciousness as the soul-image. The word *soul* is not used here in the same sense as in current religious language, but in a psychological sense, as a man uses it when he says to a woman, "I love you as my own soul," or "You are my soul mate." Jung calls this figure the *anima* in a man's case, to avoid the inevitable confusion that would result from the use of the term "soul." The corresponding figure in a woman is the *animus*. These terms are ex-

[2] *Aion*, p. 10.

ceedingly apt. For the man's soul figure has the characteristics of the feminine principle of Eros—feeling, emotion, and relatedness; while the corresponding figure in a woman, being masculine, partakes of thinking and spirit, having the quality of wind or air, of speech and of idea—it is spirit in that sense (Latin, *animus*—Greek, *anemos:* wind or breath). Like the shadow, these figures tend to be personified and to be projected to someone in the outer world. They may also be projected onto a figure of history or romance, or experienced as an inner image appearing in dreams, fantasies, or visions. If there is a lack of distinction between the elements of the psyche, as happens not infrequently, the ego personality may be contaminated by the contrasexual elements, and this produces a condition that Jung has called identification of the ego with the anima or animus, as the case may be.

The contrasexual elements in a personality lie at a deeper level in the unconscious than the shadow and indeed they are only partly within the personal psyche itself.[3] In greater part they belong to the unknown inner world, the "not-I" of the collective unconscious, that impinges on us, though we cannot contain it. But as the anima and animus are also connected with the personal psyche, they act as intermediaries between the personal parts of the psyche, the "I," and the not-personal region of the inner world beyond the personal psyche, much as the persona acts to relate the individual to the outer world. They partake of the nature of archetypes to a much greater degree than the shadow, which as we have seen also covers and partly conceals the archetypes of the brother and companion as well as those of the devil and of evil. In the gradual development of consciousness, such as occurs in the course of a psychological analysis, these figures become ever more differentiated, and the individual learns to distinguish them from his real "I." This understanding leads to a most important increase in consciousness—to a growth of freedom in

[3] See Diagram IV.

the outer life and a growth of insight and depth of understanding of the more profound aspects of life in the inner or
subjective sphere.

Our knowledge of these hidden and usually unconscious
aspects of the psyche is based on empirical observations, and
the formulations and theories that have resulted are not accessible to direct experiment or proof. But the facts are available to anybody who knows how to look for them, and they
have been clearly seen by artists, novelists, dramatists, phi-
losophers, and other observers of human experience and behavior over the centuries. The theories and the systematic description, however, come from psychologists, in particular
from Jung. He pointed out that materials stemming from three
sources give rise to the anima or animus and to their special
characteristics. These characteristics are to a great extent quite
general, as might be expected, since they belong in such large
measure to the collective unconscious realm. But is the anima
(or animus) the same in everyone, or is it individual?

Let us consider the three sources from which the anima
(or animus) comes. First, there are the experiences that a man
has had of feminine beings. These give him a certain knowledge of women and how they behave. The most important are
the experiences with the mother. They impinge upon him
even before he becomes conscious, and they have an enormous
influence in molding his attitude towards and expectations of
women, usually lasting all his life. He may expect all women
to be like his own mother or react negatively to those who do
not resemble her. A man may search all his life for a woman
exactly like his mother, and may be unable to relate to any
actual woman because he is never able to find one who exactly resembles her. This was the case with a certain man who
married a girl his mother had pointed out as a suitable
match, though as a matter of fact he did not care for her at all.
He was always very resistant to her, because she was not at all
like his mother. Since he was quite well to do, he used to

spend his free time looking for a woman who *was* like his mother. He would get on a train and, if he saw a girl at the far end of the car who had ankles like his mother's or the particular type of curly hair that his mother had, he would watch her and get off the train when she did, regardless of the fact that he might have a through ticket. He would follow women in the street, hoping that they would prove to be like his mother. If he saw a woman who in the least resembled her physically, he would go in pursuit of her, but he never could make up his mind to address her. He lived and died pursuing the image of his mother but never catching up with it. It was a tragic situation not only for the man but also for his poor wife, who was left at home to manage as best she could without him.

Behind the mother lies the *mother archetype,* the typical picture or image of "Mother" that each of us carries within him and that leads each individual to expect from his actual mother a response to his own need, really that she should be the complementary reciprocal—the opposite—of his childness and dependence. This image is of course colored by the experience of the actual mother, but it can and does exert a deep and far-reaching influence on everyone, even on those who have known no personal mother. If the personal mother does not correspond adequately to this inborn image, the child will feel neglected and deprived, and may develop a negative relation to his actual mother, even though she is doing her best for him. These difficulties are especially apt to occur in cases where mother and child are of different psychological types, so that mutual understanding is difficult.

This situation is repeated over and over again in myths and fairy tales where the children are living as the adopted children of the woodcutter, although their real parents are the king and queen. This is a motif that is found in all countries, and it is one that occurs in the fantasy of many, many people in whom we would not expect it. For instance, a man who came to me as a patient was convinced in childhood that his parents were not really his parents. He had been shown a tombstone on which was the name of his father's first wife, and he was immediately convinced that he must have been this woman's son. As a matter of fact, he was not; she had died long before his birth. But he was sure that the woman at home had been foisted on him as his mother, and that he really had a much better, a much more desirable mother who had somehow been taken from him. Such a person lives in the fantasy that life would be ideal *if only* he could find his real mother. It is a fantasy that is extremely common, though it does not usually emerge into consciousness so clearly as in this case. It is the hunt, the search for the archetypal image.

After the mother, the sisters and other female relatives help to mold a man's image of woman, and all his encounters with girls and women also play a part in forming his anima image. For example, there was once a man who fell in love at the age of seven with the little girl who sat in front of him at school. She had golden pigtails. He was entranced by this beautiful golden-haired girl. His image of woman always had golden pigtails, and he hunted for her constantly until he came to analysis and finally discovered what the trouble was.

The second source for the anima image stems from the feminine elements within the man's own psyche. Because of these he has a certain tendency toward, or capacity for, feminine attitudes and behavior arising from within himself. These of course vary greatly in strength in different men. In the very masculine man they are quite recessive; in others they may be so evident that the man takes on a quite feminine appearance and manner; this is one cause of homosexuality. But as the feminine elements in a man are weaker than the masculine ones and are also inferior as compared to the masculine elements, they correspond to an inferior type of feminine function. This does not imply that women and the feminine principle are inferior to men and the masculine principle (a question none of us is in a position to decide, since we are all biased by our own sex and psychosexual make-up). Clearly, however, the feminine elements in a man are or represent the inferior parts of himself, just as the masculine elements in a woman represent the inferior parts of her psyche, with the result that their functioning is also inferior and generally has a negative quality. In addition to the feminine elements that function from within himself and give him at least a hint of how a woman feels, the masculine elements within a man also give him a certain instinctive knowledge of woman. For instance, a man knows instinctively how to behave towards someone of the opposite sex, just as male animals know how to approach a female in a way that is likely to be acceptable to her, an entirely different way from the one in which he approaches a male; that is, he has a certain knowledge of what will please her—he "knows" what she is like. A similar instinct guides the human being.

There is a third source from which the anima acquires its characteristics, that is, the inherited knowledge of the ancestors, who have experienced "the way women are" throughout the ages of life on earth. This means not the way women are in themselves, for that will remain forever a mystery to men, but rather the way they are in relation to men. (What they are in themselves remains a secret. Women's mysteries, and men's, as well, are performed secretly. In primitive societies they lie under the strictest taboo and may not be revealed to members of the opposite sex; infringement of this taboo is generally punished by death.) These countless experiences of the opposite sex have created an image of womanhood in the man's unconscious psyche that influences his behavior and may be experienced by the individual man as an inner image or picture of his soul-figure. It may be observed in art forms, poetry, romantic literature, and mythology, as well as in the individual's projection upon the loved woman; and in its highest manifestation it has given rise to the images of divine figures: Ishtar of Babylon, Isis of Egypt, the Magna Mater of

Syria, Aphrodite, Hecate, Demeter, and Persephone of Greece, the beneficent and destructive goddesses of the Orient, the Sophia of later Judaism, and the Madonna of Christianity, all of whom portray the inner image of womanhood and of the anima in its deepest and most essential form.

If we turn to the psychology of the woman, we find that the figure of the animus takes its characteristics in a similar way from corresponding sources. But whereas the anima, being feminine, partakes of the qualities of emotion and relatedness and is personal in character, the animus, being masculine, partakes of the qualities of thinking, impersonality, and spirit, leading to a concern for justice, logic, and a "cause." It is therefore relatively impersonal. The animus exerts on the woman a fascination similar to that of the anima for the man; she loves and longs for its manifestation. She may find it mirrored in or projected to a teacher or orator, a man of words and especially a "man of the Word," a role that members of the clergy are often called upon to fill. The image may be projected to a suitable man or to a quite unsuitable one, one who only *promises* to dispense wisdom, while actually suffering from an afflation that deceives only the woman obsessed by her animus. The false aspect of such a man may be quite obvious to another man, who cannot think why women fall for such pseudo wisdom. Men see through him and may be quite aware of the falsity of his claims to be a guide. There is, of course, a considerable temptation for a man who has a certain facility with words, a "gift of the gab," to use it to get converts and followers, perhaps for personal prestige, power, or money. Just so the woman who has the gift of attracting the projection of the man's anima image may use it for personal advantage. In such a case, other women are usually quite aware of her motives and despise or hate her accordingly, while men are much more easily taken in.

The anima image, when it is hypostatized and projected, gives rise to the images of the Magna Mater or the Sophia.

So, too, the animus is sometimes seen as a divine or semi-divine Master of Wisdom, an ideal figure of father, teacher, protector, and guide. A man or god of power, perhaps a Hercules; a man of the powerful word, the Logos; or a suffering savior—any of them may catch the projection of the woman's animus.[4]

In considering the anima and animus, we must always keep in mind that these figures stem from a very deep source in the unconscious and are only partly available to consciousness. In addition to being parts of the personality, they partake of the nature of the archetypes. Jung has called them border phenomena, standing at the junction of the personal and the collective unconscious. We can describe them only to the extent that they are manifested in consciousness; we cannot delimit them completely; and so we are dependent, as we really are in all psychological investigation, on empirical data.

After discussing the impossibility of getting the average person to realize his projections to his mother or father, for example, Jung continues:

I mention all this just to illustrate the order of magnitude to which the anima/animus projections belong, and the moral and intellectual exertions that are needed to dissolve them. Not all the contents of the anima and animus are projected, however. Many of them appear spontaneously in dreams and so on, and many more can be made conscious through active imagination. In this way, we find that thoughts, feelings, and affects are alive in us which we would never have believed possible. Naturally, possibilities of this sort seem utterly fantastic to anyone who has not experienced them himself, for a normal person "knows what he thinks." Such a childish attitude on the part of the "normal person" is simply the rule, so that no one without experience in this field can be expected to understand the real nature of anima and animus. With these reflections one gets into an entirely new world of psychological experience, provided of course that one succeeds in realizing

[4] See Diagram IV.

them in practice. Those who do succeed can hardly fail to be impressed by all that the ego does not know and never has known. This increase in self-knowledge is still very rare nowadays and is usually paid for in advance with a neurosis if not with something worse.[5]

The anima and animus function in life in three ways, corresponding to the three sources from which they derive. First, the anima is projected to a woman in the external world, the mother first of all, then the sisters and friends; the animus is projected to the father, brothers, and so on. Finally, in each case, the soul-figure may be, indeed always is to some extent, projected onto the wife or husband. This projection is especially strong when a man and woman have fallen in love. In addition, the anima or animus can be said to influence every relation between men and women to some extent, depending on the degree of consciousness they have individually achieved. For it is unconscious elements that are projected, not conscious ones.

Second, the feminine elements in the man's own psyche produce certain reactions of a feminine type in himself. These usually show themselves as moods, of which resentment is the commonest. When a man is not up to a situation, when he cannot deal with it adequately by means of his developed ego, he falls back on inherited patterns of behavior, latent in the unconscious, and so the anima within him is brought forward, as it were, to fill the gap in his adaptation, and he acts in a feminine way—an inferior feminine way. He gets angry or peevish, or is resentful that things do not go right of themselves or that someone else does not attend to them. Or he merely looks and feels helpless, with the expectation that someone—wife, mother, secretary—will come to the rescue. Indeed it sometimes seems that a man has a woman secretary just for the purpose of taking care of his anima, that is, to protect and nurse along his inferior side. In the main part of

[5] *Aion*, p. 19.

his job he is probably adequate, but in all the minor matters that he prefers to ignore, especially those that have to do with personal relations, namely, the eros side of life, he is helpless. If confronted by them, he feels pushed, abused, or he gets peevishly angry. He may even go to pieces, but the secretary, whether she is a "charming little thing" or an old and tried "dragon," comes to the rescue, soothes his hurt feelings, and deals efficiently with the intrusive demands of personal or public relations.

In other cases, if for any reason the ego itself is inadequately developed, so that the man is unable to make a workable masculine adaptation to life, his whole character may have a feminine quality. He is soft, gentle, girlish, but, since he is not a girl, there will always be, in such a case, a more or less concealed negative factor of resentment or moodiness which may show itself in subtle dishonesty, unreliability, and autoerotism. A woman who acts by means of an identification to her animus instead of in her own feminine way will be argumentative, dogmatic, opinionated, and mannish when she is unable to cope with a life situation. The woman dominated by her animus is so well known in literature and also so frequently met with in life that I hardly need to describe her further. In all cases of this kind we say that the man is identified with his anima and the woman with her animus.

The third form in which the soul-figure appears is that of an inner image. Many men know instinctively what "She" is like. Indeed, H. Rider Haggard gave this name to his portrait of the anima, and people generally know what he is talking about without further explanation. The corresponding image is not so clearly marked in a woman, partly because, being impersonal, it is more diffused, and indeed may be represented by a group of masculine figures, as, for instance, a council of men, the Fathers of the Church or State, but there are in literature several excellent examples of him, notably Heathcliff in *Wuthering Heights*, by Emily Brontë, whose sister Charlotte also drew remarkable portraits of the animus in her various books, especially in *Jane Eyre*. As a woman develops psychologically, the animus figure becomes clearer and more definite and tends to become unified. Indeed, in immature persons, whether men or women, the soul-figure is apt to be multiple. In men it may be represented by rather indefinite groups of nymphs, the sirens of Ulysses' temptation, or the flower girls of Tannhäuser's, and only as his masculine character takes form does the unified anima figure emerge. It is a little different for the woman, but with her, too, the animus tends to become unified into one or two figures. Many of the women mystics, for instance, were aware of an inner guide, personified perhaps as Christ or as one of the saints, and the control of a woman medium is usually a personification of her animus, while many women, neither mystics nor mediums, experience an inner masculine figure to whom they look for guidance and support in times of need, whether by direct prayer and meditation by an instinctive turning of their attention inward, or, if they have learned the technique of what Jung calls "active imagination," by a deliberate introversion.

The inner image in either man or woman may be the inspiration and guide on the inner journey, as Beatrice was for Dante,[6] or, as in the case of Rodin, the inspiration for a work of art. This image is for many artists the source of their creative genius, the renewal of life, the refuge in death. Similarly, for a woman, the soul-figure[7] is "dear love," master, teacher, guide on the inner journey, and heavenly spouse.

This is only the briefest outline of the subject, and it must be clear that we are dealing with a very large and complicated theme indeed. Jung has written about it extensively, and there are many other treatments of the subject. Indeed, it is hard,

---

[6] In both the *Vita Nuova* and *The Divine Comedy*.
[7] See the novel *Precious Bane*, by Mary Webb, where both positive and negative animus figures are clearly drawn.

when writing on any psychological subject at all, to avoid referring to the functioning of anima and animus.[8]

We must now take up in more detail the effects of the projection of the soul-image. The projection of the anima to a woman, or of the animus to a man, always produces a peculiar fascination and a strong emotional involvement with that particular person. Sometimes this is a one-sided involvement, but more often it is mutual, the anima of the man meeting or perhaps evoking the animus of the woman. When this happens, the two are irresistibly drawn to each other. They feel as if they had always known each other not only in this life but in some previous life as well. They are certain that each of them understands what the other thinks without any explanation, that their feelings of love are recognized and returned, that in some curious way they were destined for each other from the beginning of time. This experience is the psychological counterpart of the Chinese myth of the Great Mother who ties a boy and a girl together with an invisible cord before their birth. A well-known example of this kind of falling in love at first sight is dramatized in Wagner's *Tristan and Isolde*, where the enchantment came from drinking a love potion meant not for Tristan but for King Mark, the intended husband of Isolde. So powerful was the spell that Tristan went against his sacred obligation as a knight, while Isolde, too, violated her whole code of honor in forsaking her husband for

[8] The reader is referred to Jung's *Two Essays on Analytical Psychology*. His "Concerning the Archetypes with Special Reference to the Anima Concept" gives a very clear though rather short account of the archetypal aspect of the anima. In *Psychological Types* he gives a long description of the "soul-image." This book was published in 1923, when the terms *anima* and *animus* were not as yet in general use. Many examples of how these figures function in real life are given in my *The Way of All Women*. Perhaps, since this book is a good deal simpler than Jung's, the concepts may there be more readily grasped. Almost all of Jung's books are written primarily for the specialist. He said to me one day that he wrote as he did in the expectation that his pupils would interpret his material and thought to the general public, a task for which he himself simply did not have time.

her lover. The conflict between their conscious sense of what was right and the compulsion of their love was so great that Tristan paid with his life, as did Tannhäuser when caught in a similar conflict. These dramas clearly portray how powerful the projected image of anima or animus can be. The Chinese myth referred to above tells how the Moon Mother, the Goddess of Eros, joins a boy before his birth to a girl who is his counterpart, compelling them to search for each other so that they may be united. They are destined to find each other during their lifetime on earth; they are meant for each other; they are soul mates. The *Zohar*,[9] one of the Jewish sacred writings, has a similar myth according to which two souls destined for each other in heaven must find each other on earth and marry. Only in this way can there be a perfect marriage. For such a marriage reflects and *enhances* the marriage in heaven of the "Ineffable Persons," that is, of Jehovah and Elohim. The *Zohar* further says that sexual union should take place on the Sabbath when it must be "by consent and with joy," for then God is correspondingly united to his chosen people. There is a similar idea in Hindu marriage, where the union of husband and wife accompanies, almost produces, a simultaneous union of the god Shiva with his consort, Shakti, on which the continuous creation of the universe depends. An echo of this same idea occurs in the marriage service of the Church of England, where one of the final prayers says, "O God, who hast consecrated the state of matrimony to such an excellent mystery, that in it is *signified* and *represented* the spiritual marriage and unity betwixt Christ and his Church . . . that this man may love his wife according to thy Word (as Christ did love his spouse the Church). . . ." From these examples it is obvious that the projection of anima and animus is of the greatest importance as a psychological experience, for through it the union of a man and a woman on earth is accompanied by, or even brings about, the union of

[9] A. E. Waite, *The Holy Kabbalah*, pp. 396-98.

the masculine and feminine potencies or principles in heaven. In psychological terms, we would say that through the human experience of love not only are a man and woman united in consciousness, but at the same time the cosmic or collective principles of masculine and feminine, logos and eros, are united in the unconscious. This is the mystery that the alchemists called the *coniunctio,* the union of opposites.

We have already seen how important it is for an individual to become united with his shadow, giving it a place in the totality of his "I." That process is for the most part quite a painful undertaking. Here the union with the soul-image is shown as ecstasy and joy, and we are told it has far-reaching results, even enabling a corresponding union to be effected in heaven, in the unseen world of the inner "not-I."

We have now to consider the effect of the projection of the anima and animus in real life. The myths and teachings just quoted show that, in some cases, the union of the two on earth is accompanied by a union in heaven or, psychologically put, by a union of psychic elements within the individual's own unconscious. But the outcome is not always so fortunate. When a man falls in love he sees, in the woman who has attracted the projection of his anima, his ideal, his soul-image, and he is convinced that this is what she is really like. It is as if he re-created her, this earthly fallible woman, making of her a goddess of beauty and goodness and power. He may literally create a statue, an image, as Pygmalion did. But when the image comes to life, she may reveal herself as very different from his dream woman. For the anima is *not* a concept: the anima is filled with life; she is autonomous; she is She-Who-Must-Be-Obeyed. Because man is blind, however, he rarely sees this quite obvious fact, and the cloak of the anima may fall on an unsuitable woman. If the individual is psychologically undeveloped and has done little or nothing to make the shadow conscious or to realize, let alone meet, his moral problems, the anima or animus will work in a negative fashion, so that what is undesirable, being projected, will appear desirable, or will exert an irresistible fascination. To the individual who has projected his anima onto a woman, she may seem to be possessed of all the virtues. Even in a case where there may be more insight into the character of the enchanting one, the man may find himself impelled to seek the woman who so attracts him, much as the moth is lured by the flame, and frequently the outcome is similar: he gets badly burned. The same is true of the woman who finds herself attracted to an inferior man, whom she may even have reason to suspect is a charlatan. She falls under a spell, as Trilby fell under that of Svengali in George Du Maurier's novel.

The projection of anima and animus then results in a mutual entanglement. On its overt side, this may be either positive or negative; that is, either the two persons may fall in love, or, on the contrary, a mutual antagonism may develop which might well be called "falling in hate." For a mutual antagonism can arise between a man and a woman that is just as much based on the constellation of unconscious factors as is the falling in love that seems to come about by magic. In myth this may be the result of drinking a magic potion, of eyes meeting in a special glance, or of falling under a spell. To the bystanders it may be quite evident that the two are indeed bewitched. "One can't see what got into them." "How can they be so blind to the qualities of each other?" In such phrases the family and friends marvel at the blindness of the little blind god and at his power to bewilder his victims, a power that completely prevents them from heeding the warning of parents and friends. For to them it seems they have fallen into heaven.

Strangely enough the emotions aroused even in such a mistaken fascination are not all an *ignis fatuus*. For although the partner may be far from being the marvelous creature he or she appears in the lover's eyes, the fact remains that the experience of intense love, even though it is for an unworthy or unsuitable object, may have a most favorable effect on the lover. For the time being, he is transformed not only in his inner feelings, his subjective experience of himself, but also in his outer demeanor. It is not that he is blinded or deluded; he is transformed by the emotion he experiences, regardless of whether the object is what he believes her to be or not. And in those few weeks or months, while the in-love period lasts, he may grow and mature enormously, changing from a self-absorbed youth into a man. Similarly the girl may grow overnight, as it seems, from a dreaming child into full womanhood. What has happened? Obviously something that up to this time has lain deep in the unconscious, dormant within the personality, has wakened to life, and the result is most favorable to the individual's development, even though later, when the spell is lifted, the illusion dissolved, grief and loss and bitterness may be the aftermath. For by this experience the anima and animus have been awakened to life, as in the story of the Sleeping Beauty, when at the kiss of love not only did the princess wake up, but the life spirit itself, which had lain under an enchantment, was suddenly aroused and took on new vitality. The palace and even the countryside began to live again. At this point in actual life, the anima and animus start to "live into" the conscious situation instead of remaining merely possibilities in the unconscious. I have used the expression "live into" in order to try to convey the sense that the experiencing of these unconscious values is autonomous and not under the control of the conscious ego. Their awakening is something that happens to an individual entirely without his control, and often against his conscious wish. When it happens, it seems that his whole concept of life and of his chosen path will be overridden by compulsive elements that may or may not conflict with his plans for his life. An autonomous factor, a hitherto unknown *personality* has come to life inside him, and he may well find that her power and authority are indisputable. It was not without reason that Rider Haggard called her "She-Who-Must-Be-Obeyed."

When this factor is projected to an actual woman—or, more accurately, when this factor is *encountered* in a woman— and a marriage follows, a chain of events is set in motion that will move with the inexorableness of a juggernaut. For the archetypes are the architects of Fate. And it is not too difficult, perhaps, to foresee what the outcome in any particular case will be. I recall a play in which an eloping couple come out of a storm into a strange, slightly uncanny inn at night. They are obviously completely absorbed in each other. The inn-keeper, an old man sitting by the fire, gets up, without a word shows them to a room, and goes back to his seat by the fire. In the morning the sun is shining, and the couple come down in the bright light. Their illusion of love has not survived the night. Their passion is spent; the spell has been exorcised, and they find themselves complete and uncongenial strangers. They leave, and the old man goes back to the fire. But immediately there is a knock at the door, and he rises to admit a second, exactly similar couple . . . and the curtain falls.

But disillusionment is not what the two expect while they are under the spell. The "so they lived happy ever after" of fairy tales and of sentimental and juvenile novels expresses the general expectation. More mature plays and novels and many myths may tell a somewhat different story, however, as do the divorce courts. For either the two live and die still under the spell, remaining unconscious of the nature of their illusion right up to death, or a gradual enlightenment must come about. At this point real life intrudes itself into the fairy story. Reality confronts the couple and produces one of two possible effects. If the infatuation has a sufficient admixture of *true love of the object* in it for the two to be able to weather the "time of troubles" when their realization of each other's divergence from the ideal dawns on them, then a friendship, a real psychological relationship of the greatest value, will be formed. This relationship will have true love as its foundation, with tenderness and understanding for the human weaknesses of the partner and appreciation for his or her values even if these do not tally with the animus or anima image. In this case the married couple will reach old age as the ideal Darby and Joan. If, however, the two are unable to grow and mature through their mutual relationship, whatever the reason may be, each will continue to expect that the partner ought to fill the role unconsciously assigned to him. Then the projected image of anima or animus will impose a tyrannical demand on the supposedly loved one. In such a case bitterness and resentment will inevitably arise between the two, as the partner increasingly shows himself or herself to be anything but the paragon the lover supposed, to be indeed something entirely different, a human being with weaknesses and strengths not recognized during the in-love period and not valued in the marriage.

In the first case each of the partners will grow through the assimilation of the projected factors that are progressively removed from the other's shoulders, a process that relieves the other of a considerable burden. In psychological language, the anima and animus are realized step by step as an essential part of the individual's own psyche, which is consequently enriched by values formerly sensed only in projection. These qualities are now sought by the individual, and indeed they may be found within himself, not in his conscious ego, but coming to him from the "not-I" of the unconscious realm. The man begins to be devoted to the woman as she actually is, and she too begins to develop. The latent qualities in her that served to catch his anima projection consequently begin to grow, till eventually she may come to resemble in actual fact the ideal woman he fell in love with years ago. And so the wheel turns full circle. A similar development can, of course, be initiated in a man as a result of his wife's increase in consciousness. I say "can be initiated" advisedly, for psychological development can occur only as a result of growth, and that takes effort, moral effort, on the individual's own part.

In the second case, where no assimilation of the anima and animus takes place, irritation with each other, reproaches and quarrels, become increasingly frequent between the pair. They may make up after a quarrel, but they never come to a real understanding of each other. It seems as if something that they cannot control tries to bring about a separation. In a deplorable number of cases the knot is cut in the divorce court, and the two, thinking they are at last free to begin life again, only proceed to get involved in a second relationship which will surely lead to a similar denouement, unless they should have become aware in the meantime of the fact and functioning of the anima or animus. But this does not often happen.

For instance, I recall the case of a woman who came to me because her husband had become alcoholic and was rapidly deteriorating. Her story was that she had some years earlier married another man, a sober and hard-working though rather weak individual, not because she was in love with him but because he was available. She was determined to leave home at all costs because her father was constantly drunk, abused her mother, and had reduced the family to penury. No sooner had she married her sober young man than he too began to drink! She divorced him and shortly remarried, choosing this time the leader in the local temperance group. But, strangely enough, the second husband gave up his temperance affiliations and took to the bottle.

Was this just the irony of fate, or were there elements in the girl's own character that led her to choose men with this particular weakness lying latent in the unconscious, and was there something in her that elicited the man's own difficulty? This girl's animus image, like that of every daughter, had been influenced by the personality of her father. Consciously she hated his weakness, but unconsciously she was attracted to men of a similar type. This was one factor, but there was also another at work. The feminine part of a girl's psyche is just as much influenced by the mother as is the animus by the father. This girl's only experience of home life was based on her mother's reaction to a drunken husband, and there was obviously no love between the pair. It is safe to assume that the girl reacted to her husband as her mother had done to her father, so that she cannot be entirely exonerated from a share in the guilt of the situation.

Still another element enters into this picture. When a woman marries, as this girl did, for reasons other than love, she will be unable to achieve a satisfactory relation to her husband based on deep and mutual instinctual bonds. She is unlikely to be able to respond satisfactorily to him sexually, and unless her coldness has the effect of making him impotent, his sexuality will become more urgent and more primitive. In either case both will remain profoundly dissatisfied on the sexual as well as the love side of their marriage. Since the positive side of the anima and animus is frustrated in this way, a negative aspect will be aroused and projected to the partner, who will be unconsciously influenced by this powerful force that has usurped the place of instinctive love. The woman, recipient of the man's negative anima, will become fretful and nagging, or critical and domineering; the man, frustrated on the instinctual side, is all too likely to become brutal and try to get what he wants by force. Or he may turn to alcohol to forget his difficulties. This happened, not once, but twice, to this patient. Although she wanted to be married, something in her was forcing her to live alone, perhaps so that she might discover her own side of the problem and come to grips with her animus.

In this case there had been no real involvement in the first place. Both marriages had been quite cold-blooded affairs, at least on the girl's side. But even where the deeps have been stirred by a powerful projection of the soul-figure, and the man and woman are genuinely in love, the very closeness such a projection involves may work to cause a separation. Their union, however, will be based on unconscious projections and not on real love of each other as they are in themselves, and eventually they will begin to feel crushed, strangled by the insistent demand of the projections put upon each by the other. At this point the unconscious itself begins to introduce elements into the situation that push them apart, and they become estranged.

The estrangement can come about in various ways, but always it seems to be the work of the anima or animus. For instance, when the first flush of "in-loveness" has passed and the couple should settle down to the task of creating a really conscious relationship, one or both of the pair, unable to cope with this demand of the life situation, may be attracted to someone else through a fresh projection of anima or animus not unlike the first experience with the partner. They naïvely expect that this time all emotional difficulties will be resolved. But it is important to realize that, from the psychological point of view, nothing will be changed by a change of partner. Unless the individuals become more conscious of what is happening and confront their own soul-figures within themselves, the values of the anima and animus will continue to be projected. Of course, there are cases where a real difference of character between the first couple has been masked by their falling in love, and only later does it become apparent that they are too dissimilar in every way for a true marriage between them to be possible. Then, one asks, Why did they come under this spell? Why did these particular persons fall in love, if it was not because the anima and animus were touched? But sometimes, when a marriage has been arranged not on the basis of love but for some conventional or other external reason, probably with an ulterior motive (as occurs or used to occur in Europe, where quite young people were married by arrangement between the parents), and when the discrepancy in character and outlook has been masked or deliberately ignored so that it comes to light only after marriage, it is possible that the attraction to another person, not the marriage partner, may be the first constellation of any depth of the anima or animus. Then this will be the first real encounter with these soul-figures. In such a case the marriage does not come into the present consideration for, although surely the anima and animus were involved, the aspect constellated was a selfish, worldly, and superficial one, corresponding to a similar superficiality in the individual's relation to himself. A man may have remained oblivious of those deeper values brought within reach by the soul-figure. Then, when he wakes up, he may become involved with someone other than the wife in a way that corresponds to the psychological situation more usually found in marriage, and here too a time is likely to come when "lovers' quarrels" begin to occur with greater and greater frequency, and it becomes obvious that an autonomous factor in the psyche of one or both of the partners is driving them apart.

In his discussion of the effects of the projection of the anima and animus in *Two Essays*, Jung speaks of this tendency to separation. He describes what is a very common situation in marriage:

> The anima, in the form of the mother-imago, is transferred to the wife; and the man, as soon as he marries, becomes childish, sentimental, dependent, and subservient, or else truculent, tyrannical, hypersensitive, always thinking about the prestige of his superior masculinity. The last is of course merely the reverse of the first. . . . His fear of the dark incalculable power of the unconscious [constellated by both the mother image and the anima as mistress] gives his wife an illegitimate authority over him, and forges such a dangerously close union that the marriage is permanently on the brink of explosion from internal tension—or else, out of protest, he flies to the other extreme, with the same results.[10]

[10] *Two Essays on Analytical Psychology*, p. 196.

Jung enlarges on this theme in his essay "Marriage as a Psychological Relationship." This is a most valuable study. In it Jung explains how in most marriages one partner, being more mature than the other, acts, as it were, as a psychological container for the spouse. Sometimes it is the woman who plays her mother role, containing and cherishing her son-husband; sometimes the roles are reversed, and the competent and well-adapted man protects, shelters, and guides a childish wife. In either case the one contained is protected and warmed all round, while the other is warm on the inside but exposed on the outer surface, as it were. The one within remains comfortable until he or she begins to grow, and the cozy nest becomes too small. He begins to feel suffocated and starts to fight his way out to greater freedom. The one who is the container naturally resists this action, and the two enter on a prolonged struggle. But if the dissatisfaction with the marriage starts with the other partner, the container, it is usually because he feels cold and unrelated on his strong side and begins to look for warmth and understanding and comfort from someone outside the marriage. Or perhaps the marriage has become stale and dull as a result of too much domestic comfort, and someone fresh, not encumbered with children and domestic worries, may seem exceedingly attractive. The passionate and dangerous aspect of the soul-figure becomes infinitely desirable, and the spell of the anima or animus is cast over a man or woman who, till that time, has been content to play the part of the staid husband or wife of a conventionally happy marriage. He or she falls in love and becomes the victim of the turbulent emotions always associated with the projection of the soul-figure.

Naturally such a development, whether he "knows" about it or not, creates a situation of great anxiety for the one who wants only to remain cozily within. For it means that much of the attention formerly showered upon him is diverted to someone else. And so, in this case, too, conflicts and re-proaches start. The situation where the "container" rebels is perhaps more destructive than the one in which the "con-tained" begins to struggle against the restrictions of his cozy nest, for the one who wanders away in search of comfort feels guilty, while the one contained is supported by a great sense of virtue in holding to the sanctity of marriage, regardless of the discomfort, and even distress, of the partner.

This is one reason for the tendency of a close relationship to break up. There are others where, although there does not seem to be any such cause for dissatisfaction, conflicts of a very serious nature may arise between the partners. Some-thing autonomous within them brings about disharmony when consciously they want peace. Why does this autonomous fac-tor work so persistently to bring about a separation? And what is it that works so destructively? It is another aspect of the anima and the animus. Jung points out that it does not help much to patch up each situation by apologizing, deter-mining not to lose one's temper again, and so on. For such good resolutions share the fate of most of their kind. The problem cannot be solved by repression and conscious at-tempts to be good. As Jung writes:

> We would be better advised to investigate what is behind the tend-encies of the anima [to make trouble]. The first step is what I would call the objectivation of the anima [or, in a woman's case, of the animus], that is, the strict refusal to regard the trend towards separation as a weakness of one's own. Only when this has been done can one face the anima with the question, "Why do you want this separation?" To put the question in this personal way has the great advantage of recognizing the anima as a personality, and of making a relationship [with her] possible. The more personally she is taken the better.[11]

The same thing, of course, is true of the animus, as I have indicated. He, too, must be taken personally or he will dis-

11 Ibid., p. 199.

solve into a miasma of wordy generalities that only confuse the issue. For as Jung points out:

> As the anima produces *moods*, so the animus produces *opinions;* and as the moods of a man issue from a shadowy background, so the opinions of a woman rest on equally unconscious prior assumptions. Animus opinions very often have the character of solid convictions that are not lightly shaken, or of principles whose validity is seemingly unassailable.[12]

It is for this reason that the virtuous wife has, or seems to have, such an unassailable position when her spouse goes awandering. But he has a similarly unassailable conviction that his resentments are justified, an opinion about which there can be absolutely no question in his eyes. His wife *ought* to provide comfort and warmth regardless of his own behavior. He can be as bad-tempered as a bear or as cold as a saurian, but she must always be kind and loving and considerate: doesn't she know how sorely tried he is? So the anima firmly declares, and if his wife does not fulfill this role, then he has a right to sulk or get angry or seek for love elsewhere. And so "the animus draws his sword of power, and the anima scatters her poison." And the breach between the pair widens till it seems there can never be any basis for understanding.

So again we have to ask: Why does the anima or the animus work so persistently to bring about a separation? Were not these autonomous factors in the psyche the very ones that originally produced the sense of unity and caused the two to fall in love? Apparently this element in the psyche always seeks the place where the fire is. As Jung points out, the astonishing uniformity of the language of love demonstrates how general, collective, and really banal the actual situation is. Even though the lovers live in the illusion that they are related to one another in a most individual way, this is obviously not so at all. Yet to fall in love is doubtless a most significant experience. Its importance, however, lies not in the joy, even

[12] Ibid., p. 205.

ecstasy, of the condition, but rather in a different place. First it opens the way for the establishment of a real relationship between the two, one in which they can truly communicate on a deep level. It is a precious privilege to come to know another human being in this intimate way. And beyond that the experience pierces through the outer crust and reveals depths of emotion and intensity of life that would otherwise remain closed to the couple. They can no longer live their lives in the shallows, but must, willy-nilly, venture out into deep water. Apparently the anima and the animus in their true role always lead to the experience of the depths of life. For falling in love is an important experience, whether it finds fulfillment in life or meets with frustration. If, however, it is taken lightly or flippantly, the opportunity to experience the depths of life's meaning is lost. It is like the story of the angel who troubled the waters of Bethesda.[13] If no one should take advantage of the miraculous moment, nothing would happen, and the waters would resume their untroubled sleep.

The truth that the significance of life lies in our own attitude toward it is demonstrated over and over again in analytical practice. Someone comes in, and the analyst asks what is the matter. The patient replies, "Oh, really nothing much. It's hardly worth troubling you about." He then tells a story of some situation that may be rather insignificant on the surface, or may seem more important. In either case the analyst begins to ask questions, and it gradually becomes evident that this incident is not so trivial as it has seemed to be. As the patient begins to take it more seriously, the unconscious responds and brings its treasures to consciousness. Indeed, this trivial incident resembles the trivial symptom that may indicate a serious inner disease. Like the proverbial straw, it shows which way the wind is blowing. So our lives are trivial or significant according to the way in which we deal with them. Cataclysmic events do not necessarily make a significant or

[13] John 5: 4.

meaningful life, while "the daily round, the common task, can furnish all we need to ask"—though not in the way of merely creating a resigned and patient character, as the hymn would seem to suggest.

The lesson we should learn from this is that anything that stirs us deeply, whether in a positive or a negative way, should be taken seriously, not minimized, pushed aside, or dealt with either by repression or by compensation. If such a thing seems trivial, the real meaning of this bit of life has not been found. This is especially true where instinctive reactions are involved —anger; greed of any kind, whether for food, tobacco, money, or prestige; the thirst for knowledge; and, perhaps especially in these days, sexuality and love. This rule applies not only to heterosexual involvements and urges, but also to homosexual ones, as well as to autoerotic manifestations such as masturbation and fantasy-weaving, indeed to anything whatsoever that exerts an obsessive fascination or has a compulsive hold on one. If, however, a real and sustained effort is not made to discover what their underlying meaning is, naturally these instinctive impulses will have no psychological meaning, beyond the pleasurable satisfaction of the moment. For the experience of significance belongs exclusively to one who has achieved a measure of self-consciousness.

When a strong outgoing of the libido is frustrated, as it is, for instance, when someone in love meets with no response from the loved one or is jilted, or, still more, when the loved one dies, what happens? Grief, sorrow, hurt, perhaps anger and resentment, or, in the case of the death of the loved one, anger against God, loss of faith, despair—these are the result. But then two courses, two ways of taking this difficult experience, lie before one. Either one can continue to lament, hugging to oneself the sense of the cruelty of fate, and so on, *or* one can turn within and seek the meaning of this dreadfully hard experience. Usually, when this course is taken, the unconscious is immediately activated, and dreams, fantasies, or visions of deep significance rise into consciousness. Indeed, the frustration of outgoing libido is one of the commonest ways in which the journey of the soul, the quest for the treasure hard to attain, is initiated. The alchemists, for instance, tell of a lion, the greatest and most powerful of the beasts, symbol of the August sun, and of the strongest outgoing libido, whose paws have been cut off. It is frustrated in its natural outgoing, but it is this same lamed lion that is needed for the great work. The philosophic tree, the alchemists say, grows only out of the stump of the natural tree after it has been cut down. Similarly the Chinese teach that the fires of concupiscence must be turned back and forced inward if the jewel is to be formed in the center of the mandala. In Christian teaching the spiritual quest is usually started by the conviction of sin brought about when the natural outgoing of life, the roistering, unthinking, easy-going living, is checked by the spiritual teaching and by moral considerations. Only then can the spiritual life begin.

For when the outward-going of the life energy is checked, the unconscious is constellated, and the archetypes begin to manifest themselves in mythological images that portray the stages of development of the higher man, the twice-born. A new kind of psychological development is initiated, leading to the discovery of the supreme value that Jung calls the Self.

VI

THE "NOT-I" OF THE INNER WORLD:

THE ARCHETYPAL FIGURES

THE MATERIAL which must now be discussed is much more difficult and far less accessible than any we have so far dealt with. Indeed, during a psychological analysis, it is not usually encountered until the individual has himself become conscious of the distinction between the "I" and the "not-I" of the outer world and has also learned to distinguish between the ego and the shadow. That is, he must be aware, at least in some measure, of the contents of the personal unconscious.

With the discussion of the anima and animus, we have already entered the realm of the inner "not-I"—the collective unconscious, as Jung has named it. The work on the projection to others of the autoerotic elements and of the shadow, and the resulting freeing of the "I" from identification with the family and with the collective code, will have resulted in the establishment of a more or less clearly defined ego-structure. The personal psyche has by this means been separated into a conscious part under the ego and an unconscious part (the personal unconscious) personified by the shadow. The individual is now a person in his own right, with the power to choose his goal and the freedom of will to pursue it. But with the coming of a significant anima or animus involvement—that is, when the youth or maiden falls in love with someone of the opposite sex—elements of the psyche that have till then slumbered unrecognized in the unconscious awake, and forces that the individual has never before experienced and whose existence he has never suspected take possession of him. His conscious plans are interfered with, and the ability to choose his path is no longer available. For he is swept by emotions and moved by impulses that exert a compelling power over him, so that he is no longer master in his own house. But at the same time he finds himself alive as he has never been before. And as we saw in the last chapter, this startling change results from the constellation of the soul-image, which stands on the border between the personal psyche and the collective unconscious, that great and unknown world that impinges on the psyche on its inner or subjective side and whose powers have been released through the coming into consciousness of the soul-figure.

And so, we come definitely into the realm of the inner "not-I" and its manifestations. This is the realm of the collective unconscious, the vast psychic unknown world whose chief characteristic—as Jung so often says—is that it *is* unconscious; consequently we can deal with its material, its contents, its structure, only hypothetically. We can, however, be a little more definite in regard to its manifestations, as they show themselves in consciousness, that is, either in projection to the outer world or in subjective images occurring in dreams and fantasies. For the archetypes themselves are unknown and unseen. They manifest themselves, however, in pictures or images, in myths, and in what have been called by Kerényi [1] mythologems—that is, a series of myths that follow a definite pattern having a consecutive story and outcome. For instance,

[1] Kerényi, Prolegomena to *Essays on a Science of Mythology*, pp. 2-4.

the story of the hero is a mythologem; it starts with a child born in obscurity about whom there is a certain mystery, for it is rumored that his real parents were gods or kings. When he grows to manhood he performs certain feats and achieves certain ends. This whole story is the unfolding of an archetypal pattern in a particular form.

Just as the "not-I" of the outer world impinges on us and to a large extent controls us and determines our destiny—the more so the more unconscious we are—so, too, the "not-I" of the inner world has an unconditioned effect upon us if we remain unconscious in relation to it. We are then at its mercy, mere puppets of unseen and unrecognized forces. An illustration of this is the way in which the coming of an archetypal pattern into life sweeps people along. The rise of the Nazi movement is an outstanding example. Hitler was a man who was subjected to archetypal forces that he apparently made no attempt to control; and that which manifested itself in him was acted out in a very large proportion of the German people, so that they were caught up in a series of events whose outcome was inevitable. Indeed, Allen Dulles, who, during the war, was attached to the American Legation in Bern, recently stated in a television interview that he had frequently talked with Jung during the war years, for Jung, through his psychological understanding of these forces, could give Dulles an idea of what was likely to happen. Jung, therefore, without the knowledge of most people here, was of very significant aid to the Allies, because he could give a hint, at least, of which way events would turn.

But we remain puppets of these unrecognized forces until consciousness is developed in relation to them. For consciousness is a necessary prerequisite for choice, just as our first parents' exercise of free choice and the assimilation of the fruit of the tree of knowledge were connected. The knowledge they acquired was of both good and evil; that is, natural happenings were split into opposites for them, leaving them with the ability, even the necessity, to exercise choice. The natural impulse is, of course, to choose what seems to be good *for us;* but when we are aware of the opposites—that is, aware that good and evil are relative to each other—we realize that when we choose only the "good" we inevitably fall a victim to the "evil" that has been pushed into the unconscious. Not until we have undergone an experience of the collective unconscious can we expect to find a solution of this dichotomy on a new level of consciousness. But for this a *total* experience is required, one including all parts of the personality. An intellectual understanding is not enough.

Such an experience involves cutting oneself off from all the collectively accepted standards and reevaluating the life situation without the support that collective approval can give. It is an experience of isolation, of loneliness, often of despair. It has been called the "night sea journey," or the "journey of the soul," and it is the core of religious initiation and, to a lesser extent, the objective of all true education. It is invariably part of any psychological analysis that penetrates at all deeply into the psyche.

In discussing the "I" and the "not-I" of the outer world, I made use of the concept of the *Umwelt,* the own world in which each one of us lives; and I pointed out that this world contains, for us, only such things as stimulate us in either our efferent or our afferent receptors and that, while everything else that passes before us may be seen or heard, it does not register, it does not speak to us, because it is of no use to us. In the same way some people are completely deaf to everything that does not concern the "this world" life, so that it is useless to speak to them of spiritual or psychological matters which do not come within their *Umwelt.* For we remain oblivious to everything that has no meaning in our personal economy. Psychological facts have no meaning unless they are within our *Umwelt.* Now *meaning* is the key word here. On the physical plane, meaning implies usefulness for our personal purposes; on the psychic plane, meaning is the *sine qua non* of understanding. Jung writes:

> We must interpret; we must find meaning in things, otherwise we should be quite unable to think about them. [That is, they would not exist in our *Umwelt*. He says] We must resolve life and happenings, all that fulfils itself in itself, into images, meanings, concepts [he is talking here of the creative act, and he continues] thereby we deliberately detach ourselves from the living mystery.
>
> As long as we are caught up in the creative element itself we neither see nor understand; indeed we must not begin to understand, for nothing is more damaging and dangerous to immediate experience than cognition. But for the purpose of cognition [that is, for consciousness] we must detach ourselves from the creative process and regard it from without—only then does it become a picture that expresses meanings.[2]

This is true of religious experience, of active imagination, of dreams, and indeed of any experience of material that comes from the unconscious. While it is actually happening to us, we must not try to understand but must let it unfold itself in its own terms. But after it has unfolded itself, then, as Jung says, if we are to have any relation to it, other than one of wonder or awe, we must try to understand, because the living mystery is the very source of life and of life's energies, and it produces no effect on us if we merely look at such visions or such images as if they were moving on a cinema screen.

To pursue our analogy of the *Umwelt* a little further: If the boundary of our *Umwelt* is, as it were, composed of glass —a transparent and reflecting envelope, such as appeared in the woman's dream of her family at the festive dinner table, each member enclosed in his own glass case, or the other woman's dream that she was shut off from all contact with the world because she lived behind a glass screen—then we must realize that we see the outer world dimly, and frequently

[2] "On the Relations of Analytical Psychology to Poetic Art," p. 242.

it is distorted by reflections from within our own psyche. We see only those things that are behind us, that exist in either the personal or the collective unconscious as they are reflected on the glass wall of our *Umwelt*, just as Tennyson's Lady of Shalott, living isolated on her island, saw the real world only as it was reflected in her mirror. And Socrates, trying to explain this phenomenon to his pupils, used the image of a cave whose inmates faced a wall and could not turn to see the reality behind them, but could observe it only as moving shadows on the wall.

Most people, today, are convinced that they know the contents of the inner psychic world. One hears such statements as "I know what is in my unconscious." Indeed it is hard to recognize that we see the inner world only "through a glass darkly." [3] For the inner aspect of our *Umwelt* faces not the external world, but the inner one where the light of consciousness cannot reach. It is as if the inner aspect of our *Umwelt* were composed of dark glass, one-way glass. Through it we cannot see, so that all that exists and moves behind the glass wall can be seen only as it is reflected on the other side of the globe. We have many illustrations of this from religious history. Individuals who have been caught up into the unseen world invariably come back saying that they do not know what happened on the other side, though they know it was important. It is as if it were a consciousness in unconsciousness. St. Paul [4] says: "Whether in the body or out of the body, I cannot tell, God knoweth . . . [I] heard unspeakable words, which it is not lawful for a man to utter." The contents of the collective unconscious move and act and live deep within us, but we perceive them only dimly and usually in distorted guise, as they glide across the screen of the world about us.

For, as I have said above, the contents of the collective unconscious appear to us in the form of images and typical

3 I Cor. 13: 12.
4 II Cor. 12: 3-4.

happenings. These are the themes of myths and legends, and they appear today in what Jung called "big dreams," using the term that some primitive peoples use to distinguish those dreams that have a collective import from the "little dreams" that are of merely personal significance. It is as if these are typical forms in the unknown psychic hinterland that determine the pattern of psychic experience much as the typical patterns that we call instincts determine the potentialities for biological experience.

In discussing the meaning of the term *archetype*, Jung gives many examples of its use in classical and medieval literature. It occurs in philosophical and religious writings as well as in alchemy. He sums up his discussion by saying:

> "Archetype" is an explanatory paraphrase of the Platonic *eidos*. For our purposes this term is apposite and helpful, because it tells us that so far as the collective unconscious contents are concerned we are dealing with archaic or primordial types, that is with universal images that have existed since the remotest times.[5]

The word archetype is well chosen, for *typos* means something that makes an imprint. And so arche-types mean the ancient, primordial types that are impressed on the psyche as the result of the age-long experience of life that man and the animals before him have passed through. The collective unconscious is composed of, or contains, these archetypes, patterns of psychic energy, of life energy, much as the structure of the universe, so far as we know, consists of energies which we can neither explore directly nor define exactly. They are patterns, unseen determinants of psychic nature, that in themselves forever elude us. Jung [6] has compared them to the axis systems of crystals, which determine the form and structure of the crystal even while the salt is in solution and therefore consists not of crystals but of molecules or dissociated atoms.

[5] "Archetypes of the Collective Unconscious," p. 4.
[6] "Psychological Aspects of the Mother Archetype," pp. 79 f.

Consequently, while the term archetype refers to a very real fact, anything we say about it must necessarily be quite tentative. We are on much safer ground when we begin to examine the forms in which the archetypes manifest themselves. For just as the instincts can be represented in clear-cut states, such as hunger or parental protectiveness, and are also manifested in patterns of behavior, like the nesting and migrating of birds, so, too, the archetypes can be portrayed in images, such as mother or hero, ford or bridge, weapon or tool, and can appear also in the patterns of continuous action that we call mythologems. For example, the hero has a typical history and a typical task to perform; the encounter of anima and animus leads to a drama that repeats itself over and over again in real life as well as in fiction.

These mythologems are the subject of mythology, of legends, of folklore and fairy tale, and significantly enough the same themes repeat themselves in history and are to be met with as well in all significant drama and epic. They also form the theme of fantasy, whether this is the basis of great art or the idle occupation of an empty hour, and they appear in dreams and in the products of active imagination.

In discussing the collective unconscious we are on particularly difficult ground. The whole subject is peculiarly problematic, for not only is it terra incognita, being, as Jung never tired of pointing out, essentially unconscious, but in addition it presents itself to us as an undifferentiated reality where things merge into each other in a most confusing way. It appears, for instance, in dreams and visions as a dark and mysterious realm, perhaps as a primeval forest, where nothing can be seen clearly and where the traveler quickly becomes confused and lost, or, even more frequently, as the ocean where, lacking a compass, the voyager no longer knows his direction and cannot possibly know what creatures, what dangers, what treasures, may lurk in the depths. He can find his way only by the positions of the heavenly bodies or by the use of a compass, that is, he must be orientated by factors beyond the "world."

The ocean is a particularly apt symbol for the collective unconscious, for both are fluid, no one part being really separate or distinct from any other part. A drop of water evaporates from the Indian Ocean, becomes a part of a cloud of water vapor that is borne about by the air currents, and finally descends to the earth once more as a drop of rain that may fall into any river or sea anywhere on the earth. Is it now part of the Indian Ocean, or is it part of the upper firmament, or does it "belong" to the New England river into which it has fallen?

This attempted analogy gives some small idea of the difficulty of dealing with the collective unconscious, whose contents merge and separate and merge again in a correspondingly confusing manner. But just as the chemist can analyze the sample of H_2O no matter what phase it is in at the moment —salt water, vapor, rain, ice, or fresh water in a river—so the ego consciousness can "catch" and analyze a symbol image that comes from the collective unconscious in the form of dream, vision, work of art, or fantasy.

It is not possible in the present state of our knowledge to "map" the collective unconscious in any definitive way. At best we can only try to clarify certain dominant themes, leaving to the future the task of further exploration. There are a number of possible ways in which we might attempt to unravel the enigma of the collective unconscious. We might take an outstanding and universal archetype, such as the Mother, and explore its ramifications as Jung and others have already done.[7] From the size and scope of the works on this subject, it is obvious that the application of the method to every available archetypal image would demand many encyclopaedic vol-

[7] For the hero, see Jung, *Symbols of Transformation* (originally published in 1916 under the title *The Psychology of the Unconscious*); for the Feminine Principle, see Harding, *Women's Mysteries, Ancient and Modern*; Neumann, *The Great Mother*; for discussions of various important archetypes, see Neumann, *The Origins and History of Consciousness*.

umes and a whole army of research workers. Perhaps some day such a compendium may be possible, but for the present we have to content ourselves with a more modest attempt.

Here I will take a different approach and will describe very briefly certain themes that are apt to appear in a somewhat regular sequence both during the development of the individual from childhood on, and also in a similar sequence during the course of an analysis.

About this problem Jung writes:

> The archetypes are the imperishable elements of the unconscious, but they change their shape continually. It is a well-nigh hopeless undertaking to tear a single archetype out of the living tissue of the psyche; but despite their interwovenness they do form units of meaning that can be apprehended intuitively. Psychology, as one of the many expressions of psychic life, operates with ideas which in their turn are derived from archetypal structures and thus generate a somewhat more abstract kind of myth. Psychology therefore translates the archaic speech of myth into a modern mythologem—not yet, of course, recognized as such—which constitutes one element of the myth "science." This seemingly hopeless undertaking is a *living and lived myth,* satisfying to persons of a corresponding temperament.[8]

In an earlier chapter I pointed out that the external world, the "not-I" outside us, may be considered to consist of persons, things, and situations, and I stated that there exist in the psyche imprints, or archetypes, of corresponding persons, things, and situations. So in this attempt to give a brief survey of what is known of the collective unconscious I shall make use of this formulation and give examples of outstanding archetypes of persons, things, and situations.

In the development of the individual from infancy to old age, archetypal themes are activated in the unconscious in a fairly regular sequence, each in turn acting as the dominant of that particular phase of life. These archetypal themes are

[8] "The Psychology of the Child Archetype," pp. 179 f.

the correlates of the individual's life experience. So, for instance, an old man is moved by inner motives and impulses that are very different from those that determine the behavior and experience of the child, whether the individual is conscious of this fact or not.

Dr. James Henderson, an English educator, has worked out a plan by which the material of the entire school curriculum can be based on the particular archetype that is unfolding naturally within the students at successive age levels.[9] In this way the subject matter "speaks to their condition," as the Society of Friends would say, and so it has an immediate appeal and exerts a strong influence on their psychological development. Dr. Henderson points out that, in the gradual development of the young personality, dominants of the unconscious emerge in a regular sequence and that these archetypal motifs underlie the stages of psychic and character development with which every pedagogue is familiar. The child becomes involved in a progressive series of interests that can be predicted with reasonable accuracy, since they belong to his particular age group. It is even possible to make a fairly accurate guess at the age of a child or youth if one is told what his interests are. By the same token, an immature adult is classified as having the psychological age of a child of twelve, say, or fifteen, according to what interests him as well as his proficiency in learned skills. Dr. Henderson suggests that the school curriculum should be based on this knowledge of the archetypes, so that the subject matter presented to young people would be definitely related to that particular pattern unfolding within them as the correlate of their growth and development.

Dr. Henderson's study starts with the eleven-year-old group, but his ideas can just as well be applied to much younger children and to college students. Boys at puberty are

[9] *Analytical Psychology and Education.*

concerned with competitive games and the acquisition of physical strength and skill, corresponding to the hero task, while
their interest in group activity corresponds to the formation of
men's societies in primitive tribes, the archetypal significance
of such interests is concerned with the separation of the youth
from the mother and the establishment of impersonal values
and regulations to govern conduct. Adolescents begin to be
involved with members of the opposite sex and with romantic love, owing to the emergence of the anima and animus on
a new level of importance, while very small children are more
interested in animals than in people. Stories for tiny tots are
mostly about animals—"The Three Bears," and "The Three
Little Pigs and the Big Bad Wolf," for instance. This is surely
because the child himself is as yet hardly human; human self-
consciousness has not yet arisen in him, and so his sympathy,
his empathy, is caught by the animal. Once I was amusing a
two-year-old by showing him my Christmas cards. There were
many pictures of the baby Jesus, and presently we came to a
picture of the angels announcing the birth to the shepherds. I
spoke of how pleased the shepherd boys were to hear about the
new baby, and the child, after looking intently at the picture,
said, "And what do the little sheep think about it?" In fact,
I have heard this same reaction from a child on two separate
occasions.

And so the theme, the mythologem, of the animal, the helpful one and the dangerous one, is active in the little child,
who knows as yet so little of a world that is big and frightening like a fierce animal. Yet the gentle and harmless animals
have succeeded in surviving, and in the child the theme of the
helpful animal shows him, as it were, the right way to act.
When an adult is faced with an unknown and alarming situation, these same images may appear in his dreams, and if he
will pay attention to them, they may indicate a way through
the dangers that surround him.

At the time of the Indian wars, a young Sioux boy named Black Elk, during the long fast preceding his initiation into manhood, dreamed that a Chickadee Person came to teach him and to become his guiding spirit for his whole life. The story is related by Black Elk [10] in his autobiography. As was the custom, he told his dream to the assembled elders, and they realized that the message was not for the dreamer alone but applied to the entire tribe, and taught that they should follow the example of the chickadee, who is friendly and can stay with the tribe all winter because he never fights against nature but endures everything patiently. This advice was followed by the tribe, with the result that they made friends with the white man and survived when their cousins, the Iroquois, who resisted by all means in their power, perished.

A very similar theme is found in the story of Osiris and Isis. [11] On one occasion Osiris was persuaded by his hostile and jealous brother, Set, the Dark One, to lie down in a coffin. Set then slammed down the lid of the coffin and threw it into the Nile. When his sister-wife, Isis, heard about it, she went in search of her husband. She was guided by the voices of children and animals till she reached the place where the coffin had gone ashore. This helpful aspect of the animal and the child is a constant theme in the hero quest, and it could be illustrated from Celtic myth and the Arthurian legends as well as from many fairy stories, where the helpless one may be helped by a helpful animal and, by an extension of the same idea, the helpless one himself becomes the hero. For instance, in certain American Indian myths the hero who leads the people to a new land is Hare; and American Negroes tell a long saga about Brer Rabbit, the weak one who like his African counterpart outwits and overcomes by intelligence,

[10] J. G. Neihardt, *Black Elk Speaks.*
[11] Plutarch, "Isis and Osiris," tr. by G. R. S. Mead, in *Thrice Greatest Hermes,* I, 347.

not by brawn. The hare or the rabbit also plays a part in our own Easter folk customs, and even in orthodox Christian symbolism the hero, Christ, is referred to as a Lamb, who does not resist his enemies but submits to his fate.

And so we see that this mythologem is one that should be taught to the young and the helpless as a guide to behavior and should be contemplated by adults who are confronted by overwhelming and hostile forces. We have heard, for instance, how an attitude based on this archetype proved a successful guide to survival in concentration camps, as well as in natural calamities where "playing dead" may save one's life when active resistance will almost inevitably lead to disaster. This is one form of the hero myth, but there are others where a very different attitude is required. Indeed the stories of the hero illustrate the paradoxical character of all archetypes.

The Mother Archetype

WE HAVE already spoken of the mother archetype that envelops and protects the embryonic psyche of the child and of how the image in which it appears may be good, beneficent, restoring, nurturing, and protective, or, on the contrary, may be threatening, destructive, and possessive. In the latter case it will be represented as a great maw that devours the child, or a whale-dragon that swallows the hero. If he is to fulfill the hero role, the child, in order to attain full manhood, must fight and overcome the monster, even kill it.

An individual who suffers from a mother complex in its negative form will inevitably fall a victim to the crippling and suffocating qualities of the mother archetype, unless he finds and follows the hero path. Jung outlines the unfortunate results of such a mother complex and then goes on to speak of the value of the relation to the mother. He is discussing the effect of a mother complex in a daughter and says:

143

The positive aspect of the first type of complex, namely the over-development of the maternal instinct, is identical with that well-known image of the mother which has been glorified in all ages and in all tongues. This is the mother-love which is one of the most moving and unforgettable memories of our lives, the mysterious root of all growth and change; the love that means homecoming, shelter, and the long silence from which everything begins and in which everything ends. Intimately known and yet strange like Nature, lovingly tender and yet cruel like fate, joyous and untiring giver of life—*mater dolorosa* and mute implacable portal that closes upon the dead. Mother is mother-love, *my* experience and *my* secret. Why risk saying too much, too much that is false and inadequate and beside the point, about that human being who was our mother, the accidental carrier of that great experience which includes herself and myself and all mankind, and indeed the whole created nature, the experience of life whose children we are? The attempt to say these things has always been made, and probably always will be; but a sensitive person cannot in all fairness load that enormous burden of meaning, responsibility, duty, heaven and hell, on to the shoulders of one frail and fallible human being—so deserving of love, indulgence, understanding, and forgiveness—who was our mother. He knows that the mother carries for us that inborn image of the *mater natura* and *mater spiritualis*, of the totality of life of which we are a small and helpless part. Nor should we hesitate for one moment to relieve the human mother of this appalling burden, for our own sakes as well as hers. It is just this massive weight of meaning that ties us to the mother and chains her to her child, to the physical and mental detriment of both. A mother-complex is not got rid of by blindly reducing the mother to human proportions. Besides that, we run the risk of dissolving the experience "Mother" into atoms, thus destroying something supremely valuable and throwing away the golden key which a good fairy laid in our cradle. This is why mankind has always instinctively added the pre-existent divine pair to the personal parents—the "god"-father and "god"-mother of the newborn child—so that, from sheer unconsciousness or shortsighted rationalism, he should never forget himself so far as to invest his own parents with divinity.[12]

[12] "Psychological Aspects of the Mother Archetype," pp. 92-93.

At this point the archetypal theme divides and has to be considered from the point of view of the mother on the one hand and of the son or daughter on the other, just as in actual life the relation between parent and child can be and should be viewed from both angles.

Let us take up the story of the child first. He is the one who must grow and develop into maturity, when in his turn he will have to fill the role of parent. This in itself is not simple. If for any reason the child is unable or unwilling to undertake the heavy task of freeing himself from the parents and from the parental archetypes he will remain childish, undeveloped. In everyday life he swells the numbers that make up the average conventional population, whose criterion of right and wrong, of acceptable and unacceptable, is determined entirely by what the parents and the elders of the community sanction and, as a result, he is accepted by the community as by an indulgent parent. If he cannot accomplish even this degree of independence he will remain forever a child, needing a loving parent who will support him personally, finding this situation so much easier and so much more attractive than the discipline essential for adaptation to the more impersonal rule of the "fathers" of the community. In such a case he becomes what is technically called a *puer aeternus*— one who, like the youthful gods of the antique world, is always a child, forever promising a value, even a genius, that he never achieves. These youthful gods are always closely related to adoring mother goddesses, and their counterparts in actual life are also usually the darlings of unwise and doting parents. They are the "white-headed boys," who can do no wrong, at least in "mother's" eyes.

The Hero

BUT IF the urge towards self-development is stronger in the "child" he will try to gain his freedom and independence.

Again the mythologem divides into two streams. First there is the theme (mentioned above) of the helpless one and the helpful animal, leading in its deepest meaning to the development of the innocent hero, the one who overcomes not by resistance but by adaptation. Such a one, however, frequently becomes the innocent victim, the sacrificial one. This is the theme of the dying and resurrecting gods, a further development of the "puer aeternus" theme, that has its expression in the lives of many historical figures whose death has led to a resurrection of the spiritual ideas and ideals for which they died—and which exemplify the value hidden in the depths of the mother unconscious. Such an outcome is exemplified, for instance, in the saying that the blood of the martyrs is the seed of the Church. This archetype is supremely expressed in the life and death of Christ and in the teaching that by his death mankind gains eternal life—a life not in this world but in a non-material spiritual, that is, psychic realm.

But the mythologem of the hero can take another form, the emphasis falling not on self-denial and submission but on courage and struggle.[13] From the very beginning the hero is usually set apart from others. Frequently he is born in depressed and inconspicuous circumstances, though sometimes he may be of royal descent. But in that case, in the typical story, he is stolen from his parents in infancy, and often he is brought up by peasants, or even by animals (as Romulus and Remus were by a wolf), or by a semihuman ogress, harsh human beings, or perhaps a sorceress (as in the case of St. George[14]). Shortly after his birth the hero goes through a period of dan-

[13] I give a brief account of this mythologem in *Psychic Energy*, ch. 9: "The Inner Conflict: The Dragon and the Hero." Joseph Campbell has followed the mythologem through its numerous manifestations in *The Hero with a Thousand Faces*, and there is a further elaboration of it in Erich Neumann's *The Origins and History of Consciousness*, pp. 131-256, where the stages of the hero's task are differentiated.

[14] R. Johnson, *The Famous Historie of the Seaven Champions of Christendome* (1687), quoted with commentary in Harding, *Psychic Energy*, pp. 255 ff.

146

ger when the ruling powers try to destroy him. Thus Christ was threatened by Herod, Moses by Pharaoh, and Dionysos by the Titans, who in one version of the myth actually tore him to pieces, so that he had to be rescued by his father Zeus and born a second time. This is the typical story of the birth of the hero. He is then generally chased from his home and sent on a long and perilous journey. The flight of Joseph and Mary into Egypt with the infant is a typical example, and on a collective or tribal level the wandering of the Children of Israel in the wilderness follows the same pattern. This theme is exemplified over and over again in mythology. It is a typical story.

Later the hero starts to free himself from the mother, the enclosing mother archetype, by struggling against her bondage and her attraction. This actually means that he must struggle against his own desire to remain with her. For, in the final analysis, the struggle is really against his own childish desire to be cared for, protected, warmed, and cherished. This is a phase that is lived out overtly in early adolescence against the actual mother, who represents to the young person the mother archetype. The problem should be resolved during these years on the external plane, though it may persist unresolved for years even on this level, and naturally during the life span it will be encountered over and over again on an inner plane.

Young people, especially boys, begin to rebel against the rule of the mother around puberty. They struggle against her control, however reasonable and kindly it may be. They have *got* to be free—it is a passion with them. This instinctive attitude may be the cause of great suffering to the poor woman who is doing her best to understand and guide her boy while he goes through the changes and troubles of puberty. If the mother is not understanding or tolerant and, in her turn, reacts in a negative way, the situation is naturally aggravated. And if she has never been able to give her boy the love and understanding he needs, his individuality will have been inadequately nourished, and his adult self will be maimed in consequence. For if a child has not been truly loved but has been thwarted in the development of his individuality either by overindulgence and spoiling or by repressive discipline and frustration, he will be quite unable to free himself from the home, and his struggles for freedom may go on far too long, sometimes for his entire lifetime. These people become what Neumann calls "the strugglers." Many cases of adolescent rebellion and delinquent behavior are really the results of just this undernourishment. For, on the one side, the very closeness of the bond between mother and child constitutes a threat to his development, causing a backward longing for security and warmth; while, on the other, the longing for the mother depths, where renewal and life-giving water can be found, can itself be a dangerous lure, especially in youth, though it plays a very different role during later years. For the mother represents the abyss, or "chaos," to use the terms of the Chaldean Creation myth,[15] or the "depths," as in the Gnostic Chaldean Oracles. She is the abyss that contains *all*, all the unknown values of life, all the germs of future growth, and the final promise of union with the Absolute. To the old man or woman this should be the goal of all endeavor, but to the youth it can be a fascinating and entrancing mirage distracting him from his real task in the outer world.

The Father

BUT IT is not only deprivation on the emotional side of life, not only lack of mother love and understanding in the external world with consequent unrootedness in the mother depths of the inner world, that leads to these unfortunate results. So far we have spoken mainly of the mother and the child's relation to her, and it is true that this is the fundamental archetype that

[15] S. H. Langdon, *Semitic Mythology*, in *The Mythology of All Races*, V, 178. See also G. R. S. Mead, *The Chaldean Oracles*, I, 55: "[She is] source of [all] sources, womb that holds all things together."

influences not only the child but the adult as well. But the reaction to the father and to the masculine principle he represents has an influence secondary only to that of the mother.

In the days of the matriarchal culture the Mother Goddess ruled alone, and in the experience of the child the mother comes first and the father takes his place only later. But with the coming of the patriarchate the Father and the father archetype have come to hold a dominant place. The individual of the Western world is governed in consciousness by the laws of the patriarchal society in which he lives; in the unconscious, however, he may still be living under the rule of the matriarchal order, and the resulting conflict within him may seriously hamper his adapatation.

The father stands for strength, power, authority, law, right, and will-power. The archetypal images in which this principle has been expressed down the ages start with brute strength. The bull-gods of Egypt and the enormous bull statues of Assyrian art are examples. Father Zeus was such a god of strength and tyrannical power, and it was not till about the ninth century B.C., as Hesiod tells us, that "beside Great Zeus upon his throne, Justice took her seat." [16] In one of the dialogues,[17] Socrates asked of what justice might be formed. The debate did not seem to get beyond the idea that justice was represented by the will, the fiat of the person who was at the top. In spite of all Socrates' questioning, justice, as an impersonal and impartial principle, was never clearly formulated. So that Justice had barely taken her seat upon the throne of Zeus even in those days. Before that the will of Zeus, not modified by any consideration other than his own desire, had ruled; but from that time on the principle of justice and of right came gradually to take precedence over brute power. The same evolution can be traced in the case of Yahweh through the cen-

---

[16] *Works and Days*, p. 261 (Evelyn-White edn., p. 23).
[17] Plato, *Protagoras*, 322c-361c *passim*.

turies of Old Testament history to those immediately preceding the Christian era, when God becomes Father.

These archetypes not only are represented in the form that the gods assume but are to be found as well in the dreams of modern people, and they influence us in our daily lives in two other ways. First, they may be projected to someone in the environment. This does not necessarily mean that we see such a person as a god; we may not be conscious at all that this projection has fallen upon this particular man, but in our reactions to him it becomes clear that we behave towards him and feel towards him *as if* he were the most powerful or the wisest person, one having qualities surpassing by far all human limits. His words carry a weight beyond their actual value and we cannot avoid being influenced by them. We are caught as by a spell and are unable to exercise any adequate critique based on his actual accomplishment. Or it may happen that we ourselves become possessed by this powerful archetype. In that case, we act as if we had superior wisdom or authority and expect others to recognize our superiority and pay us the respect we feel to be our due.

Behind the personal father, then, stands the archetype of Father, manifested as ruler or teacher, as one having authority, symbolically the King, or as one having wisdom, symbolically the Priest—and finally as God.

And so in his struggle against the mother-rule the child, and later the adolescent, is helped by the constellation of the father archetype. For instance, in the nursery the mother's say-so is the sole arbiter of right and wrong; she makes and embodies the law. But when the child goes to school, an impersonal law begins to function. School is ruled by clock-time, the nursery by what mother says is "time"—to eat or sleep or wash or go out or come in. Nursery life is governed by the mother and by her alone. But at school the impersonal law of the father begins to replace the personal law of the mother. Logos supersedes Eros in certain realms of life, and this is of enormous help to the young person struggling for his freedom. His chief complaint against the seemingly arbitrary rule of the mother is: "It isn't fair!" He has begun to feel that Justice should also sit on the throne. This is a quality of the masculine principle.

The Group

BUT EVENTUALLY a time arrives when the law of the father comes to be as restrictive as the law of the mother had formerly been. Then a new archetype begins to function, leading the emerging individuality another step towards autonomy and further development. This is the archetype of union and cooperation that comes into play when the weak who want to be free find that by joining their forces they can gain added strength, not only against the regressive backward pull to childhood and mother love but also against the rule of the father. For while in the past the rule of the father has helped them in their struggle against the mother-rule, now, in its turn, it begins to hamper their free creative energies by insistence on the authority of established order.

This development is exemplified historically in the founding of the Greek *polis*, the city state. For then the masculine principle began to assert itself over against the mother-rule of the archaic matriarchal period, and a culture was developed in which the masculine principle and virtues were emphasized and enhanced by the emergence of homosexuality and its social acceptance. The effect of this was to foster masculine values and, also, to provide a basis of emotional gratification by means of which individual men could free themselves, in some part, from their dependence on the matriarchate and mother love. But man's purpose and determination are weak in view of the power woman exerts over him by virtue of his physical needs and his desire for love and comfort, a fact that Aristophanes satirized in his comedy *Lysistrata*, in which the heroine persuaded the women of Hellas to refuse to sleep with their husbands unless they put an end to the great war and returned home, as they promptly did!

So, too, youngsters in their teens, who are rebelling against both the lure of mother love and warmth and the dominance of father authority and the security it gives, form groups, societies, and gangs. The need to satisfy their growing sexual urge without running the risk of falling again under petticoat influence, on the one hand, and the further need to satisfy the longing for warm human relationship by closer ties of friendship, on the other, may result in the appearance of homosexuality among them. If the period of struggle so characteristic of early adolescence is unduly prolonged, the homosexual phase of instinctual life may also persist.

The emotional aspect of this period manifests itself in the development of the gregarious instinct. Teenagers form groups largely because the sense of belonging in a group of their peers tends to compensate for the loss of the family tie. Such groups can be helpful, wholesome, and valuable, leading to the development of group spirit, co-operation, and the investment of personal interests and desires in a collective ideal or goal, or they can be destructive, all the negative qualities being let loose with the sanction of the group, while the social morals and family codes are replaced by the code adopted by the group for its personal ends and gratification.

Just as the idea of father and mother presupposes a child, so the pattern of "group" or collective presupposes a "one"; the "many" is offset by the "one," the leader, whom all the rest follow. It is said that in the Alps contests or duels are fought among the cows of a herd till one emerges as victor over all the rest and becomes queen. Each year the queens of the various herds fight it out till one is acknowledged as supreme and is so accepted by all the herds of the district. A flock of hens, too, establishes a social hierarchy in what Clyde Allee,[18] the

[18] *The Social Life of Animals*, pp. 176-208.

ecologist, who worked it out, called a "pecking order" in which one hen lords it over all the others and may peck any of them. The others, according to their place in the social order they have established, are allowed to peck all those beneath them, but not any above. At the bottom is one unfortunate individual whom all may peck, but who may peck none, who thus becomes the butt of them all. But, and here is a very interesting point, if she gets to the point where she can stand it no longer and rebels, she does not peck the one next above her. No, she must undertake the most heroic task and peck the leader. If she wins in the resulting battle, then she in turn is acknowledged as queen of the flock. So we see that one and the same archetype rules in the social animals and in man. For in human society a similar law (or archetype) holds good, and in any group of human beings a leader will sooner or later emerge. So constant is this law that we usually take account of it ahead of time. The first act of a committee is to appoint a chairman; of a democracy, to elect a president; of a school, to appoint a teacher, and so on. These are conscious acts, and the leader appointed has well-understood functions and limitations. But in a situation that has *not* been consciously arranged, the unconscious brings about a somewhat similar result. A crowd, for instance, especially one in which emotions run high, as in a group brought together because of a stirring of unconscious elements common to all its members, quickly degenerates into a mob, and sooner or later one individual will become the spokesman for the whole group. He is usually the one in whom the emotions are strongest and most unconscious; the mob spirit takes possession of him, and he voices the unconscious or partly unconscious wishes of the crowd. His words inflame the others, because he dares to say openly what they have hardly dared to admit to themselves. They then throw off all the conscious restraints of the father, that is, of the socially accepted mores and conventions, and surrender themselves to the impulses that surge up from the darkest depths of the unconscious. The leader becomes a rabble-rouser, a prophet, perhaps a Hitler.

In other cases the leader who voices the unrealized longings of a group may invoke quite different impulses, for the emotions stirring in the unconscious may be redemptive instead of destructive. There will then arise a spiritual leader, perhaps even a Messiah. This was very clearly shown in the century immediately preceding the Christian era, when in the whole of Judaism and in the antique world as well the longing for a savior became manifested.

Hero and King

AND SO the archetype of the hero and his typical story and adventure leads into that of the leader and of the king, who also has a typical story and a typical fate. For when the hero has succeeded in his fight against the established powers, represented by the king, he becomes king in his turn and enters a new cycle, where constructive effort must replace the fight for freedom. Because this is an extremely difficult transition to make, many a one who has been successful in the hero fight finds it impossible to change his attitudes and become a constructive leader in the new era. As king he must now build and organize, and institute reforms, and as he grows older his revolutionary and dynamic drives give way to conservative habits and values. Such a man is naturally concerned to protect what he has created. Gradually the king who was once a reformer becomes the symbol of the established order, and a new generation arises that feels stifled under the restraints of those very laws that the formerly revolutionary king enacted. Soon a hero will come forth to do battle with the ruler, thus freeing the members of his generation from the sense of oppression that prevents them from creating anything of their own. Then "the king must die," [19] a mythologem of which the King of Nemi [20] is a typical example. For this is one of the basic archetypal patterns of life. It lives itself out in a cyclic pattern corresponding to the seasons of summer and winter or the rhythm of day and night.

Anima and Animus

IN THE development of consciousness in the individual the hero rebellion usually takes place before the constellation of the anima image has occurred as an entity apart from the mother image. As soon as this new archetype begins to function the entire psychological orientation changes. Around the age of fifteen, boys begin to be aware of girls as different from themselves—strange, attractive, and desirable. New emotions begin to stir in them, and part of their interest is diverted from the "group" of their peers to a single, personal, emotional interest in a particular girl. This is a happening of the greatest moment, for here for the first time an individual relation must be created with someone outside the family, outside the gang, someone who is different from himself, strange, unknown, exciting. Childhood friendships may have been warm and satisfying to youngsters, but they do not touch the depths of emotion that this experience touches. The earlier friendships are usually with someone of the same sex, so that the mechanism of identification gives each a sufficient understanding, or appearance of understanding, of the other to form the basis for a companionship and friendship satisfying at that age. But with the coming of the projection of the anima and animus, an entirely new level of experience is opened up—one that demands and produces a big jump in psychological development.

[19] Cf. Mary Renault's novel, *The King Must Die.*
[20] Frazer, *The Golden Bough*, chap. 1.

And so the young people enter the phase of anima and animus psychology mentioned in an earlier chapter. At this point the whole psychological scene changes. Up to this time the boy has been struggling against both the all-embracing and possessive mother and his own backward longing for love and protection. But with the constellation of the anima image a new factor comes into the picture. To win his beloved he must free himself from the mother tie. In actual life the young man wishing to marry must normally leave home and apply himself to work so as to make a home for his bride and the children of the future. Then the young couple will have to take upon themselves adult responsibilities, and in their turn assume the role of parents. The hand of the clock has moved round—full circle—and a new cycle begins.

In order to free himself from his bondage to the mother, the youth must conquer his childish dependence and his desire to be loved and cared for without effort on his own part. The myths invariably represent this transition in the form of a battle, a fight against the mother in the guise of a monster, usually a dragon. That is to say, it is not the personal mother, the actual woman, who must be overcome, but the mother archetype. Usually this dragon has imprisoned the beautiful damsel and keeps her shut up in a dungeon, that is, in the unconscious. It is to free this maiden that the hero has to undertake his heroic task. The damsel is, of course, the anima, and the myths show quite clearly what the psychological condition of the youth on the threshold of life is. For while he has struggled against the paternal rule and has probably gained for himself a measure of both inner and outer freedom and a more or less conscious ego personality—he has gone away from home, to college or to a job, or has perhaps been called up into the army—and while he feels himself to be independent, very much a man, free to do exactly as he pleases, yet the question remains: How free is he really in the *emotional* realm? Does he still look for father's support, financially and socially; does he still expect the kind of love and protection he had in childhood from his mother, regardless of whether or not he does anything to deserve it? In a time of difficulty, can he face the problem like a man, or does he look for some way out, either by evading the issue, running home for help, getting drunk, or in some way acting like a child rather than like a man? If he does so, it indicates that his anima—that is, his feeling side, the ability to relate without going to pieces—is still under the power of the mother-dragon.

Then if, instead of playing around, satisfying his physical urges by casual and promiscuous contacts where he has no responsibility and can walk out if things do not go as he likes, he falls in love, the situation changes. New emotions are evoked, new and entirely unexpected *energies* become available, and these can provide the incentive for a truly heroic feat. In the myths this is represented by the dragon fight. It is not a fight against the actual mother. It is the dragon who must be killed and dismembered, not the mother. Here is one of the most serious fallacies of Freudian teaching. For many of the Freudians take this symbolism literally and teach that children should be allowed, even encouraged, to "act out" their resistance against the actual mother, and to express their negative feelings against *her* by breaking a mother doll and pulling it to pieces. Someone has even invented a doll with breasts that can be pulled off and limbs that can be disarticulated just for this purpose. Some therapists not only permit these acts of mayhem and matricide, but encourage them or even suggest them to children who have no such obvious impulses, on the theory that it is "normal" to have such secret feelings against the mother. A little child surely needs to achieve a measure of freedom from dependence on his mother, but he must accomplish this by acquiring some skills for himself, not by severing his relation to his mother or by rebelling against wise guidance and discipline. The dragon fight belongs not to childhood but to late adolescence, and then it is not to be directed against the actual mother. However, if there has been a too close bond between mother and child, whether because of love between them, or because of possessiveness on the mother's part that has kept the child dependent, then negative reactions will certainly be constellated in the child, giving rise to repeated struggles between the two. Apart from such an unfortunate strengthening of the mother-tie, most sons have to go through a very painful period of overt resistance against the mother, and she too has to face this "time of troubles" and accomplish the "sacrifice of the son," a myth discussed in my *Woman's Mysteries*. But with good will on both sides and with increasing insight, a relationship of greater affection and deeper understanding can usually be established on the new footing, gained through the victory of the son: a victory not just over the mother, but far more significantly over his own backward longing for his childhood's paradise.

In the stories of the dragon fight the dragon is killed by the hero and the imprisoned maiden is released. The young people then marry. The maiden is the anima, his soul-image that heretofore has remained projected to his mother, or to *the* Mother, and must now be rescued so that the youth can develop a relation to his own soul and to the eros values she represents.

In actual life, when the youth has overcome his own childishness and has freed himself from his tie to his mother sufficiently to be able to fall in love and to marry the girl of his choice, the values formerly embodied in the mother will be transferred to the loved one, and the problem of his release from the mother bond and his achievement of true freedom, that is, the differentiation of the "I" from the "not-I" of the inner world, will have to be taken up on a new and more conscious level.

We must consider now the corresponding experience of the girl. It was pointed out in the second chapter that in growing up the girl has a different problem from the boy. He must separate himself completely from the mother to follow the masculine road, while the girl comes to womanhood not by going over to the masculine side, but by assimilating the feminine spirit embodied in the mother, usually by identifying with her. Just as the awakening of sexuality in the boy initiates his struggles against the mother, so too a change begins at puberty in the girl. Usually she stops being a tomboy and begins to be interested in her own appearance; something in her turns her towards making herself attractive to the male, and she usually suffers from recurrent moods of a heavy, sultry, languorous dreaming, frequently associated with her monthly periods. As F. W. H. Myers writes:

> Lo, as some innocent and eager maiden
>   Leans o'er the wistful limit of the world,
>
> Dreams of the glow and glory of the distance,
>   Wonderful wooing and the grace of tears,
> Dreams with what eyes and what a sweet insistence
>   Lovers are waiting in the hidden years.[21]

At such times she becomes immersed in fantasies and day dreams of a lover, a strong man, perhaps a cave man, who will make love to her, possibly abduct and rape her, and bear her away to an imagined heaven of sensuality. This is one reason why the Victorians took such care to guard young girls with chaperones and duennas, for the girl who has such dreams, or unconscious urges, is usually entirely unaware of what the reality would involve. Our adolescents today are somewhat protected in that they are not kept in such abysmal ignorance of the "facts of life" as the older generations were, but the promiscuous sexuality of young people so common today is evidence that mere knowledge is not an adequate safeguard.

The myth of the girl abducted by the dragon, awaiting her release by a hero who fights and overcomes her jailer, repre-

[21] *Saint Paul*, p. 19.

sents the emergence of the youth from childhood, but it also represents the psychological condition of the girl in whom sexual instinct is awakening, who does not as yet realize the significance of the changes going on in herself. She is, indeed, in thrall to the Mother unconscious. Mother Nature follows her age-old way and the girl can remain blind to what is occurring within her. She is a helpless victim of unconscious instinct that holds her prisoner until a lover accomplishes the heroic deed and releases her. For the girl thus captured by the dragon of instinct cannot escape by her own efforts, but must await the arrival of the hero who defeats the dragon and releases her, not to a life of her own but to become his spouse. This myth does not concern woman as she is in herself, but woman in her role of anima to a man. She can remain totally unconscious of herself and her own potentialities as an individual while still carrying for him the image of his soul figure. A similar unconsciousness can prevail in adults. But it is not usually realized that when a woman gives herself over to her instinctive impulses to live only as the man wants she plays the part of anima to him and fails to develop a true individuality of her own. The ordeal is not the same for the girl as for the boy. He must fight to achieve manhood; she must find a feminine way to come to womanhood.

In the myth of the dragon fight the theme is of the rescue of the maiden by the hero, whose ordeal and victory show the way by which the youth emerges from childhood and gains his manhood, and also wins his soul, his anima, represented by the maiden. The girl's part in the mythologem is depicted in corresponding stories where the accent falls on *her* experience and she must release herself by her own effort instead of waiting passively to be rescued by a hero-lover. The abduction and rape of Persephone by Pluto [22] is a classic example. Persephone was abducted as a young unopened bud of woman-

---

[22] Kerényi, "Kore," in *Essays on a Science of Mythology,* pp. 150 ff. (Torchbooks edn., pp. 101 ff.).

hood, the Kore, but when she returned to the upper world she came as a mature woman. She then replaced her mother, Demeter, becoming in her turn "The Demeter," "The Mother," while in the following year a new Persephone underwent the abduction and rape.

The myth of Amor and Psyche [23] contains similar material, but it is further elaborated. In his book on this theme, Erich Neumann analyzes the story and demonstrates the kind of ordeal the girl must go through in order to reach womanhood. For the pattern of feminine initiation, corresponding to the boy's initiation rites, leads not only to release from the bondage to mother and childhood, but in some cases leads on to the ordeal of the inner journey and the discovery of selfhood.

The story is that Psyche, the youngest and most beautiful of the king's daughters, incurred the jealousy and anger of Aphrodite, or Venus, because of the admiration, even worship, her beauty had evoked in the community. In revenge Aphrodite demanded that she be given as bride to a monster. She was led out to a precipitous cliff and left to await his arrival. Amor, or Eros, Aphrodite's son, saw her, fell in love with her and, replacing the monster, bore her away to a paradise in the dark. But she was forbidden to look on him. When she disobeyed this command she lost him, for the *dream* of love is not love and can be enjoyed only in unconsciousness. From this it is clear that the initiation into womanhood is different from the initiation into manhood. For while the boy must engage in a conscious struggle against his own childishness and inertia, the girl must submit to the law that makes her a vessel of life and bearer of the seed of the future, a submission that means a sacrifice of her personal autoerotic wishes as drastic as that demanded of the youth by his initiation into manhood.

When interpreted from the masculine point of view, the

[23] The tale of "Amor and Psyche," from Apuleius' *The Golden Ass*, is given in Neumann's book.

myth states that the man must kill the dragon and rescue the maiden, that is, rescue his own anima; but if it is interpreted from the feminine angle, it speaks of *her* task. The girl is sucked down into a languorous and sensuous sleep, being drugged, as it were, by the dragon's poison. Her first act must be to gain some light on her condition; this happens when she begins to love an actual man, instead of merely desiring *a* man whose sole concern is to fulfill her instinctive needs. In the myth, when Psyche dares to light a lamp and sees that it is Amor who lies beside her in the nuptial bed, she falls in love with him, but he flees from her. As a consequence, before she can be reunited with her loved one, she has to undertake the four labors imposed on her by Aphrodite, the mother of Amor.

In real life this is a not infrequent outcome of a liaison based on mutual attraction and sensual pleasure, in which, although the man and the woman have projected the soul-figure to each other, there is little real relationship. The affair is carried on with more or less abandon and delight, while the couple agree mutually that it is to be entirely free—no commitments, no consequences! But then one of them, usually the woman, begins to be personally involved with the partner; glimmerings of real love enter the picture and she finds she is emotionally caught. She begins to press for a true relationship. She wants to bring this clandestine affair out into actual life. Immediately the partner takes fright, and like Amor he flies away. For genuine love, as apart from mere involvement, means commitment, responsibility, real life, and that is most alarming to the still childish and autoerotic individual. If he has not already won his freedom and slain his dragon, he will have to undertake that arduous task now. And the woman, too, will have a long hard road to travel, and labors corresponding to Psyche's to perform, if she is to be able to deal with the situation. These labors correspond to the heavy task the man must accomplish to win his manhood: for example, the twelve labors of Hercules, or the ordeals of Ulysses. The man must accomplish them by his own masculine strength, while the woman has to gain the aid of the helpful animals, representing her instinctive femininity.

The above account might suggest that these things happen only once—as though the youth had one encounter with the dragon and slew him once and for all. But, of course, this is not so. In the myth the dragon is a magic beast and recovers from what seem like mortal injuries, even from dismemberment and death. And so he has to be met again and again. In actual experience the struggle for freedom and independence has to be undertaken time after time during the individual's life. The child of three or four rebels against being treated as an infant; he reaches seven or eight and again a time of struggle, that in turn is not definitive, begins. At puberty it is engaged in with greater energy and greater resistance against authority, because of the awakening of the sexual instinct and the coming awareness of the greater world with all its challenges and rewards. And later, when the anima or animus image is evoked, the struggle is renewed with increased seriousness and intensity. Later still the adult will inevitably be confronted by critical situations in his life that ever and again challenge his courage and his strength and test his mettle. They bring him the opportunity to become more truly an individual, but this involves overcoming himself as well as facing the ordeals life presents to him.

In the inner life, too, very similar struggles are lived on a psychological plane, and may be represented in dream images that portray what is actually occurring. For life is lived in cycles. A problem that is met and dealt with on one level will be encountered again on the next turn of the spiral. The myths represent archetypal patterns, and these are like the formulations of psychic laws that reflect themselves endlessly in one form after another, in one phase after another.

The basic myths of mankind are many, corresponding to

the many archetypal themes in the unconscious, while each individual life is short, so that it is impossible for all of them to be embodied or experienced in one lifetime. Indeed, Jung has suggested that each individual life is based on a particular myth, and that we ought each to discover what our own basic myth is, so that we may live it consciously and intelligently, co-operating with the trend of this life pattern, instead of being dragged along unwillingly. He never elaborated this idea, and I should be put to it to bring forward enough evidence to substantiate it, but I have observed from time to time how in an individual one mythological theme repeated itself again and again, so that it might be possible to say that the lives of these people exemplified a particular mythological theme.

For instance, certain people's lives illustrate and demonstrate the myth of the "hero" or the "leader," others that of the "savior," others again that of the "mother"; in others we can observe the story of Ulysses, or of Isis and Osiris, or perhaps of Phaëthon, who tried to drive the sun chariot of his father Helios and perished for his hybris.

These patterns can be seen recurring in the lives of certain people, who remain totally unconscious of what they are living. But if the individual becomes conscious in relation to the archetypal trend that underlies his life—his fate—he can begin to adapt himself to it consciously. The outer fate is then transmuted into the inner experience, and the true individuality of the man or woman begins to emerge. This is an important step in the quest for the Self.

An example of such a change is given in T. S. Eliot's *The Family Reunion*, which was mentioned in an earlier chapter. There, when the hero became conscious of himself and accepted his own shadow, the pursuing Fates became the guiding spirits.

But let us go back to the myth of the dragon fight and explore what actually happens in real life when this crucial ordeal has been met, and the youth has won his spurs. In the myth he marries the maiden, and in real life he marries the girl who has caught the reflection of his anima. For with both the youth and the maiden, it is the coming of love, that is, the projection of the soul-image, that initiates the new stage of struggle, a struggle not against imprisonment or outer authority but against the childish and autoerotic elements within the individual himself. In its outer life-aspect, the development that is initiated by the projection of the anima or animus leads to confrontation at close quarters with another individual, a situation that inevitably involves effort if a psychological relationship is to be created through a growing understanding and appreciation of another human being. For one must become conscious of the fact that one is not oneself the only "I" in the world, all others being but persons in one's dream. During marriage it gradually dawns on one that the beloved is also a person in her or his own right and is not just the God-given embodiment of one's own soul image. In other words, one comes into a realm where consciousness of the object is possible, indeed indispensable, if the marriage is not to go on the rocks. This is the stage in the development of consciousness depicted in Tantric Yoga as the heart level, where for the first time a light is lighted in the heart, so that one is no longer dependent only on reflected light, but can at last see directly; that is, one sees through the projections to the reality of the other person and at the same time becomes aware, dimly and fleetingly at first, of the god within, whose guiding light makes it possible for one to see beyond one's own ego, to see the other as from the inside, that is, to see him or her as also a whole person.

When the other person is seen in this new light, one inevitably begins to realize that in one's earlier view much entered into the picture that did not really exist in the outer situation. The other person, perhaps, seemed supremely lovely, good, desirable; he or she carried, in fact, an almost divine aura and divine values. But if the partner is to be recognized as truly human, with all the weaknesses and limitations that implies, this optimistic judgment must naturally be recognized as illusion. What then becomes of that glorious image with which the partner had been endowed? Is it *just* an illusion and nothing more? If so, the coming of relationship would indeed have to be paid for dearly. Do we have to come out of the "land of faërie" into the prosaic everyday world, merely disillusioned? This is not what the myths and legends tell us, for they say that with the marriage of the woodcutter's son and the shepherdess another marriage also takes place: the prince and princess are released from the spell under which they, too, have lain and can now be united. This means that when two people who have been in love and under a spell finally meet in their human reality and come to love each other, the values of the anima and animus, removed from their projections in the outer situation, can be assimilated to live a conscious life within the psyche. Instead of being projected to another person, they become available for psychic development.

The gradual assimilation of these superior values, formerly projected to the object of one's love, results in the opening up of that region of the unconscious that is personified by the image of the soul-figure, and so the opportunity to embark on the journey towards the goal—the unknown goal—of psychic or spiritual life, confronts one. This is not the only entrance to that road, but it is a very common one.

What happens if an individual has no chance to separate out the projections of anima or animus through a lifelong relationship, as one can do in marriage? Supposing the projection is forcibly checked because the loved object is inaccessible or perhaps dies, what happens then? After such a blow many people fall into a depression and see no further possibility of fulfillment and satisfaction in life. But, if they were to take a different attitude towards the disappointment of their hope for outer fulfillment, the inner realm might be opened up much earlier in life than in those more usual cases where the projection can be assimilated in easy stages. This was the case with Dante, whose vision of heaven and hell resulted from the frustration he encountered in his love for Beatrice.

In cases of this sort the unconscious is activated by the back-surge of the libido, and archetypal images appear once more in the dreams. An inner union of anima and animus may be portrayed, a sort of sacred marriage, technically called the *coniunctio*,[24] and in all likelihood this will be followed by the image of a child, possibly of a pregnancy and birth, representing a rebirth of the personality.

If, however, the path of love runs more smoothly for our imagined couple, the man and woman, who formerly played the part of children in real life as well as in their subjective experience, have now entered into adult responsibilities, and in the natural course of events they will soon become parents in their turn. The coming of a baby constellates the parent-child archetype once more, but now the roles are reversed. The erstwhile child must perforce view the problem from the point of view of mother or father and a different mythologem will be activated in consequence, one in which the happening is viewed from the opposite side, the side of parent.

And so we see that the "child," like so many archetypal images, is paradoxical. For a child in a dream can represent childishness, helplessness, lack of will-power, autoerotism, dependence, and so on, and it is frequently taken to signify these qualities, which for the adult are of course regressive. But this is not the only significance of "child." When Jesus said to his disciples that unless they became like little children they could not enter the kingdom,[25] he certainly did not mean that

---

[24] Jung, "Psychology of the Transference," pp. 167 ff.; *Mysterium Coniunctionis, passim.*
[25] Matt. 18: 3.

they must become childish. He surely meant that they must become child-*like*, innocent of worldly or egotistic striving, full of wonder and interest, able to play, to experiment, to accept the new and untried. The alchemists were so impressed with this truth that they even said that, while their opus was an arduous task which like woman's work was never done, at the same time it was like child's play. In *Splendor solis*,[26] an alchemical treatise that shows in pictorial form the entire process of the transformation resulting from the alchemist's "great work," there is a picture showing little children running about with pin wheels, playing leapfrog and ball, while over the nursery door is an alembic, whose neck is encircled with a golden crown, implying that this kind of play is part of the royal work and is necessary for the transformation.

And so when the figure of a child appears in a dream it may signify, not that the dreamer is acting like a child, but that the moment has come when the individual is touching an untrammeled and free creative spirit arising from the depths of his being, so that he can, perhaps, release himself from the bonds of conventional thought and the habit of years and allow the free flow of creative energy to transform his life. In this way the child would represent a rebirth of the individual, a new chance, and the hope of a future life. Jung writes:

"The child" is therefore *renatus in novem infantiam* [reborn into a new infancy]. It is thus both beginning and end, an initial and a terminal creature. The initial creature existed before man was, and the terminal creature will be when man is not. Psychologically speaking, this means that the "child" symbolizes the pre-conscious and the post-conscious essence of man. His pre-conscious essence is the unconscious state of earliest childhood; his post-conscious essence is an anticipation by analogy of life after death. In this idea the all-embracing nature of psychic wholeness is expressed. Wholeness is never comprised within the compass of the conscious

[26] Solomon Trismosin, *Splendor solis* (1582), pl. XX, reproduced in Jung, *Psychology and Alchemy*, fig. 95.

mind—it includes the indefinite and indefinable extent of the un-conscious as well.[27]

The elements of the individuality that are not accepted by society and are not acceptable to the external world or to our own idea of ourselves are repressed and disappear into the unconscious. This is inevitable, if one is to learn to be an adult, a responsible member of society. But if, in order to meet the requirements of the environment, too large a part or too dynamic a part of the individuality has been repressed, then, sooner or later, the individual will come into conflict within himself, or develop a neurosis. If such a person goes to an analyst, he may find, to his dismay, that he is represented in his dreams as a child, dressed, perhaps, as he was at three or four, or riding in the baby carriage of his infancy. But the child in the dream may not represent the dreamer himself; instead it may be his own child, perhaps a newborn infant, to which, strangely enough, he has given birth, indicating the birth of the hero-figure. Or the dreamer may be searching for a lost child, whose recovery brings unutterable joy, meaning that something lost in his childhood is about to be recovered.

And so it is obvious that while "child" can mean regression to childishness and infantility it can also represent a new beginning, the birth of a psychic value with a potentiality for growth and development that the ego-personality had lost.

Things and Situations

IN THE outer world a myriad things exist of which we en-counter only a tiny fraction during our personal lives. And of these very few really enter our *Umwelt.* However, an en-counter with any one of them, animate or inanimate, will in-evitably create a "situation," in the psychological meaning of that term. For an encounter demands a reaction on the part

[27] "The Psychology of the Child Archetype," p. 178.

of any conscious being. Even a decision to do nothing in relation to the object, whether this is a person or a thing, is actually taking part in a situation, and on the psychological plane the object and the subject are both changed by the encounter. This corresponds to the discovery of the nuclear physicists that the mere observation of subatomic particles alters their behavior.

And so consciousness of any object in the outer world creates a situation that has to be dealt with. This is also true of an encounter with archetypal symbols in a dream. For, as such symbols contain energy, a dynamic relation is set up between the dreamer and the psychological fact expressed by the symbol.

We have so far considered archetypal images that correspond to persons in the outer world. There are naturally many others that could have been chosen as examples, but Mother, Father, and Child, and their amplifications, represent the most fundamental and universal themes. When we come to consider the archetypes of "things" we are confronted by an intermingling multitude of images no less extensive than the images of persons. Natural objects—tree, forest, mountain, spring, river, ocean—have many aspects in the outer world and endless ramifications of meaning in the archetypal world. The same can be said of cultural objects, such as house, cup, bridge, tool, and vehicle.

In my original division of all outer experience into the three categories of persons, things, and situations, animals were to be included among "things," and so the archetypes of animals must also be classed in this category, although, true to its character of undifferentiation in the unconscious, the distinction between animal and human is not as clearly defined as it is in the outer world. For instance, in mythology we meet with such figures as the Sphinx and the centaur, while even a god may be half human and half animal, like the Egyptian goddess Sekhmet, or may change, like Vishnu, from one form to the other. In folk tales we meet with such figures as werewolves, bat-men, and trolls, while in fairy tales we are not surprised to find a wolf disguising himself as the grandmother of Little Red Ridinghood.

Water may serve as the example of a natural object that occurs frequently in unconscious imagery. Jung interprets water as the source of life; the fluidity of unconscious symbolism is also illustrated by the image of water in its many transformations. For water, as the ocean, is the place of the origin of life; it is the life sap of all living things, which must drink of it daily. It is cleansing; it can dissolve many things; it can transform itself as vapor or ice into an airy or a solid form. As river it serves man for a road or way, and for transportation; as flowing it symbolizes change-in-continuance, and so the flow of life or of time. As ocean it expresses undifferentiation and infinity, that is, the unconscious. These few thoughts merely serve to indicate the endless variety of interrelated meanings concealed in the archetypal image of water.

Cultural objects show only slightly less variation and richness of meaning. A house, for instance, as it appears in dreams, might be taken to represent shelter or containment, and with this meaning can appear in many forms, corresponding to the many attempts man has made to adapt to external conditions. So his shelter may be a den, a cave, a primitive hut, a modern house, or even a palace. In its negative aspect house can represent prison and confinement. Or the house of the dream may represent the dreamer's psyche. In this case the living rooms correspond to the conscious part of his psyche, while the cellar and attic contain contents that have fallen into the personal unconscious. Jung [28] tells a dream of his own in which he found an unknown lower floor in his house and under it a cellar, and beneath that a cave containing the remains of primitive and archaic man. And he explains that when he dreamed

[28] *Memories, Dreams, Reflections,* p. 159 (English edn., p. 155).

this dream he realized that the unconscious was not merely the receptacle of forgotten and repressed elements from the conscious, but that it also had a far older and more primitive layer, the collective unconscious. In other dreams it may be found that, in addition to articles discarded by the dreamer and his immediate ancestors, the attic may contain ghosts. These may be either ancestral ghosts, like those in Gilbert's *Ruddigore,* or uncanny intruders who have taken up their residence in the "top story" unknown to the owner of the house. This is such a typical image of a state of partial possession by unconscious elements that we speak of an individual as having "bats in the belfry" when we mean that strange ideas have taken possession of his mind. The ancients spoke frankly of possession by devils or demons in such cases and undertook drastic rituals to drive out the evil spirit, while the medicine man of primitive tribes treats the sick in mind or body by just such methods of exorcism. In the Roman Catholic Church a ritual of exorcism is still provided to expel the evil spirit in cases judged to be due to possession.[29]

Another dream that is by no means uncommon deals with a similar problem. The dreamer discovers that his house is connected by a hidden door with a companion house totally unknown to him. In his dream he is lured by curiosity to investigate this strange "double" of his abode, a theme that was elaborated by Robert Louis Stevenson in *Dr. Jekyll and Mr. Hyde.*

The variations on the theme of house are endless. For instance, instead of being a personal abode, the house may be a collective building, perhaps a theater. This is the place where the typical stories of man's life are shown, that is, the mythologems are presented to consciousness. And in the dream the dreamer may discover that he has to play a part in such a theater, and not infrequently arrives at the theater only to discover to his consternation that he does not know what play

[29] *Rituale Romanum,* "Ritus exorcizandi obsessos a daemonio."

is to be presented or what his role is to be. This is a typical anxiety situation, and it has the characteristic ambivalence of all archetypal images. For it can mean either that the dreamer has been neglecting to prepare himself for some part that he must play in his life—some impending change, such as puberty, marriage, or death inevitably brings—or that in his present dilemma he must trust himself to the situation, when "it will be given him what he shall speak." That is, the dream may be indicating that he must rely on the functioning of psychic instinct, on the unfolding of the archetype within him. And so the "object," theater, leads into the "situation" of ordeal, namely, the necessity to act as best one can.

But this does not cover every possible meaning of "house." For the house may be church or temple, namely, the "house of God," when, as in the theme of parent and child, the individual is led over to an attitude that transcends the personally oriented one. He is brought to the realization that he is in the presence of God, of a transcendent reality, and that some service or ritual is about to be performed which will have as its purpose the establishment of a relation between the ego, that is, himself, his "I," and the tremendum that men call God, that is, the "not-I." So that again the symbol of an object leads over into the archetype of a situation.

Cultural objects, such as tools or weapons, obviously express an intention to act, and so they, too, lead over into the archetypes of situations. For instance, cup, plate, and spoon suggest eating, while cooking vessels give the idea of transformation. Spade, hammer, ax, or pen imply the intent to create something new, while a weapon implies either destruction or self-defense. But here again the intent may spread into further realms. A sword, besides representing aggression, may be a symbol of power, such as the sword of state, and it frequently appears in dreams as an instrument of cutting or discrimination. If we turn to the imagery of the alchemists we find that for them the sword was a weapon of division. In one illustration of the alchemical treatise *Splendor solis,* a man is represented dismembering another with a sword. Dismemberment was one of the processes that the alchemists were instructed to carry out on the basic substance, the *prima materia.* That here it is a man who is being dismembered clearly indicates that the later alchemists (this is a sixteenth-century work) understood that the *prima materia* was man himself, or his ego. This drastic procedure was undertaken in order that the parts that had been wrongly put together in the first place might be reorganized in a new and better way. The parts were then put into a cooking vessel or an incubator, and after prolonged heating a new creation emerged—the imperfect and ignoble substance transformed into a perfect or noble form. And so the scene of the dismembered man is followed by one where he is seen sitting in a sort of steam cabinet, as in a womb, where he is obviously being put together again.

In another old picture,[30] the alchemist is shown about to sever the cosmic egg with a sword and so divide it into halves, obviously a pair of opposites. If we can judge by the man's expression, this operation was accompanied by great anxiety and fear. Thus the image of tools and weapons, like that of the river and the house, leads over into the archetypes of situations. Already we have mentioned that when the libido is frustrated it flows back and activates unconscious images. But libido is energy, and so the images of persons and things occurring in fantasies and dreams are not static but active and appear in a moving relation to the situation. Dante's vision was not merely of heaven and hell as static images; it spoke of a journey and a guide, indeed, of a *Way.* For when the outgoing libido is frustrated in life it flows back into the unconscious; images of the *Way* may appear in the individual's dreams, and he is led step by step towards a goal.

On the way he will meet typical—arche-typical—situa-

[30] From Michael Maier, *Atalanta Fugiens* (1615), reproduced in Read, *Prelude to Chemistry*, pl. 17.

tions which he must deal with as best he can. But he is not alone in his quest, for, just as Dante was led first by Virgil and later by Beatrice, and as Isis [31] was guided by the voices of children and animals, so the modern seeker will find helpful figures on his inner journey. It may be a helpful animal or a child or perhaps an old man or woman who gives him advice and acts as guide on the journey. These are themes that are met with not only in mythology but in many fairy tales and legends as well.

But the goal of his journey is usually unknown; and, just as in the theater dreams referred to above, the individual must look for guidance as he goes along. He cannot know it all beforehand. This journey cannot be accomplished by intellectual understanding or by self-willed choice. The saying *solvitur ambulando* (it will be resolved walking) is a practical guide of great value here.

As the individual progresses on his way, symbols of the goal usually begin to appear in his dreams. The goal may be represented as the treasure hard to attain: as a jewel, the pearl of great price, for instance, or as the celestial city of *The Pilgrim's Progress*. Or it may take the form of a flower, a living, growing being that forever reproduces itself. The celestial rose of *The Divine Comedy* is an apt example, corresponding to the Buddhist conception of the Buddha seated in the lotus. The treasure may also be represented in a more abstract form, a circle or sphere signifying wholeness, completeness, or perhaps a mandala, representing a resolution of the opposites. The World Clock was the form this archetype took in the dream of a modern man that Jung has discussed.[32] But, in whatever form it appears, the goal, the center, has a numinous quality. It is fascinating and powerful, it has lifegiving and death-dealing powers, it is immortal, beyond good

[31] G. R. S. Mead, *Thrice Greatest Hermes*, I, 283.
[32] *Psychology and Alchemy*, pp. 194 ff.; "Psychology and Religion," pp. 65 ff.

and evil, and, as Jung has pointed out, it has all the attributes of a God-image. This does not mean that it *is* God, but that it is an image, a type or imprint of supreme value. It is, in other words, a psychic content, a content of that great unknown psychic realm of the collective unconscious that corresponds to an image of God. Can we perhaps say that, as God created man in his own image, so the image of God lies deep within the psyche of man, waiting for man himself to turn consciously towards it so that it may be established as an acknowledged and consciously accepted ruler of his life? [33]

These speculations bring us close to the problem connected with the psychological aspect of metaphysical reality that we must consider in the last chapter. I need hardly point out that this is a very difficult subject, one full of pitfalls as well as of thorns and prickles, and I venture to bring it up with a good deal of misgiving. What I have to say will naturally be quite tentative and must be approached not with the intellect or with rational thinking, for it can be grasped only with that new kind of thinking that Jung has called "symbolic."

[33] See Diagram VI.

VII

THE PSYCHOLOGICAL ASPECT

OF METAPHYSICAL REALITY

IT IS WITH considerable diffidence that I approach the subject of the psychological aspect of metaphysical reality, because, as Jung writes, "The psyche cannot leap beyond itself. It cannot set up any absolute truths, for its own polarity determines the relativity of its statements." [1] For "if the dynamic conception of the psyche is correct, all statements which seek to overstep the limits of the psyche's polarity—statements about a metaphysical reality, for example—must be paradoxical if they are to lay claim to any sort of validity." And as we saw in the last chapter archetypal images are always paradoxical.

The reality of the nonphysical realm does not, however, depend solely on dogmatic statements regarding its nature, for these have surely arisen from the direct experience of human beings: seers, prophets, and religious teachers. And similar experiences are encountered today that have a dynamic effect, changing the psychic climate in which a man lives. Jung points

[1] *Memories, Dreams, Reflections*, p. 350 (English edn., p. 322).

out at the beginning of his lectures on the subject of religion that his point of departure is "the psychology of the *homo religiosus*, the man who takes into account and carefully observes certain factors which influence him and, through him, his general condition." These factors are what Rudolf Otto called the *numinosa*, dynamic agencies or effects not caused by an arbitrary act of will. And Jung further stated that in his lectures he would deal with "facts which demonstrate the existence of an authentic religious function in the unconscious" and would bring forward examples of "the religious symbolism of unconscious processes." He went on to explain that as a psychologist he found himself obliged to deal with the psychological experience of *homo religiosus*, but did not feel called upon, nor indeed competent, to pronounce on the nature of the metaphysical realities to which these psychological experiences refer.[2]

I myself approach this subject from the same starting point. I shall consider *only* the psychological aspect of the numinous experience and shall not speculate on the problem of what lies behind or causes the psychological happening, though I may be obliged to use terms such as "god" in order to connect what I have to say with the age-old human experiences that have been designated by such terms. Obviously the source of such experiences does not inhere in the ego. They arise spontaneously from an unknown and unseen source which psychologists call the unconscious and which in religious terminology is the spiritual realm.

In his introduction to Otto's *The Idea of the Holy* John W. Harvey writes:

> [Dr. Otto] is concerned to examine the nature of those elements in the religious experience which lie outside and beyond the scope of reason . . . but which none the less as "feelings" cannot be disregarded by any honest inquiry. And his argument shows in

[2] Jung, "Psychology and Religion," pp. 9 f. and 6.

the first place that in all the forms which religious experience may assume and has assumed . . . certain basic "moments" of feeling . . . are always found to recur. All genuine religion exhibits these characteristic reactions in consciousness. . . . We are shown that the religious "feeling" properly involves a unique kind of apprehension, *sui generis,* not to be reduced to ordinary intellectual or rational "knowing" . . . yet itself a genuine "knowing," the growing awareness of an object, deity.[3]

In his autobiography Dr. Jung describes experiences of this nature that came to him, overwhelmingly, beginning in early childhood and recurring at intervals all through his life, right into old age.[4]

Otto points out that it is impossible to define this kind of experience in intellectual or rational terms, but he does attempt to differentiate its characteristics. He calls the experience itself *numinous,* and points out that it has the characteristics of (1) awefulness, often expressed as dread or "shuddering"; (2) overpoweringness or majesty, such as Job experienced when confronted with the magnitude, the power and inscrutability, of God's creation; (3) energy or urgency, expressed in the Old Testament as the wrath of Yahweh and frequently symbolized by fire. Harvey adds: "The primary fact is a confrontation of the human mind with a Something, whose character is only gradually learned, but which is felt from the first as a transcendent presence, 'the beyond,' even where it is also felt as 'the within' man."[5]

It is obviously very important, then, when dealing with these dynamic elements of subjective experience, to differentiate between what is the "I" that Harvey calls "the human mind" and what is the "not-I" in this inner realm that Harvey speaks of as a "transcendent presence" beyond man though perhaps felt as within him. For identification of the "I," the

---

[3] Otto, *The Idea of the Holy,* introduction, pp. xiii ff.
[4] *Memories, Dreams, Reflections,* for example, pp. 30 ff. (English edn., pp. 42 ff.).
[5] Otto, *The Idea of the Holy,* introduction, p. xv.

ego, with these strange and powerful contents of the unknown psychic world produces a most serious inflation, an inflation that can lead to insanity. Indeed a special term, religious insanity, is used to describe these cases in which the sufferer not infrequently identifies himself with one of the divine figures. These numinous factors may be experienced subjectively as vision, inspiration, voices, and so on, or at times they may be projected to some object in the outer world. We saw in the last chapter that not only the anima or animus might be encountered in projection to a human being, but that other archetypes could be projected in a similar manner. For instance, the hero, the savior, or the devil could be encountered in some human being, who seemed to possess the powers of the archetypal figure they seemed to embody. Or the individual could act the part of such a figure, being himself identified to or possessed by the archetype, so that in his own eyes, if not in actual fact, he would be a hero or a savior, a leader or a sacrificial victim.

In primitive society a similar phenomenon exists much more generally. At least we recognize it more easily because, having outgrown its grosser manifestations, we can observe it in others and recognize it for what it is, while those who are still under its spell are incapable of recognizing the nature of their own illusions. This is the phenomenon that Lévy-Bruhl called *participation mystique*, which I have discussed in an earlier chapter.[6] It is a most useful term, denoting the relation of primitive man to objects in his surroundings about which he has peculiar feelings because to him they seem to be possessed of a quality or spirit called "mana," after a Melanesian word (or, by other primitives, *mulungu* or *wakonda*).[7] These terms, and others as well, refer to the same experience of force, energy, spirit-power felt to be possessed by or to emanate from the object in question. To primitive man such an

[6] See above, pp. 38-40.
[7] Cf. Jung, "On Psychic Energy," pp. 61 ff.

object is taboo, sacred-dread, and he surrounds it with rituals and precautions of various kinds, petitions it for aid in his need, and, indeed, acts towards it as if it were a religious object. And so the early missionaries translated the terms "mana" and "mulungu" as "God." But that translation is not quite correct. For while mana and mulungu represent spirit-power, psychic energy, felt to reside in or to emanate from a tree, animal, or rock, the objects are not gods even to the primitive man, and we know that the magic effect they have upon him is due to a projection of an unconscious psychic content into the objects. Some part of the man's psyche that is *not* conscious to him is "found in" or, as we say, "projected into" the "mana-containing" object.

When a primitive man is unable to think out a problem for himself, but has to ask his tree, or his snake, or his fetish-object for advice, he is really consulting a part of his psyche that is not located within himself but is found only in the projection to the tree or other object. Such an object is, of course, taboo—sacred-dread—and no one may injure it or even touch it without doing serious damage to the man for whom it is sacred. In some cases the projection has actually involved the man's soul or his life, so that if the tree should be cut down the man himself would die. To us this seems like the crassest superstition, but the same mechanism persists and is still effective among civilized people, and we can even observe it in ourselves at times. For instance, when an individual has to perform a difficult task, such as giving a lecture, he may form the habit of playing with some small object, he may jingle the change in his pocket or twist the button on his coat or indulge in some similar foolishness, and find himself quite unable to proceed if this play should be denied him. If one day he had no money in his pocket, or if the long-suffering button should at last come off and get lost, he too would be at a loss to go on. Dependence on an "amulet" of this kind is particularly apt to occur in neurotic personalities. In Wouk's novel *The Caine Mutiny*, the captain's dependence on his play with little steel balls was used to great advantage as showing his increasing mental deterioration. But the psychological mechanism is not always so pathological.

In an earlier chapter it was pointed out that a peculiar sense of *myness* sometimes inheres in certain of our possessions. This is an illustration of *participation*, and when it is very strong, giving rise to compulsive reactions the individual is unable to control, it points to the probability that his excessive reaction is more than mere possessiveness or egotism. For it seems as if the object possesses something essential to him, so that interference with it by another is tantamount to interference with the very core of his being. Obviously when this happens something that should be a part of oneself is really outside, glimpsed, felt, but not possessed. Of course it is not really the object as such but something much more subtle, namely, the psychological value the object represents, that produces such an uncontrollable effect. When his tree talks to the primitive man it is the man's own thinking that is projected, that is, the power of thinking he needs, that he "ought" to have, that he might have, did it not lie dormant, out of reach in the unconscious. The tree may represent or contain his very life, or the numen that speaks out of the tree may represent the voice of God, as in the case of Moses [8] when he saw the bush flaming without burning up, or as in an Egyptian picture [9] of the goddess Nut as tree numen, manifesting herself to her worshipers as the life energy of the tree.

These are instances of psychic factors that affect the individual but are unknown to him. He is completely unconscious that they originate from and belong to the realm of the psychic "not-I"; that is, they are subjective factors, and because they are unconscious they are encountered in projected form in the outer world.

[8] Ex. 3: 2.
[9] Harding, *Psychic Energy*, p. 176.

When the primitive man finds numinous qualities in a sacred animal or tree he usually has a peculiar sense of relation to that object. It is his own particular object of reverence and may not even be sacred to someone else. This special sense of personal relation to the sacred object may be compared to the irresistible influence on certain people of particular objects, such as an amulet that is believed to protect from danger or infection, a mascot that is supposed to bring good luck to a military unit, or a fetish that is essential to one's feeling of well-being. Sexual fetishism is a well-known example of this compulsive dependence. On a religious level, the veneration of relics of the saints, icons, sacred pictures, or the cross is an example of such an influence. In medieval times the cross was not merely a reminder, which could call to mind or evoke a conscious will to follow a vow or something of that sort. Rather, it was used to evoke a spirit power thought to inhere in the cross itself. It was employed in this way in the exorcism of evil spirits, because of the belief that they would pay attention to the significance of the cross and be unable to defy an order enforced by its display. There are many tales of evil spirits shrinking in fear and slinking off at the sight of the cross. The crusaders used their swords as weapons of power in the same way. The hilt of the sword was formed by a crossbar, and they believed that if, when they went into battle, they held their swords hilt upward, so displaying the cross, the Saracens would be unable to fight against them but would fall back before their advance. Although the Saracens, being Mohammedans, did not share their faith, the Crusaders were still convinced that the cross had this "magic" power regardless of whether the opponent believed it or not. The "power" inhered in the numinous character of the cross itself; that is, it had mana.

In the case of fetishes, amulets, and so on, the sense of power that originates from unknown factors within the individual's psyche is peculiar to himself alone, but in generally recognized symbols like the cross, the power obviously comes from a source operative in the psyches of all who are similarly affected by the mana-object, that is, from the collective unconscious common to them all. In the case of the cross this would apply to all persons in the Christian tradition.

The fact that the numinous quality does not inhere in the object but arises from within the individual's own unconscious psyche is attested by the sense of subtle connection he has with it. And it is further attested by the fact that, when the individual becomes conscious of the psychic factor that has been projected and has assimilated it, so that the outer object is no longer the container of the projected material, then the object becomes just an object in the outer world, having its own value only, and it is no longer able to exert a magic or mysterious power.

This is the psychological reason, perhaps, for some of the strange initiation rites that were practiced by the Knights Templars in the twelfth and thirteenth centuries. After their initiation they were required to "spurn the cross," sometimes by spitting on it, sometimes by treading on or over it. Now, of course, these acts were not intended as sacrilege, though they were so construed in the trials that took place in 1309. But repeatedly the members of the order stated that while they had spat on the cross it was *ore non corde* (with the mouth, not with the heart). The stepping on or over the cross is explained by Bothwell-Gosse [10] as a ritual of entering the center, formed by the crossbars. But there may be a further psychological explanation for this strange practice. It might well have been intended to demonstrate that the power the cross represented had really been assimilated by the knight as a result of his initiation. It was a test, an ordeal that searched his very soul. If he was truly an initiated one, then the cross of wood was only a material object to him. The ritual must

[10] *The Knights Templars*, pp. 41, 88.

have had to do with the psychological assimilation of the significance of the cross. Otherwise, these deeply religious men
could not have performed an act so repugnant to the feeling of
the times. The ordinary man simply could not have done such
a thing; he would have died of fright.

So far we have been considering the projection of unconscious elements to actual concrete objects that exist in their
own right in the outer world. When we come to examine the
images and figures that appear in dreams or visions, in fantasies and works of art, the same mechanism of projection is
at work, although the objects that carry the projection are no
longer concrete external realities. They are real, indeed, and
can produce effects very similar to those experienced in *participation mystique*. Inasmuch as they are inner objects, however, inner images only, we speak of them as symbols. If these
symbols are felt to have an objective reality, or to refer to an
object having an individual substance, then we speak of an
illusion (or delusion) or of a hypostasis,[11] rather than of a
projection. For then the subjective experience of the inner
image has been projected into a realm that is conceived of as
a real place and its denizens are regarded and treated as distinct personal beings.

For instance, in *The Divine Comedy* Dante writes *as if* the
figures in his fantasy were objectively real. They were real to
him, of course, but their reality was a subjective and psychological one. The fact that in many cases Dante used actual
persons to serve as the characters in his poem means that the
qualities he was dealing with were to a certain extent hypostatized for him, whereas in Bunyan's *Pilgrim's Progress*
the figures who personify the qualities his pilgrim encounters
are given names representing the attitudes they personify. But
when Bunyan comes to speak of heaven he projects his vision-

[11] Hypostasis: distinct individual substance; a phenomenon or state of
things conceived of as a real substance; a real personal subsistence—a
personality.

ary ideas into a quite concrete form. Dante shows more insight, for his Celestial Rose is obviously a symbol and is not conceived of as a concrete reality.

In speaking of Dante we can say that he writes "as if" his figures were really the actual persons whose names they carry. But we do not know how far he was consciously aware of that "as if." And even today there are those who consider psychological or spiritual realities to be of the same nature as concrete reality. Obviously the worshiper of an idol or a statue does so. When I was in Mexico I went to the cathedral of Guadalupe and there saw the famous picture of the Black Virgin. She is also represented in the form of a statue, which is enclosed in a glass case, and I witnessed a little scene that showed me why this was necessary. An old Indian came up with his wife. He evidently had pains in his neck and shoulders, for he rubbed his hand over that part of the glass that corresponded to the Virgin's neck and then rubbed his own neck. This he did repeatedly, evidently hoping to transfer the healing power of the Virgin from the statue to himself. For him the mana, the spiritual power, called Holy Virgin, was identical with the statue. It was the most primitive psychotherapeutic clinic I have ever attended. Not so very long ago, the majority of ordinary churchgoers thought of heaven as a concrete place situated "up there," and thought, too, of God in anthropomorphized form, as if he were a manlike being. Today, although the ordinary churchgoer would deny that he thought in these terms, he would probably be at a loss to tell in what form he now conceived of the deity and of heaven.

Man's conception of deity has obviously changed and developed during the course of the centuries. Yet his sense of the divine has always evolved out of his actual experience of the numinous. Even the inspiration of the prophets and saints came to them as an inner, that is, as a *psychological* experience, and the insights they gained have been transmitted to us in wisdom teachings and dogma, but always through the medium of human beings. The unknown source of such experiences is unconscious to us, and all intimations and experiences from that unknown source must perforce come to us from the unconscious—not the Freudian unconscious, which Jung calls the personal unconscious, but a much deeper and broader region, available to all men, namely, the collective unconscious. This statement does not imply that God is *only* psychological, though the statement that God is spirit would be capable of such an interpretation, but it does say that our *experience* of the numinous *is* a psychological experience and that the form in which it is clothed is a symbol, an expression of an unknown reality.

The form that the *numinosum* takes for the individual man and the mythologem in which it is expressed for a people depend on the stage of psychological development that has been achieved. For if such an experience is to become conscious at all it has to be experienced and expressed through the medium of the conscious functions, that is to say, through the ego-consciousness, and its form is necessarily modified and limited according to the psychological capabilities of the man to whom the experience has occurred. This is so even though it is of the nature of the numinous experience to transcend our conscious capacity to grasp or comprehend it. St. Paul, for example, confessed his inability to describe his visionary experience or even to realize it himself consciously, for it was of the nature of *ecstasis*—a going out from oneself.

And so to one man God is good, a father concerned with his child's welfare; to another he is a cruel tyrant, or is entirely indifferent to the fate of his creation. If we glance over the history of religious development throughout the centuries we get a glimpse from the psychological angle of why this is so.

In the earliest days of recorded history, as in the case of

187

the most primitive peoples today, god or the gods were not concerned with man at all. In the Babylonian religious myths [12] the whole drama took place among the gods: good and evil were embodied in heavenly beings and underworld demons, and the war between the constructive and the destructive powers was played out in that otherworldly sphere. Man did not have any part in the struggle, for he did not yet exist, that is, the drama took place entirely in the depths of the unconscious. When man at last appeared on the scene in the Babylonian story, he was created, we are told, with the sole purpose of serving the gods. Now the account of these happenings was not transmitted to mankind by gods who were persons and could tell their own story. Indeed, at that time the gods were only potencies. The myths originated within the psyche of man; the knowledge of them happened to him, as vision or fantasy or dream coming from the unconscious. At this stage of man's development the drama was played out by creative and destructive forces, potencies, that had no direct relation to man at all—that is, the drama took place entirely within the unconscious. But the drama was really a happening within man himself; it represented the condition of his own psyche, not his conscious psyche, but his unconscious; and it was his attempt to depict, *to make conscious to himself*, the forces that ruled the world. It was his first attempt at a "scientific" explanation of the world about him, and within himself as well, since the "I" and the "not-I" were quite undifferentiated. He was swayed by powers and compulsions over which he had no control, which went their way as unconcerned as a tornado, about which he could do nothing. For him the sense of psychic potencies and the experience of numinous forces and of the battle of the opposites were projected into the forms of gods and demons, who appeared to him in hypostatized form.

---

[12] See, e.g., *The Fight between Bel and the Dragon*, tr. E. A. Wallis Budge with the assistance of Sidney Smith. See also Harding, *The Parental Image*, chaps. II and III.

By this personification the Babylonians sought to account for the effects under which they suffered, effects that seemed to emanate from beings outside themselves.

So long as this psychological condition prevailed man was not responsible for good and evil. He could exert no influence on the course of events. At first, according to the myth, he was not there at all. That is to say, his consciousness was not there. When man did come on the scene, the sole reason for his creation was that he might bring sacrifices to the gods. Now, the interesting thing is that, though of course we do not accept this explanation as factually valid, the stories do correspond to the gradual awakening of consciousness in the modern infant and young child, who is morally and psychologically in a world ruled over by gods in the form of parents, whose ways and actions he cannot possibly understand and in whose power he lies quite helpless. And from time to time we also find that in individuals who are in conflict, feeling themselves quite impotent in the face of some superior power, images arise from the unconscious in dreams and fantasies that correspond to the situations depicted in these early myths. The symbols in which they are clothed are very powerful, fascinating, perhaps terrifying—that is, they are numinous, and they throw a light on the psychological condition of the dreamer by representing the inner problem or conflict with which he is confronted. We are obliged to recognize that, although the forms of the gods as represented in such myths no longer carry *for us* the validity and numinosity they did for the ancient peoples whose gods they were, all the same these stories do express *a* truth—a *psychological* truth—that was valid for them, and is still valid in certain instances for modern people, though not of course as hypostatized fact. The stories form a mythologem, that expresses in dramatic form a truth, and often a wisdom, which would otherwise be inaccessible to our understanding.

When we come down the centuries to Greek times there has apparently been a considerable change in the gods. That means, of course, not that transcendent deity as such has changed, but that man's psychological condition has changed, a change that is mirrored in the development of his conception of the gods. Man is now much more aware of the movements of the forces in the unconscious. The gods, though once represented as animals—Zeus as a snake, Athene as an owl, Aphrodite as a dove, Dionysos as a bull, and so on—[13] now have not only a human form, but human thoughts and emotions as well, even the beginning of moral scruples, though the conception of guilt is still quite remote. But they are concerned only with their own affairs and have very little to do with man, except as he represents a pawn in their own game. In the *Iliad*, for instance, the gods are involved with the Trojan war as a kind of sport, each backing his own hero whose victory or defeat is of importance to him only as it raises or lowers his prestige in the continual struggle for place on Olympus. As Tennyson puts it,

> Like Gods together, careless of mankind.
> For they lie beside their nectar, and the bolts are hurled
> Far below them in the valleys and the clouds are lightly curl'd
> Round their golden houses, girdled with a gleaming world:
> Where they smile in secret, looking over wasted lands.[14]

But then the Hebrews, with their religious genius, came on the scene, and God really became involved in his creation; he was no longer "careless of mankind." His doings in heaven receded farther and farther from man's consciousness and concern and his dealings with man took possession of the stage. God became concerned with his people, with a particular chosen people representing the unit that, in the eyes of the Hebrews, was of supreme importance to God. He was not yet concerned with individuals, but for a few notable exceptions— namely, the ancestors of the family chosen for his experiment

[13] See Jane Harrison, *Prolegomena to the Study of Greek Religion*, pp. 431 ff.; see also Harding, *Women's Mysteries*, p. 49.
[14] "Song of the Lotos-Eaters."

and the seers and prophets who had the ability to hear and convey his messages to his people. Beyond that the people were regarded and treated as a group, who must serve him and fulfill his purposes. Quite early in the story, however, man began to deviate by disobeying God's command and making a free choice, thus taking upon himself some part of the burden of moral responsibility. Yet throughout all the early centuries of Hebrew history guilt and innocence were concerned only with obedience and disobedience. If a man had not committed certain specified acts, if he had not disobeyed the actual law, he was innocent of guilt. The negative confession of the Egyptians was still the criterion of righteousness. This confession, made in a set form at the judgment of the deceased, is given at length in Chapter CXXV of *The Book of the Dead*, where the particular sins the deceased declared he had *not* committed are enumerated. For instance, he declared he had harmed no man, had not injured his family, had committed no evil in a holy place, had not kept evil companions, and so on, going on to the confession that he had not stolen the milk of children and had not raided cattle.[15] That is, for the Egyptians disobedience was *the* sin. Sin was equated to transgression. There is an interesting point here, for we are not told that Adam and Eve were directly or spontaneously conscious that their nakedness was a cause for shame. It was only after they had eaten the magic fruit that this fact dawned on them. Their first sense of shame or guilt was concerned with this and not with their disobedience. The magic quality of the fruit is another example of mana—and when they had eaten it its power was magically transferred to themselves, so that they now had to distinguish good and evil apart from the dictates of the lawgiver.

The struggle between good and evil, started by the theft of the fruit of the tree of knowledge in Eden, did not really

15 E. A. Wallis Budge, introduction to *The Egyptian Book of the Dead*, pp. clxv ff.

come to full consciousness until the dispersion. Then a new stage of consciousness was initiated and man began again to see visions, as he always does at such transition points in his inner history. And the mythologem started to unfold a stage further. This new stage is portrayed in the Book of Job. God and his opposite Satan begin to struggle for the possession of man. But now they both recognize that the outcome of their dispute, of their own struggle for sovereignty, depends on the part man will play in the ordeal. Man has come to hold a very different place in the drama; the heavenly beings are for the first time really related to and dependent on him and his actions; in fact, everything depends on him. Will God win, or the devil? In psychological terms this means that man has begun to question God's dealings with him. He dares to question the justice of the punishment inflicted on him in the dispersion! For was it not the ancestors, the fathers, who had disobeyed God, who had sinned, not just the current generation? They were being punished for the sins of the fathers that are to be visited upon the children. We are dealing here not just with individual trespass, but with inherited guilt, original sin. And that surely is the term for evil in the unconscious, evil as a principle, not guilt for personal transgression. Psychologically speaking, this is a most important differentiation, whether or not it bears the same significance theologically. For transgression is a matter of personal misdoing, while original sin belongs to our inheritance, and we do not have the same personal responsibility, psychologically, in regard to it. From the psychological point of view, it must be treated differently. And surely as Christians we also make such a distinction when we pray for forgiveness for our trespasses, our transgressions, but continue by saying "Deliver us from evil," implying that it is in the hands of God whether we shall be delivered over to evil or saved from it.

Evil is here represented as a spiritual power—*The Evil*—much as we speak of *The Good* meaning good as a power, a spirit, or in psychological terms, a principle. *The* Evil does not mean man's sins any more than *the* Good means man's good works. We might almost read the Lord's Prayer as saying "Deliver us from the Evil One"—from Satan—but of course in these enlightened times we do not like to personify the evil one.

If man is subject to evil in this sense, then his sins, or his sinfulness, are not just a matter of his own actions. Rather, the evil stems from the unknown regions of the spiritual world, that is, evil is a principle of the unconscious, of the collective unconscious, that we encounter in the psychological experience of the *numinosum*. Although we *are* responsible for our relation to it, we are not responsible for its existence.

And so we have the story of Job, written when these ideas were just beginning to dawn on man. Jung [16] has analyzed this drama from the psychological point of view, although, as he himself recognized, it could also be interpreted differently. The drama starts with a scene in heaven where a dispute takes place between God and Satan, reminiscent of the much earlier Babylonian myths concerned with the relations between the good and the evil gods. In the Babylonian story man does not exist. In the Hebrew story man exists, but in the first act of the drama God and Satan are the only characters. Man is merely a pawn; the world is only the arena for the struggle between God and Satan.

Job did not fail as a result of his most unjust persecution. One would therefore expect the story to end, as Jung points out, with Satan paying his wager, for God had won the bet. But that is not what happened, for a most unexpected change had taken place as a result of this experiment. The experiment was intended to decide the rulership of the world. Instead God's own attitude came under scrutiny. Neither God nor Satan had considered Job as a living and potentially evolving

[16] "Answer to Job."

being. They had dealt with him as the behaviorists might with an animal. In their opinion a dog is a good dog or a bad dog, and while a suitable test will decide whether he is the one or the other, conceivably giving a final answer as to the dog's temper, it could not be expected to produce consciousness in the dog. But in the Book of Job the outcome is different. Satan falls out of the cast, and the further stages of the drama are played out between God and man. And, as Jung has pointed out, this marks a most important transition in the development of man's psychology.[17] Modern man may be said to have begun at this point.

For now at last it was realized that God and man are relative to each other. A most significant step had been taken in the recognition that God—*as we conceive Him*—or, shall we say, our conception and our experience of God, are psychological phenomena, and are relative to the stage of psychological development and of consciousness we have attained.

In a sense, of course, this is a well-known fact. Everyone recognizes that the saints and holy men of whatever religion have had an inner experience of the numinous different from that of the ordinary religious man. But the implications of this fact are not always realized. For if our conception of God is relative to our own psychological capacity to comprehend or even to experience the inner intimations from the unconscious, then it is obviously quite futile to argue about the truth or falsity of anyone else's conception of the deity. It is an area where the conception someone has, or the image he perceives with his inner eye, is for him an absolute—as absolute as his perception of some object in the outer world. And it is entirely useless to argue against it. It will remain operative within him until or unless he has a further revelation from within.

But here we come to another aspect of the problem, for

[17] Ibid., p. 381.

the *conception* we have of the deity is not constructed of conscious ideas and thoughts, and certainly not of "infantile wishes," as Freud would have us think, though naturally these ideas modify and may be the main source of our consciously held creed. Our inner conception, the secretly held belief that influences our thoughts and motivates our actions, is not a consciously built-up construct. No, it stems from the *Urgrund* of our psyche, the collective unconscious, and is formed by the innate patterns of psychic functioning present in every human being, the archetypes. And when Tertullian [18] says that the soul of man is naturally Christian he is affirming for Western man a truth that analytical psychology can verify. We live in the Christian epoch, and the dogmas of Christianity have actually expressed the condition of Western man's unconscious throughout the last two thousand years. These same mythologems and symbols can be found in the psyche of Western peoples whether they are consciously Christian or not.

And just as the cultural patterns of behavior, both physical and mental, can help to fashion specifically human ways and actions by example and by exercise, so, too, the appropriate archetypal patterns, embodied in myths, religious stories, folk tales, and fairy tales, act as molds for the developing psyche. This is an important element of education.[19] A knowledge of the archetypes can and should be used in the planning of a school curriculum, so that the appropriate themes may be made available to the young people in the best and most illuminating form that the creative genius of the centuries has produced. In this way the archetypes are experienced by them in their most helpful form. Jung [20] himself has pointed out how important it is for children to be told legends and fairy tales, and for adults to be made familiar with religious myths and dogmas, because they constellate the archetypal pat-

---

[18] *Apologeticus*, xvii (Migne, *PL*, I, col. 377).
[19] See James Henderson, *Education and Analytical Psychology*.
[20] *Aion*, p. 169.

terns and give to man a sense of the meaning of life. For he then realizes that his life, small and insignificant as it is in its personal aspect, is a necessary part of the unfolding of Life itself. He becomes consciously a part of history, and realizes himself as a carrier of life and of the life-spirit, as Jung expresses it:

> . . . the world exists for us only in so far as it is consciously reflected by a psyche. *Consciousness is a precondition of being.* Thus the psyche is endowed with the dignity of a cosmic principle, which philosophically and in fact gives it a position co-equal with the principle of physical being. The carrier of this consciousness is the individual . . .

whom, at the end of "The Undiscovered Self," Jung calls

> the individual human being—that infinitesimal unit on whom a world depends, and in whom, if we read the meaning of the Christian message aright, even God seeks his goal.[21]

In man this life-spirit is expressed and in him, as in the forefathers, it continues to evolve. God is revealed in him in a new form, and such a revelation is always accompanied by an outpouring of energy—fire, the spirit. For when his image is brought to life in the living individual man, it is as though God were incarnated again in human form—his image revealed through this particular human life.

From what has been said above it is clear that the image of God that we experience within ourselves, as well as its representation in the dogmatic form enshrined in a religion, will be susceptible to change. Indeed, if man's psyche is to develop, if his consciousness is to grow clearer and brighter, the image of Divinity will inevitably change, as the writer of the Epistle to the Hebrews obviously realized when he began his letter with the words: "God, who at sundry times and in divers manners spoke in times past unto the fathers by his prophets,

[21] "The Undiscovered Self," pp. 271, 305.

hath in these last days spoken unto us by his Son." [22] This was a thing that had never happened before, so that a new era was inaugurated with modifications and even radical changes in the then current form of religion. For a new revelation of God's image implies that the old image that has been held sacred by the fathers will inevitably have to be superseded. The old image is overthrown or discarded, and this is an act of sacrilege or of iconoclasm. It is obviously a heinous sin from the point of view of the old order. A new understanding of religious truth has generally been regarded as heretical at first, even if some or all of the revelation is later incorporated into the dogma and teachings of the Church. For to be the recipient of a new understanding puts one into the position of Adam in Paradise. His act of disobedience was a dire sin, punished by ostracism from God, but out of it came the knowledge of good and evil which could have been acquired in no other way. Everything that man could wish for to satisfy his physical needs was provided in Paradise—but not everything on the side of the life of the spirit. For everything was provided except the right to make a free and conscious choice, that is, to exercise that freedom of the will that is a *sine qua non* of the "I," the conscious ego. And this was denied man by the Good God, who had yet given him the capacity, the potential capacity, to exercise free will. And so we see that if consciousness were to be achieved at all, the theft of this knowledge was necessary. It is the necessary sin, the *felix culpa*. For one cannot have freedom of choice given to one!

This story is repeated in the lives of most people who embark on the road to individuation, that is, the achievement of wholeness. Indeed, it might almost be considered the portal that guards the way—on one side is innocence and the safety of the sheepfold, on the other the vale of tears, insecurity, adventure, hardship, *and* increasing awareness and inner dig-

[22] Heb. 1: 1-2.

nity. The necessity to make a choice of which way we shall go brings us face to face with the problem of the paradoxical nature of sin: sin as wrong and sin as the necessary precursor of awakening to greater consciousness. Surely we have here the very germ of all conflict and of tragedy—and also of consciousness!

Sin is first encountered as disobedience, a transgression of the law. Initially the law is an entirely external code: the law of the parents, the law of the land, the code of society, and so forth; obedience to this law, with the consequent discipline of the autonomous desires of the individual, is the first step in the differentiation of the "I" from the "not-I" by which the *autos* begins to develop into the ego. Only later does a breach of the law of society begin to be felt as morally wrong. This marks the beginning of a new level of consciousness and the birth of a moral sense, a change that is essential for the development of the ego. But when we have eaten of the tree of knowledge—the knowledge of good *and* evil—we may see that the good, represented by the law of society, does not always work for good, and it can only be bettered by a transgression of the given law. If we follow this course we inevitably become guilty, as our first parents did. Their act, however, was the beginning of consciousness, and out of it came the possibility of a true morality transcending mere obedience.

But this does not dispose of the deeper implications of the problem, for sin may also be due to a transgression of the inner law. In considering this aspect of the problem we must differentiate conscience, or the inner voice that Freud called the superego and that is the counterpart of the law of society, from the voice of a superordinated value inherent in each individual. Jung called this the Self, avoiding the use of metaphysical terms, but in the products of the unconscious it is usually personified in the form of a divine image, and it is symbolized, for instance, as the Christ within or as the indwelling Holy Spirit. To deny this voice, to reject the call of this inner value, is one possible interpretation of the saying that the sin against the Holy Ghost shall not be forgiven. And from empirical experience I can say that whenever an individual with whom I have been working has, even for a short time, denied this voice and gone his own egotistic way, he has fallen into despair or has met with some external disaster, even though his choice was in accordance with what most people would consider the right and moral way. If he saw what he was doing and changed his attitude, things would begin to go well with him. But of course he then had to carry the burden of having gone an *individual* way, instead of subscribing to the general view of what is right and what is wrong, and this is a heavy burden!

So we see that, on one side, sin can be the violation of a man's deepest value, while on the other it is an indispensable means by which the "I" is differentiated from the group and from unconscious identity with nature and society. Sin marks the beginning of consciousness and also the beginning of history. For there is no history of our first parents in Paradise, nor is there any history of the preconscious infant.

We have been talking as if it would inevitably be good for a man to find his deepest core. But what about the teaching that the heart of man is incurably evil? And do we not, as a matter of everyday experience, have bitter evidence of the evil in mankind? Then there is the argument that, as God is both all good and all powerful, it follows that all evil must come from man. But here is a stumbling block. In this case God is not all powerful for, even if God allowed man free choice to do good or to do evil, at the creation of the world an all-good God could create only good. Who then created the evil?

And so as psychologists we have to consider the problem of good and evil on two levels—as Conrad did when he followed his story of "The Secret Sharer" by "Heart of Darkness," in which he considered evil not just as personal sin but as a daemonic energy rising from the depths of the unconscious in a power-driven man. For sin in the form of trespass, or transgression, is a matter of the conscious "I"; while good and evil as principles, or powers, spring from the collective unconscious; they are, as it were, the concern of the gods, and man suffers them. They come upon us in the form of compulsions, of temptations to evil deeds, or perhaps as impulses to good ones. At times we see them as good and evil forces, or as spirits, possessing demons—using the terms with which more naïve civilizations would have styled such invasions from the unconscious. At such times they may indeed possess us, so that we act and think and feel compulsively, regardless of our conscious wish and intent.

There is a very instructive Hindu myth dealing with this subject that is, I think, well worth study. The story is that Golden Garment,[23] a demon, undertook the most strenuous yogic discipline and practiced severe ascetic self-control for a number of years in order to acquire merit. When he had accumulated what he felt was an adequate amount of merit, he went to Brahma, the highest god, and demanded a reward for his work. As the merit was so large in amount, Brahma could not refuse him a boon and asked what he wanted. Golden Garment asked to be granted the boon that he could never be killed with any weapon, either inside a house or outside a house, or by man or beast. Brahma did not like to give such a far-reaching boon but, having promised, he could not refuse. So Golden Garment went away, and being, as he thought, completely invulnerable, he proceeded to enslave and exploit mankind. At last the cries and laments of men began to rise to the gods as they reclined on Mount Meru, and one after another they tried to answer the plea for help. But the boon was too powerful; none of them could do anything against the tyrant.

[23] Zimmer, *Myths and Symbols in Indian Art and Civilization*, p. 180 n.; Keith, *Indian Mythology*, p. 123. See also Harding, *Psychic Energy*, pp. 212 f.

Finally Vishnu, next in rank and power to Brahma, agreed to see what he could do. So he transformed himself into a monster, half man and half lion, and hid inside the pillar of Golden Garment's palace. When a great feast was in progress, he suddenly split the pillar apart, fell on Golden Garment, and tore him to pieces with his talons. For, as he was neither in nor out of the house, was neither man nor beast, and used no weapon but only his talons, he evaded the conditions of the pact and succeeded in destroying Golden Garment.

Now Golden Garment was himself a half-god, being one of the demons. He is a representative of absolute evil, for his asceticism was performed with a power motive, not a religious one, and the use he made of his power was for the exploitation of the world. He could not be overcome by men, not even if the entire world had united against him. He could be conquered only by one of the gods. Absolute evil corresponds to and must be met by absolute good. Man suffered from the conflict of the gods, he was exploited, but he took no part in the struggle of good and evil. Brahma, the supreme god, sat on the top of Mount Meru. He was above the dichotomy of opposites. The lesser gods, though not entirely "careless of mankind," could do nothing to help men until one of their number became at least half human. But Vishnu was exempt from human suffering. While he had compassion for man's distress, he himself did not suffer. He was above the battle.

Although the Hebrew genius saw God as interested in human beings—Abraham and his seed—he was not conceived of as father of the individual man until, in the revelation of Christ, God himself became man. One result of this was an enormous increase in the dignity of man: man became in very truth a son of God. But this brought with it a terrific sense of guilt and personal responsibility. For man now had to take a conscious part in his own fate. His sense of responsibility expanded to include more than himself and his own welfare. God was no longer just what was good for the individual, evil not merely what was bad for the individual. Good and evil were beginning to be realized as principles. Man could no longer be judged solely on the basis of the Egyptian "negative confession." His worth, his value, could not be measured simply by his obedience or disobedience to the law. Indeed, the sense of what constitutes morality had changed and is constantly changing, even today, as consciousness increases.

To the Christian man God is no longer Yahweh, the Judge. The judgment scene in heaven makes sense to us only when we realize that the court is the court of our own consciousness. The judge is represented by the form our own experience of the *numinosum* has taken. For God becomes man, not, like Vishnu, a superman invulnerable to human ills, but "one like unto ourselves." "For we have not a high priest that cannot be touched with the feeling of our infirmities, but one that hath in all points been tempted like as we are," [24] "one made perfect through suffering." [25]

To each generation the dogma of its religion expresses the ultimate truth. A historical survey such as was outlined above should at least enable us to formulate the question whether the dogmas of the Christian religion may not be one of this long series of attempts to formulate ultimate truth, as it is conditioned by our own state of psychological development. Jung once remarked that "God spoke once, two thousand years ago, and he has not been allowed to say another word since." [26] Of course he spoke in this arresting way in an attempt to make people realize their tendency to become bound in their own conceptions, leaving no room for any further development on the religious and psychological planes. Dostoevski, in *The Brothers Karamazov*,[27] puts a very similar statement into the mouth of the Grand Inquisitor, who used it as an

[24] Heb. 4: 15.
[25] Heb. 2: 10.
[26] In an unpublished lecture, 1923.
[27] Book V, ch. V (Penguin edn., I, 288 ff.).

unassailable argument to justify the claim of the Church that it had absolute authority in matters of religious belief, and should rightly persecute and kill all heretics.

The Christian teaching goes beyond the idea of Christ as sacrifice for the sins of humanity. His crucifixion between the two thieves, of whom one went to heaven and the other to hell, indicates that he was suspended between the two opposites. His sacrifice was connected with this dichotomy, not just with sins as trangression, misdeeds. And when, before his death, Christ spoke of sending the Holy Spirit to dwell in man, he was surely foretelling a time when his own spirit, his own imprint, his image, would inhabit and be found in the psyche of man.

The archetypal symbol that Jung calls the Self is one form of this image, and it will become operative in the individual to the extent that he becomes conscious of it and voluntarily submits his ego to its direction. His conception of the deity will change and grow as he experiences the power, beauty, and value of this archetypal image and brings his own wishes and ego desires into accord with its superordinated authority.

It is strange to us to speak of an evolution of religious conceptions and objects of veneration. We are brought up to believe that the revelation of the Christian dogma is a final one. But when we begin to study the teaching of the New Testament from the symbolic point of view we find that much of the meaning has been overlooked or deliberately suppressed by orthodox interpretation and is in need of reexamination today. Such a reevaluation corresponds to a kind of psychological evolution—an evolution not only of the individual's conscious personality, but of his conception of God as well. Scattered throughout Jung's works [28] are many discussions of

[28] See *Psychology and Religion: West and East,* particularly "Answer to Job," "Psychoanalysis and the Cure of Souls," and "Psychotherapists or the Clergy"; *Aion,* chapters on the Christ Image; and *Memories, Dreams, Reflections,* chap. XII.

biblical passages showing how a deeper psychological understanding reveals a new and arresting meaning that is applicable to the psychological condition and the problems of twentieth-century man. And, interestingly enough, the hidden teaching this reveals corresponds amazingly with the findings of depth psychology.

Why are we so unwilling to accept the idea of evolution in religious ideas? In another field, that of biology, we recognize that a gradual change and an increasing adaptation of the living organism towards its environment takes place. But even in this realm we are apt to say with great confidence that man is at the peak, is the topmost form. In considering the animal kingdom we recognize that any one species may be superseded by another more capable of adaptation and therefore having a greater capacity to survive, not only because of physical changes but still more through the acquisition of mental or psychological powers. With the advent of man our attention becomes concentrated on the further steps in the evolution of man himself, not on his possible replacement by a more developed species. And when finally twentieth-century man arrives, with his physical structure and mental equipment and the *given* qualities of his psyche, our evolutionary curiosity comes to a halt. If you ask the twentieth-century man what the next step in evolution is likely to be, he is dumfounded. Are we not the apex? Further change in organs? Impossible! Improvement, perhaps, but *new* organs—absurd! And this attitude is particularly firmly entrenched in the realm of religion. "As it was in the beginning, is now and ever shall be" refers to the transcendent God, surely not to man's limited conception of Deity. As for change in man himself, that is relegated to the after-death state.

The nature of the after-death state, or the idea of it, has also undergone an evolutionary change. It was at first thought of as a continuation of the present life, in an improved, indeed a perfect, form: the happy hunting grounds, the fields of Elysium. Even the Christian heaven is not so very different. But although golden streets, crowns, harps, and so forth are not really very appealing, when further questions are asked the answers are not at all illuminating. The skeptics of Christ's own day questioned him about this in their absurd proposition about the woman who married six brothers in succession. But the Sadducees were the materialists of that day. Christ's answer really tells us very little, for he substituted for a concretized proposal a symbol that was equally absurd to his questioners, who did not believe in the existence of angels.[29] When he said this, he brought in a further argument, namely, that the God they worshiped called himself the God of Abraham, and made the statement that the living God must be a God of the living, not of the dead.

The Roman Catholic Church goes further than this and teaches not only of reward and punishment, of heaven or hell, but also of an intermediate state of *reform* in purgatory. By this teaching a distinction is made between forgivable or remediable sin and unforgivable or irremediable sin—that is, between trespass and evil.

Another conception of such an intermediate state following immediately on death comes from the Mahayana Buddhism of Tibet.[30] According to this teaching the dead go immediately into the Bardo, the intermediate state, where they meet certain typical experiences for which the initiated have been prepared during life. The reactions of the deceased to the test situations he meets determine whether he shall go to heaven or to hell. Both these realms are conceived of as if in a series, corresponding to the "circles" of Dante's vision of the beyond. The majority of people, in the Buddhist view, miss their chance of heaven and yet do not fall as low as hell. Instead

---

[29] "In the resurrection they neither marry nor are given in marriage but are as angels in Heaven." Matt. 22: 30.
[30] Evans-Wentz, ed., *The Tibetan Book of the Dead*, pp. 85 ff., and Jung's psychological commentary.

they gradually approach the earth and so are reborn, gaining another chance for further development. For, like us, the Buddhists believe that development can take place only in this world. However, I am now concerned, not with that aspect of Buddhist doctrine, but with the nature of the experiences encountered in the Bardo.

Our knowledge of this teaching comes from the instructions that are given to the dying man and are continued after his death. The teacher, the guru or the household priest, remains with the dying man, and then with the dead man for forty-nine days, and instructs him in the significance of the experience that he is going through during that period. The instructions to the dead consist of a repetition of the teaching he received in his initiation, teaching designed to guide him now that he is face to face with the figures of gods and demons of whom he learned in life. He meets first the beneficent gods, then the destructive ones, and in each case he is reminded: "Recollect, O Nobly-Born, these are but the manifestations of your own thought forms." That is, he is taught that the gods and the devils are symbols, formulations, embodying psychological factors in his own psyche—not in his personal psyche, but rather in the nonpersonal part of the psyche, more often thought of as the *inner world*.

This teaching gives us a clue to the understanding of the relation between psychology and religion. Religion deals with the symbol-image—corresponding to the embodied deity, if one may use such a term. For those who have little psychological development the personification is complete. For the primitive, the peasant, and the psychologically immature among us, the symbol-image is completely hypostatized. This is true whether "images" and statues are used or not. Even the Protestant movement that made such strenuous efforts to cleanse the Church of "idol worship" succeeded only in destroying a form in which psychological elements could be housed. Because no more appropriate "house" was found for them they escaped into the world, so that an even darker era of superstition supervened, with witch-burnings, blue laws, and so on. For the evil of the unconscious was now projected not to images or idols but to *persons*.

Yet throughout the centuries there have always been enlightened men and women who conceived of God as Spirit and worshiped in spirit and in truth. They have approached the *divine*, the *numinosum*, as an inner experience, that is to say, as a psychological experience. And just as the enlightened Buddhist is taught that the gods, whether beneficent or destructive, are the concretizations of his own thought forms, so the supreme values must be realized by us as coming to us from the great and unknown inner world, modified for each of us by and according to the structure of our own individual psyche.

This insight really corresponds to the Christian message that, because of the incarnation of God in a man who voluntarily paid the required price, the Spirit of God, his image, could as it were be incarnated also in the ordinary man, so that God need no longer be regarded as far away in the heavens but could also be experienced, contacted, psychologically, as the poet says, "nearer than hands or feet." [31]

Through a sincere and humble approach to the unconscious, the God-image may perhaps become accessible to us, even though God Transcendent remains hidden in the depths of the Unknown, for, as Jung has repeatedly said, each generation formulates the ultimate truth of life in terms that are meaningful to the individuals of that generation, terms that correspond to the numinous experiences they have personally had. But whether these formulations appear to him as gods, or whether they present themselves as psychological experiences, they are one and all only *symbols* of the unknowable reality and should not be taken as the truth itself. In these days

[31] Tennyson, "The Higher Pantheism."

we have discarded and discounted the experience of the ancients. A time will come when our ideas in their turn will doubtless be considered superstitious by our descendants, in the light of the new truth that will have become accessible to a younger generation.

The experience of an inner value that may be clothed in the form of a God-image or of some other numinous symbol, perhaps as the reconciliation of opposites, has a powerful and awe-inspiring quality. These symbols obviously represent a value that far surpasses the best achievements of the conscious ego, the empirical man, with his contradictions and inadequacies. And yet this value is experienced as arising within the psyche, in dream or vision. It is surely important, then, to try to clarify the relation of such experiences to the representations of the Transcendent Deity, the Ultimate Source of being, as it is expressed in religious terms.

Since we have seen that the aspect of this supreme value changes as man's consciousness grows, we are obliged to conclude that the expression and form in which the divine figures are experienced in any given religion are in some way relative to man's own psychological development. In every age mankind has believed that his conception of deity was true and the only possible truth—a belief that he has held fanatically, frequently being willing to die or to kill in order to hold this paramount truth inviolate. But a later generation finds itself obliged to question the validity of this conviction. Perhaps it would be possible to conceive of God Transcendent, the Ultimate Source of all things, as being only reflected in the numinous archetypal symbol experienced by the individual within his own psyche, where, one must in all modesty allow, this experience is not absolute but is surely modified by one's own subjectivity. Perhaps this same Reality that appears in the heavens in a particular form, not only for one individual but for all who subscribe to the same religion, is also a reflection. On this assumption the divine personages of dogma, the deities of a particular religion, will be realized as reflections of the Transcendent Reality, and not the reality itself. In other words, the divine figures would then be conceived of as hypostatized forms of a Transcendent Reality reflected in the heavens and also experienced by the individual man in his innermost communion with the inner "not-I" of the inner psychic world.[32]

The ordinary individual may experience a symbol of wholeness, but the attainment of the reality symbolized is another matter. For as Jung [33] points out, the very fact that our psyche is a dynamic system means that we can experience value only in polarized form, that is, as a tension or a flowing between opposite poles. Absence of such polarity would mean a static uniformity that could have neither meaning nor power, that is, it would produce in us neither consciousness nor growth and development. It could result only in a sterile condition of unconsciousness.

From our human experience we cannot say that the unconscious is only good. The Transcendent Reality must perforce be paradoxical, beyond good and evil. This polarity might be represented as spiritual above and chthonic below, corresponding to Jung's formulation of the two poles of the psyche, that he calls "psychoid." [34] Thus the sphere of the Transcendent Reality would be experienced by man in two opposite aspects, like the polar regions of the earth: a Cloud of Unknowing above and an Abyss of Unknowing below.[35] To us the former appears as good and desirable, the latter dark and evil, though to the ancients the chthonic realm, while undoubtedly dark and fearsome, was not necessarily evil.

Contents of the collective unconscious come from both

---

[32] See Diagram VI.

[33] *Memories, Dreams, Reflections*, p. 350 (English edn., p. 322).

[34] "On the Nature of the Psyche," pp. 176 f., 183 f.

[35] See Hans Jonas, *The Gnostic Religion*, p. 182, where he quotes from *The Gospel of Truth* (Malinine, Puech, and Quispel edn., 22: 23), which speaks of the "depth of Him [the Father] who encircles all spaces."

realms. They appear in our dreams in many guises. They all have this in common: that they are numinous; but not all of them are psychologically valuable, not all lead to development, to wholeness. Some are definitely destructive, definitely evil, like the harmful gods of the Bardo. The fact that the symbols in which these powers are clothed are numinous is not necessarily a guide to their value. A systematic and conscientious exploration of the unconscious can and frequently does lead to an experience of a numinous nature, which is mediated to consciousness by means of symbols, symbols that may be encountered in dreams, in active imagination, or in visions. The numinous power of the "not-I" may manifest itself in compulsive and unwilled thoughts, feelings, and desires. Some of these things may be valuable, others destructive.

What test, then, if any, can we apply that will evaluate such experiences? They certainly come from a psychic realm that has to be classified as belonging to the "not-I," the "not-I" of the inner world, that is. For they neither come at our behest nor depart at our command. They are not under the control of the ego, and their very numinous quality compels us to assign them a superordinate value in the inner psychic world. They may function in a constructive life-giving way or be quite destructive in their effects. That is to say, the symbols in which they are manifested and their development clearly show the workings of good and evil as principles or, as St. Paul designated them, principalities and powers, or, as the Gnostics of the first centuries of the Christian era called them, "thrones and angels," and so forth. And for this reason it is exceedingly important to determine, if possible, whether the conscious ego, the "I," can do anything in regard to this dichotomy of good and evil in the unconscious. That it cannot control these forces we have seen, and we therefore have to conclude that the "I" is responsible neither for their existence nor for their appearance in its unconscious material. St. Augustine said he thanked God that he had not made him responsible for his dreams! But the individual *is* responsible for the attitude he takes towards these innate drives. He can choose the good and eschew the evil—provided he knows how to discriminate between them. When in his life situation an individual is faced with the kind of conflict that results from the constellation of two ways, two paths, two opposites, and finds himself quite unable to choose between them, he may turn to the unconscious for guidance. His dreams or active imagination may produce a symbol that can give him a clue to the solution of his problem. He must then observe how the symbol acts in the context of the dream. Is it a symbol of reconciliation of the opposites, that is, does it tend towards wholeness, or is it leading rather to destruction? Does it lead to an inflation of the ego, that is, to hybris, or does it give rise to feelings of humility and awe? What associations and amplifications cluster around it?

Often the mythologem that parallels the dream symbol will give a clue to its import in this particular case. For instance, I remember a man,[36] who was competent and had been successful in a position of responsibility, who came to me because of a neurotic disturbance that had led to public disgrace and the consequent loss of his job. He told me this very distressing story and related how he had struggled with his problem over and over again, and how each time his good resolutions had given way before a particularly trying situation, until the final calamity had occurred. We had not been working very long together when he dreamed that he was a naked infant lying in my lap and that I was about to give him a bath in the tub. Naturally this dream image was a very embarrassing one and disturbed him a good deal. But it really did express the situation he was in. He had been stripped of all prestige and

[36] Cf. Harding, "What Makes the Symbol Effective," *Current Trends in Analytical Psychology*, pp. 11-12. Some of this material was presented before the first International Congress of the International Association for Analytical Psychology, 1958.

self-esteem. He was like a naked infant in his mother's lap. I asked him for his associations. To myself he associated that, while I was not his actual mother, yet I had been a sort of spiritual mother to him, in that although he had confessed all his weakness and shame to me I had not rejected him. The dream said that I was going to give him a bath. He said a bath was to wash off the dirt, and then associated dirt to guilt, so that the bath would be a sort of baptism to cleanse him from dirt, from sin. This was to take place in the tub, which he said was a container like the womb where the embryo floats in the waters of birth. So the idea of rebirth was directly indicated.

In the next dream, which occurred two or three weeks later, he found himself standing on the street, gazing at a procession coming toward him. He realized that the procession was in honor of some great personage, and he had the uncomfortable feeling that he was not worthy even to look on this great man, let alone take part in the demonstration. He stepped down into the areaway of the building where he was standing so as to be able, unobserved, to see the procession go by. He suddenly realized that it was in honor of the Christ. As the procession passed him, the Christ turned and looked at him with a smile of recognition and a gesture that he should join the procession.

Now that man had had no religious education to speak of. He had heard of Nicodemus [37] and of the question of being baptized and born again, but he had never heard the story of Zacchaeus,[38] who climbed into a sycamore tree to watch the great rabbi go by, feeling unworthy to make any direct approach to him because he was a publican, a tax collector, ostracized by the Jews for being a collaborator with the Romans. But Jesus called to him to come down and entertain him at his house. After supper Zacchaeus made his confession and

[37] John 3: 1-13.
[38] Luke 19: 1-10.

promised restitution, as my patient had done in his analysis. And Jesus said to him, "This day is salvation come to this house, for the Son of Man came to seek and to save that which was lost." My patient did not know this story—this mythologem—and yet he dreamed it, and he too felt himself accepted. He was able to turn over a new leaf, to begin again and build himself a new life.

The archetypal pattern may come to an individual from the unconscious in a symbol of transformation like this of the dream, bringing with it a clue to the way of salvation for the particular dreamer. It brings not only a clue, but also the energy to follow the clue. For such a symbol is *numinous* and the creative energy of the *numinosum* is made available for conscious use through such a subjective experience.

When an individual has been blessed with a numinous experience of a symbol of transformation, how can he ensure that it really functions in his life, so that its life-giving promises will be fulfilled? How can he be sure that it is not a wishful fantasy that will fade away again, like a mirage, and disappear into the depths from which it arose? What are the conditions that must be met by consciousness, by the "I," if the transcendent symbol that comes from the "not-I" is to have a constructive and healing effect on the psyche as a whole? There are four conditions that have been recognized as essential for spiritual healing under many religious disciplines, but I want to formulate them in psychological rather than in religious terms.

The *first condition* is that, whether the individual is suffering from a neurosis, an emotional conflict, or some other psychological disturbance, he must be keenly and deeply aware of his need for healing. In religious terms he must have a conviction of sin, not just of *a* sin, but of sinfulness, of uncontrollable sin. St. Paul called it "the war of my members," meaning that he suffered from unbearable conflict; when he willed the good, evil was present with him. So the first condition is that the individual must be conscious of his *need*.

The *second condition* is that he must have done all he possibly can to deal with his problem, must have explored every avenue open to him, must have tested his conscious attitude, must have sought out and, as far as possible, have dealt with his shadow involvement in the situation, and must have realized that the problem is indeed beyond the power of his conscious ego—that he is utterly unable to resolve the difficulty by will power or by conscious effort.

This is the point that in religious terms has been called the giving-up of the self. In analytic practice it is often symbolized by the death of the ego, or by dreams of mutilation, dismemberment, or death. But such dreams are invariably followed by symbols of renewed life, for energy cannot be destroyed. It is a case of "the king is dead, long live the king!" If the attitude is right, and the ego is willing to be sacrificed and to submit to a higher authority, then the symbols of healing begin to appear in the dreams, but if the attitude is wrong, then disastrous symbols take over the stage.

So the *third condition* is that the symbols arising from the unconscious must be realized as truly belonging to his own condition and must be explored and handled from that point of view. They are not static, but move within him, unfolding their message from one dream to another, and so map out a way that he must follow. At the same time they release the energy latent in the unconscious that has power to produce a fundamental transformation of his personality. But—and here we come to the *fourth condition*—unless he allows himself to be moved by the happening and unless he experiences the full affect connected with it, he will not be radically changed. If he merely views his dreams as an interesting show, like a motion picture, nothing will be accomplished. The unconscious process may play itself out; the dreams may contain marvelous symbols; the whole drama of salvation may be enacted by the figures of the unconscious, but unless its meaning is seized by the conscious "I" and used to direct the life, the entire process will subside without affecting the psychic condition.

For the part played by the affect is very important. Intellectual understanding and appreciation of the aptness, the beauty, and the awe of the symbol process do not bring salvation. It is only emotional participation in the happening itself that can transform an idea or a hope into a reality.

Should destructive symbols arise, instead of healing ones, these, too, must be taken seriously and applied by the dreamer to himself in their full import for, unless he changes his wrong conscious attitude, they will indeed produce the negative and destructive effects their sinister connotation threatens.

For when an individual has come into direct relation to the collective unconscious through his analysis, the symbols he encounters are the very ones that actually pertain to his condition, and they can reveal the secret way in which the unconscious is moving to bring about his completion—his wholeness, which, the *Gospel of Truth* states, remains *in potentia* with "the Father," that is, is already existent as a potentiality in the hidden depths of the unconscious, waiting only until error is overcome to be restored as it was intended to be. In psychological terms, this means that the Self is restored to its rightful place as center of the psyche; in religious language, the image of God is restored to its original place within man.

VIII

CONCLUSION

WHEN THE DEVELOPMENT of consciousness has progressed through the process outlined in the foregoing chapters, the "I" will have been gradually differentiated from both the "Not-I" of the outer world and the "Not-I" of the inner world. As a consequence, since people in the outer world will have gained in value and significance and the denizens of the inner world will also have been recognized as separate from the "I," it will become possible to establish a direct relation between the "I" and the "Not-I" of both the outer and the inner environment.

Because it contains unconscious elements as well as conscious ones, the ego can no longer claim to be the center of this enlarged psyche. A new center, called by Jung the Self, comes into view, but it is seen only in symbolic form. It is a symbol of the wholeness of the individual and at the same time a symbolic expression for that inner image that carries the numinosity of a God-image and has done so throughout the ages.

But this is, of course, a long hard road, and to follow it involves the investment of a great deal of energy and attention directed to one's own psyche. Today many people feel that the search for individuation, concerning as it does the psychological welfare and development of one person only, may be merely selfish and quite insignificant in a world threatened with possible extinction. Would it not be better, the ordinary man argues, to preach to the multitude rather than to spend so much time and energy on oneself?

A vision such as that of Job certainly points in a different direction. For the outcome of the struggle between God and Satan for the rulership of the world was shown to depend on man. If only one man, Job, could stand firm under the most terrible tortures in his allegiance to God, that is, to the good, then Satan's claim to be Prince of this World would be disproved. Does this, perhaps, give us hope as to the outcome of the present-day situation where once again the powers of evil and of darkness are in battle array against the powers of light? In the vision of the author of the Book of Job the outcome depended on the constancy and courage of *one* man. This man not only held firm, but through his ordeal he gained insights that initiated an era of enlarged consciousness. On a former occasion when a somewhat similar test was used the outcome was different. I refer to Abraham's [1] plea for Sodom. God agreed not to destroy the city if ten righteous men could be found there, but apparently the ten were not forthcoming, and Sodom was destroyed. We should never forget that the world is made up of individuals, and that the one thing within our reach is our own development: it should not be neglected however much it may cost.

The history of religious development and the evolution of metaphysical ideas point to the conclusion that good and evil are not to be considered absolute, but relative to the state of

[1] Gen. 18: 23-33.

man's consciousness, as Job's ordeal forced him to recognize. The psychological advancement of mankind and the progress of civilization can be achieved only by an increase in consciousness and in individual responsibility. Not the triumph of "the good," but rather the discovery of a totality, beyond good and evil, should be the goal. When looked at from the point of view of ego-consciousness, such a solution is, of course, an impossibility. But a symbol may arise in the dreams and visions of an individual, representing a reconciliation of the opposites. Such a symbol is transcendent, usually of a quite paradoxical nature, and always carries the value of a numinous experience.

Symbols of this kind can never be exactly described, nor can the value they represent be definitely stated, because they contain more than conscious man can formulate with his mind. The promise, for instance, that in the Kingdom of Heaven the lion shall lie down with the lamb is a paradoxical formulation. For the lion, if he retains his natural quality as lion, must eat the lamb; otherwise he will not fulfill his lion nature. And if he is deprived of his lion nature heaven can hardly be called heaven for him. The ultimate truth is always a paradox. Though it is beyond description, it is yet experienced in the form of a symbol—a symbol of a totality that embodies the deep and mysterious, the unknown meaning of the paradox of life. It is not merely an *idea*, but an experience of numinous character, and one who has had such an experience can echo Jung, who said: "I do not have to believe; I know." [2]

[2] Television interview by John Freeman, British Broadcasting Corporation, 1959. See F. Fordham, "Dr. Jung on Life and Death."

APPENDIX

Although the diagrams in this section give a tentative map or plan of the psyche, they do not purport
to give a final or absolute statement of its structure
and relations, such as an architect's drawing gives
of a building. The psyche is largely an unknown
quantity, especially in its deeper layers. It cannot
be seen and can be explored only indirectly. These
diagrams are an attempt to give a visual conception
of the present state of our knowledge about this ter-
ritory. They are tentative projections not unlike the
diagrams of molecular structure drawn by physicists, and they must be so regarded. They may have
to be replaced in whole or in part whenever a new
insight renders our present knowledge obsolete.

DIAGRAM I

General Scheme of the Psyche

Diagram I shows a general scheme of the psyche, whose gradual development is discussed in the first four chapters. The large circle represents the personal psyche of the individual, divided into a conscious and an unconscious part. The conscious part is ruled over by the ego, the "I" of the individual. This is represented by a small circle. The unconscious part of the psyche, the personal unconscious, is similarly focused in a center called the shadow.

The individual inhabits two worlds: an outer one, the external world, and an inner one, the collective unconscious. Both these worlds are experienced as objective by the subject, in spite of the fact that the unconscious is within him.

The impact of the outer world on the individual results in the formation of a protective skin or mask, the persona. This is a system, or function, of adaptation that only approximately represents the genuine personality. It is an aspect of the individual that is modified to meet the expectations of the environment, and he presents it to the world as if it were a true and complete picture of himself.

In a somewhat similar way the part of the personal psyche that is turned away from the outer world to encounter the inner realm is both protected from and connected with the contents of the objective or collective unconscious by means of a function composed of the contrasexual elements of the individuality. So a man has a system of inner adaptation of a feminine character, called the anima, while a woman has a corresponding masculine adaptation, called the animus. These elements of the psyche make up the soul-figure.

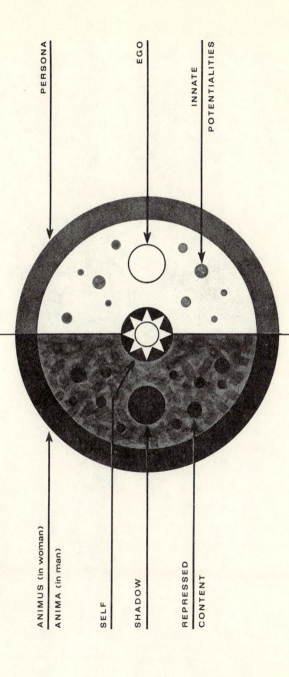

Diagram I: General Scheme of the Psyche

DIAGRAM II

The Child's Psyche

The large circle represents the psyche of a young child. At birth a child is not without psychological content; he is not a *tabula rasa,* a slate on which nothing has as yet been written. For he contains potentialities of future development that are peculiarly his own. His psyche resembles a psychological egg. One fertilized human ovum appears to be just like any other, but one, nonetheless, will develop into a boy, another into a girl; one into a genius, another into an idiot. Although in their first beginnings these potentialities are not apparent, they cannot be altered.

In the psyche similar potentialities (indicated by dots) also exist. When a child is confronted by the persons, things, and situations in his environment, he will act in a characteristic fashion. These impinge on him from without. But at the same time there is within him an unconscious expectation of what the environmental elements should be, resulting from the inborn patterns laid down in the unconscious by the ages of human experience of the world, namely, the archetypes, the unconscious patterns or dominants of the psyche that correspond to the patterns of instinct on the physiological plane. These are represented by the circles on the left.

The child, because of the nature of his own inner feelings, soon begins to show characteristic reactions. At the age of two to three years, he begins to call himself "me" or "I." This is the first recognition that he is a conscious and separate individual. It represents the earliest sense of "I-ness," really a somatic "I-ness," the "I" of my body, my instincts, my desires, called the *autos.* When the relation to the parents is positive, the child's reaction will be "I love," "I *want* to be loved," even "I *expect* to be loved," "I *demand* to be loved." But if the atmosphere of his home interferes too much with the sense of "I-ness," if, for instance, the parents are either too enclosing, too embracing, too indulgent, or, in contrast, if they are indifferent and cold, the reverse reactions appear, expressed as "I hate," "Leave me alone," or "Don't touch me."

Very similar reactions occur in regard to things, and may be expressed in such words as "I love my doll," "Naughty chair to hit Baby," and so on. It is the same with situations. Very early in his life the child finds that he is under discipline: "Now is the time to go for a walk," "Now you must go to sleep," and so forth. At first, perhaps, there is absolute compliance, but shortly the child begins to have his own ideas on the subject. Either he is willing to comply or he begins to resist. He is thus subjected to pressure from within as well as from without. But, as the external world is bigger and more powerful than he is, he gradually learns to adapt himself to its demands, and to wear a mask, the protective layer or skin that Jung names the *persona.*

Only when he encounters an assent or a dissent from the environment does a child become aware of being an "I," someone *other* than the per-

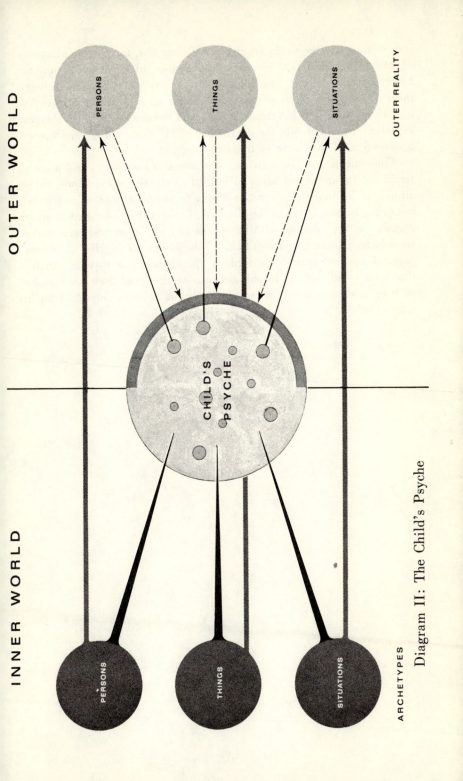

OUTER WORLD

INNER WORLD

OUTER REALITY

PERSONS

THINGS

SITUATIONS

CHILD'S PSYCHE

PERSONS

THINGS

SITUATIONS

ARCHETYPES

Diagram II: The Child's Psyche

sons or things in the world around him. Before this, the psychic substance of the child pushes out, like the pseudopodium of an amoeba, into the parent or other object, producing a sort of psychic continuum between them. It is as if a piece of him were outside himself, in the object. Not only his personal self but the archetypes and the images in which they are expressed also enter into the continuum of "I" and "not-I," and are experienced as if they were *in* the outside object.

Consequently, all the individual's relations to the outer world are contaminated by archetypal material from the collective unconscious. In his attitude to his parents he reacts not only to his actual mother and father, but to the inborn image of the Great Mother and the Great Father, which contain the very essence of Mother-ness and of Father-ness, and unconsciously he expects his parents to fulfill the assigned role. His "child-ness" requires a counterpart, expressed as "parent-ness," a psychic situation that leads to all sorts of trouble between children and their parents. For no man or woman is only parent, and no child remains only child for his entire life.

DIAGRAM III

The Shadow

The large circle again represents the psyche. The sense of "I-ness" that starts as the *autos* develops little by little as the child's sense of outer reality increases, till the ego is formed. This is a real center of consciousness. But in order to meet the world and the demands it makes on him, the individual develops the mask known as the persona. Before this can be done the unacceptable elements that are present in the psyche, and function unrestrictedly through the *autos,* must now be repressed into the background. The result is that the psyche is divided into two parts: a conscious part represented by the ego, and a relatively dark unconscious part that Jung calls the *personal* unconscious. In the diagram the right half of the circle is the conscious part of the psyche and the dark half to the left is the personal unconscious. The large area to the right of the circle represents the outer world, the area to the left, the collective unconscious world.

The contents of the personal unconscious consist of those elements of the psyche—aggressive impulses, sexual and other instinctive desires, and so on—that are not acceptable to the individual's particular environment and mores, together with those things he prefers to forget —his mistakes and blunders, his negative feelings and unadapted impulses. In addition those things that have not had sufficient energy content to catch his attention fall into the unconscious. They are not actually repressed, but they drop below the threshold of consciousness into the personal unconscious. Eventually these things together form a secondary personality, which Jung calls the *shadow.*

Because the shadow is unconscious it tends to be personified and projected, with the result that persons in the individual's environment become "cloaked," as it were, with his own dark and inferior qualities and contents. The shadow may also figure in his dreams as a person having these qualities. Such a person will be of the same sex as the individual because the shadow is part of the personal psyche.

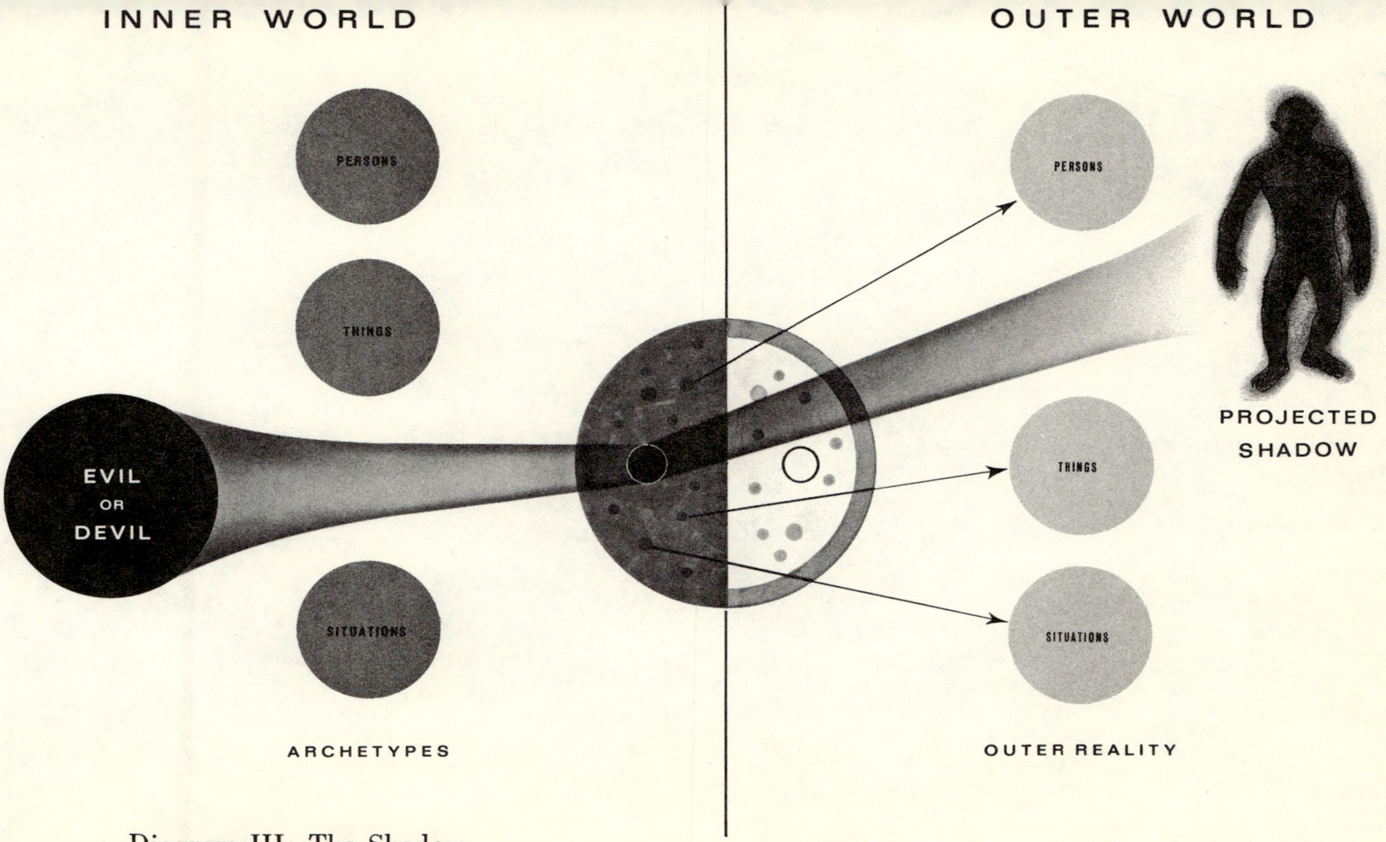

INNER WORLD

OUTER WORLD

PROJECTED SHADOW

PERSONS

THINGS

SITUATIONS

OUTER REALITY

PERSONS

THINGS

SITUATIONS

ARCHETYPES

EVIL OR DEVIL

Diagram III: The Shadow

DIAGRAM IV

Anima and Animus

Again the large circle represents the personal psyche, divided into a conscious and an unconscious part, including the persona, ego, and shadow described in the previous diagrams. These are all parts of the personal psyche. The present diagram represents the relation of the individual to the contrasexual elements in his personality. These form the soul-figure that lies at the threshold between the personal psyche and the collective unconscious. In a man's case this is the *anima*, in a woman's, the *animus*. Like the persona, the soul figure connects the personal psyche with the "not-I" of the collective world, but here it is the inner, not the outer, world.

The man's situation is represented in the upper half of the diagram; the woman's, in the lower half.

The form of the anima in any particular man is modified by the experiences he has had with his mother and with the other women he has met, but in its essence the anima is a universal figure, which has been formed by the human experience of Mother and of all other aspects of womanhood, whether mother, witch, mate, seductress, beloved, virgin, or harlot, that have impinged on man from the very beginning of time. All these elements enter into the image of the anima that a man experiences in himself, perhaps merely as an inner state or reaction, possibly as an emotion, but more likely as an instinctive body feeling. As the elements of the psyche of which the individual is unconscious tend to be personified and projected, the image of the anima will be projected upon some woman in the external world who has aroused the man's emotions. To him she will seem to be endowed with qualities that come from all these various layers in the collective unconscious. When this happens, the woman on whom the anima has fallen will exercise an undue, even an unconditioned, influence over him, whether she wishes to do so or not.

In the woman's case, her soul figure, the animus, is modified by her experience of her father, brothers, and men friends. But behind these more superficial influences the archetypes of Father, Husband, and Man exert their power. Man as brute, as authority, as wise man, as king, even as God—all these affect her relations to men in the external world. One on whom the projection of the animus has fallen may seem to her powerful, wise, cruel, protective, lustful, or indifferent and impersonal. The actual man she meets may be endowed in her eyes, and in her emotions, with any or all of these contradictory qualities, while at the same time he is irresistibly fascinating.

For these reasons, it is obviously most desirable for the individual to become aware of the anima, or animus, as an inner psychic reality and to make a relation to this element of his own being, so that he

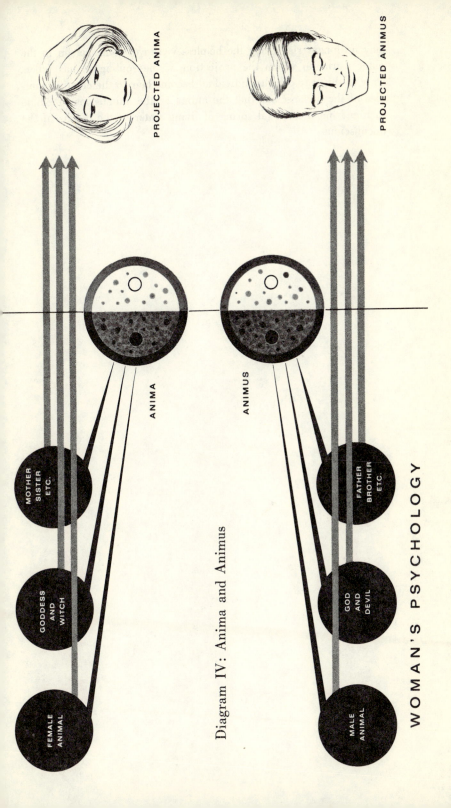

Diagram IV: Anima and Animus

WOMAN'S PSYCHOLOGY

PROJECTED ANIMA

PROJECTED ANIMUS

ANIMA

ANIMUS

MOTHER
SISTER
ETC.

GODDESS
AND
WITCH

FEMALE
ANIMAL

FATHER
BROTHER
ETC.

GOD
AND
DEVIL

MALE
ANIMAL

may no longer risk being the helpless victim of some person in the outer world on whom the projection of the soul-figure has fallen. Only in this way can the individual become heir to the creative energies of the unconscious that the anima or the animus may mediate to him from the eternal spring of living water in the depths of the unconscious.

DIAGRAM V

The Archetypal Images

The archetypal images occur in a series reaching farther and farther back into the depths of the unknown, the collective unconscious. Behind the parental images will be found the Great Mother and the Great Father, the Queen, the Sybil, the King, and the Priest; and beyond these the antique goddesses and gods. Still farther back are the animal forms of divinity—cow, lion, bull, snake, dragon, and so on. Behind that the archetypes are expressed in abstract formulations existing in such a remote and inaccessible region of psychic life that they cannot be personified. They are not near enough to human consciousness to be recognized as having either human or animal qualities. They are experienced as psychic patterns or determinants, and they lead down to the region of life that Jung has called *psychoid*.

A very simple mandala represents this layer of the unconscious where the opposites are brought together, and a reconciliation between them is at least suggested. Behind the mandala there is a star or a sun, which is simply an idea of something eternal, immortal, so far away, yet so luminous, that it cannot really be depicted at all. Deep within the psyche of man there lies a content of the collective unconscious of transcendent nature. When it is activated in a human psyche, it arouses awe, wonder, fascination, and dread. In other words, it is numinous. The experience of such an image exerts a powerful influence on the individual. It is as if he had tasted living water, which has power to heal the soul and release the creative energies of the unconscious. In all ages the images in which this experience has been embodied correspond in symbolism and in power to the forms that have been used in dogma and other religious writings to represent the deity. Jung, therefore, designated this supreme symbol as a God-image, corresponding to a new center of consciousness, called the Self.

Like the anima and the animus, these images may be projected to the outer world. In such a case some person will be endowed with their qualities and mana. Or an individual in whom they have been constellated may become identified with them and so be inflated with material from the collective unconscious. Finally, these archetypal images may be experienced in hypostatized form "in the heavens." In this case it is not possible to determine whether the psychic patterns of the collective unconscious are primary or whether they are the reflections in the psyche of a transcendent reality.

OUTER WORLD

PERSONS

THINGS

SITUATIONS

INDIVIDUAL PSYCHE

ANIMA ANIMUS

GREAT MOTHER GREAT FATHER

GODS AS ENERGY

ANIMAL GODS

INNER WORLD

RECONCILIATION OF OPPOSITES

STAR OR SUN SOURCE OF LIFE

SCHEME OF THE COLLECTIVE UNCONSCIOUS

Diagram V: The Archetypal Images

DIAGRAM VI

The Relation of the Individual to Metaphysical Reality

Diagram VI is an attempt to illustrate the relation of the individual psyche to the unknown and unknowable source of creative energy experienced in the confrontation with the *numinosum*.

In experiences of a religious nature this numinous factor is designated as God, and, as we have seen, the images in which this experience is expressed have changed and developed during the course of the centuries, being embodied in one archetypal form after another. Such images have always had two aspects—an upper spiritual one and a lower chthonic one, corresponding to the psychic structure of man, who can become conscious only by means of a polarity.

Throughout the ages men have worshiped their particular god, feeling that their conception of deity must be the only right and true one, the final revelation. Subsequent generations, however, having received a new revelation, have regarded the earlier representations as inadequate, if not definitely false. Usually they have considered the former gods to be idols, which it was their duty to break.

However, even today there are to be found in the collective unconscious many images that correspond to the gods of the ancients, and these images may still have a numinous character. They correspond, indeed, to the many forms in which God revealed himself to the fathers (Heb. 1:1). Today the image of the Self carries for us the earmarks of a god-image, not only in its numinousness but also in the many associations that cluster around it. It seems unavoidable, therefore, in searching for a formulation that may express the paradox of changeability and immutability, of predestination or fate and free will, of life-giving and death-dealing powers, and so on, which such images contain, to postulate a "Transcendent Reality," from which there arise not only the forms of deity seen in the heavens and of devil or antichrist in the abyss, but also those of the god-images found within the objective psyche.

If this suggestion is valid, it will follow that the form of deity revered in any given religion will be a *reflection* of the Transcendent Reality, rather than that reality itself; similarly the Self, discovered in the unconscious, will also be a reflection of Transcendent Reality. And in each case the form these images take will be dependent on the degree of development of the perceiving individual.

The individual "I" can be related to the Transcendent Reality—the Cloud of Unknowing above and the Abyss of Unknowing below—in one of two ways, by means of one of two disciplines. The first is through a religious experience of the divine image, as it is represented and interpreted in the dogma and teachings of a religious formulation; the second is through a direct contact with the subjec-

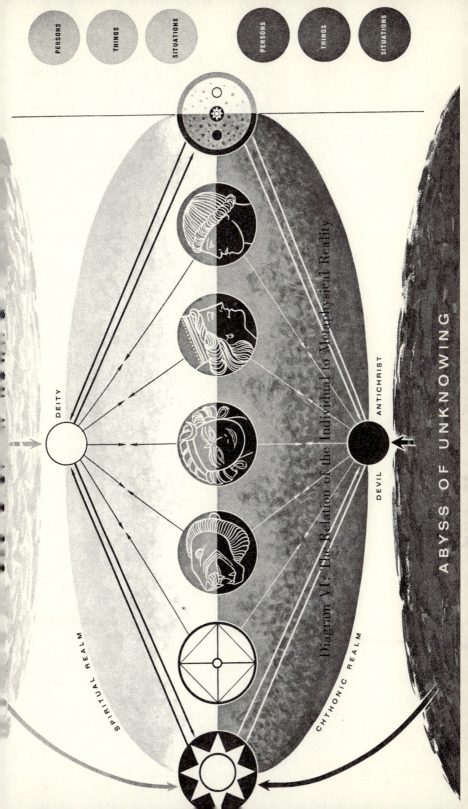

PERSONS THINGS SITUATIONS PERSONS THINGS SITUATIONS

DEITY

ANTICHRIST

DEVIL

SPIRITUAL REALM

CHTHONIC REALM

ABYSS OF UNKNOWING

Diagram VI: The Relation of the Individual to Metaphysical Reality

tive experience of the Self, that does not depend on any dogmatic formulation but arises spontaneously from within the psyche. The latter way has the advantage of being direct and individual, but, as it is unsupported by the sanction of a church or by the *consensus omnium,* it suffers from serious disadvantages. The man who elects this way must face the inevitable doubts as to its validity and the inevitable loneliness of one who follows an individual path.

LIST OF WORKS CITED

LIST OF WORKS CITED

ADAMSON, JOY. *Living Free: The Story of Elsa and Her Cubs.* New York, 1961; London, 1962.

ALLEE, WARDEN CLYDE. *The Social Life of Animals.* New York, 1938; London, 1939. Rev. edn., under title *Cooperation Among Animals*, New York and London, 1951.

ARISTOPHANES. *Lysistrata.* For tr., see *The Complete Greek Drama*, ed. by Whitney J. Oates and Eugene O'Neill, Jr. New York, 1938. 2 vols. (II, 809-59).

BOTHWELL-GOSSE, J. AIMÉE. *The Knights Templars.* (Golden Rule Lodge No. 21, Transaction 1.), Paddington, London, 1912.

BRONTË, CHARLOTTE. *Jane Eyre.* London, 1847. 3 vols.

BRONTË, EMILY JANE. *Wuthering Heights.* London, 1847. 3 vols.

BRUNER, JEROME SEYMOUR. *On Knowing: Essays for the Left Hand.* Cambridge, Mass., and London, 1962.

BUDGE, SIR ERNEST A. T. WALLIS, tr. and ed. *The Egyptian Book of the Dead.* 2nd edn., revised and enlarged. London, 1949. 3 vols. in 1.

——. *The Gods of the Egyptians; or, Studies in Egyptian Mythology.* London, 1904. 2 vols.

——, with the assistance of SIDNEY SMITH. *The Babylonian Legends of the Creation and the Fight between Bel and the Dragon, as Told by Assyrian Tablets from Nineveh.* London (British Museum), 1921; 2nd rev. edn., 1932.

BUNYAN, JOHN. *The Pilgrim's Progress.* (World's Classics.) London and New York, 1923. (Orig., 1678.)

CAMPBELL, JOSEPH. *The Hero with a Thousand Faces.* New York (Bollingen Series XVII) and London, 1949. (Paperback edn., Princeton, 1972.)

CONRAD, JOSEPH. "The Heart of Darkness." In: *'Twixt Land and Sea Tales.* (Uniform Edition of Works.) London, 1923. (Orig., 1902.)

——. "The Secret Sharer." In: *Youth . . . and Two Other Stories.* (Uniform Edition of Works.) London, 1923. (Orig., 1912.)

DANTE ALIGHIERI. *The Divine Comedy.* Tr. by John Aitken Carlyle, Thomas Okey, and Philip H. Wicksteed. (Modern Library.) New York, 1932.

——. *The New Life* [*Vita Nuova*]. Tr. by Dante Gabriel Rossetti. New York, 1901.

DOSTOEVSKI [DOSTOYEVSKY], FYODOR. *The Brothers Karamazov.* Tr. by David Magarshak. (Penguin Classics.) London and Baltimore, 1958. 2 vols.

DU MAURIER, GEORGE. *Trilby.* London, 1894.

DUNNE, JOHN WILLIAM. *An Experiment with Time.* London, 1927. 2nd edn., New York, 1938.

ELIOT, THOMAS STEARNS. *The Family Reunion.* London and New York, 1939.

EVANS-WENTZ, W. Y. *The Tibetan Book of the Dead; or, The After-Death Experiences on the "Bardo" Plane.* London, 1927. 3rd edn., with a psychological commentary by C. G. Jung, London, 1957.

FORDHAM, FRIEDA. "Dr. Jung on Life and Death," *The Listener* (London), 62:1596 (Oct. 29, 1959), 722-25. (A report of a television interview with C. G. Jung by John Freeman, British Broadcasting Corporation, Oct. 22, 1959.)

FRAZER, SIR JAMES GEORGE. *The Golden Bough.* Abridged edn., London and New York, 1922.

GILBERT, SIR WILLIAM SCHWENK. *Ruddigore; or, The Witch's Curse.* In: *The Savoy Operas.* New York and London, 1926.

Gospel of Truth, The. See GROBEL; see also MALININE.

GRAY, L. H., ed. *Mythology of All Races.* Boston, 1916-28. 12 vols. (Vol. V, Semitic, ed. by S. H. Langdon; Vol. VI, Indian, ed. by A. Berriedale Keith.)

GROBEL, KENDRICK, ed. and tr. *The Gospel of Truth: A Valentinian Meditation on the Gospel.* Tr. from the Coptic, with commentary. New York and London, 1960.

HAGGARD, SIR HENRY RIDER. *She.* London, 1887.

HARDING, MARY ESTHER. *Journey into Self.* New York, 1956; London, 1958.

——. *The Parental Image.* New York, 1964.

——. *Psychic Energy: Its Source and Its Transformation.* 2nd edn., New York (Bollingen Series X) and London, 1963. (1st edn., subtitled *Its Source and Goal*, 1947. In the present work, the 2nd edn. is cited.)

——. *The Way of All Women.* New York and London, 1933.

——. *Women's Mysteries, Ancient and Modern.* New York, 1935; rev. edn., 1955.

HENDERSON, JAMES. *Analytical Psychology and Education.* (Guild of Pastoral Psychology Lecture no. 87.) London, 1955.

HESIOD. "Works and Days." In: *Hesiod, The Homeric Hymns, and Homerica.* With English tr. by Hugh G. Evelyn-White. (Loeb Classical Library.) London and New York, 1920.

I Ching. The German tr. by Richard Wilhelm, rendered into English by Cary F. Baynes. Princeton (Bollingen Series XIX), London, 3rd edn., 1967.

JAMES, WILLIAM. *The Varieties of Religious Experience.* London and Cambridge, Mass., 1902.

JOHNSON, RICHARD. *The Famous Histories of the Seaven Champions of Christendome.* London, 1616.

JONAS, HANS. *The Gnostic Religion: The Message of the Alien God and the Beginnings of Christianity.* Boston, 1958.

JUNG, CARL GUSTAV.* *Aion.* CW, 9, ii.

——. "Answer to Job." In CW, 11.

——. "Archetypes of the Collective Unconscious." In CW, 9, 1.

——. "Concerning the Archetypes, with Special Reference to the Anima Concept." In CW, 9, i.

——. "Flying Saucers: A Modern Myth." In CW, 10.

——. "Marriage as a Psychological Relationship." In CW, 17.

——. *Memories, Dreams, Reflections.* Recorded and ed. by Aniela Jaffé. Tr. by Richard and Clara Winston. New York and London, 1963 (differently paginated).

——. *Mysterium Coniunctionis.* CW, 14.

——. "On Psychic Energy." In CW, 8.

——. "On the Relations of Analytical Psychology to Poetic Art." In: *Contributions to Analytical Psychology.* Tr. by H. G. and Cary F. Baynes. London and New York, 1928.

——. "Psychoanalysis and the Cure of Souls." In CW, 11.

* CW = Collected Works, for which see list of relevant volumes at end of entry. For works not yet published in that edition, reference is made to currently available versions.

Jung, Carl Gustav (*cont.*). "Psychological Aspects of the Mother Archetype." In CW, 9, i.

——. *Psychological Types.* CW, 6.

——. "Psychology and Religion." In CW, 11.

——. "The Psychology of the Child Archetype." In CW, 9, i.

——. "The Psychology of the Transference." In CW, 17.

——. "Psychotherapists or the Clergy." In CW, 11.

——. "The Stages of Life." In CW, 8.

——. "Synchronicity: An Acausal Connecting Principle." In CW, 8.

——. "The Undiscovered Self." In CW, 10.

——. *The Collected Works.* Ed. by Gerhard Adler, Michael Fordham, and Herbert Read; tr. by R. F. C. Hull. Princeton (Bollingen Series XX) and London, 1953- . 18 or more vols. The vols. cited in the present work are:

5. *Symbols of Transformation.* 1956.

6. *Psychological Types.* 1971.

7. *Two Essays on Analytical Psychology.* 1953.

8. *The Structure and Dynamics of the Psyche.* 1960.

9, part i. *The Archetypes and the Collective Unconscious.* 1959.

9, part ii. *Aion.* 1959.

10. *Civilization in Transition.* 1964.

11. *Psychology and Religion: West and East.* 1958.

14. *Mysterium Coniunctionis.* 1963.

17. *The Development of Personality.* 1954.

——, and C. Kerényi. *Essays on a Science of Mythology.* New York (Bollingen Series XXII), 1949. (Also pub. as *Introduction to a Science of Mythology,* London, 1950. Paperback edn., Princeton, 1969; Kerényi's essays are cited in this edition, Jung's in CW 9, i.)

Kazantzakis, Nikos. *The Last Temptation of Christ.* Tr. by P. A. Bien. New York, 1961.

Keith, A. Berriedale. *Indian Mythology.* See Gray, L. H.

Kerényi, C., see Jung, and C. Kerényi.

Langdon, S. H. *Semitic Mythology.* See Gray, L. H.

Lévy-Bruhl, Lucien. *How Natives Think.* Tr. by Lilian A. Clare. New York and London, 1926. (Original: *Les Fonctions mentales dans les sociétés inférieures.* Paris, 1912.)

Maier, Michael. *Atalanta fugiens.* Oppenheim, 1618.

Malinine, Michel, Henri-Charles Puech, and Gilles Quispel, ed. *Evangelium Veritatis.* Zurich (Studien aus dem C. G. Jung-Institut, VI), 1956.

MEAD, G. R. S. *The Chaldean Oracles*. Vol. I. (Echoes of the Gnosis, vol. VIII.) London and Benares, 1908.

——. *Thrice Greatest Hermes: Studies in Hellenistic Philosophy and Gnosis*. London and Banares, 1906. (New edn., London, 1949.) 3 vols.

MUSMANNO, MICHAEL A. "Man with Unspotted Conscience." A review of Hannah Arendt's *Eichmann in Jerusalem* (New York and London, 1963). *New York Times Book Review*, May 19, 1963.

MYERS, FREDERIC W. H. *Saint Paul*. London and New York, 1905.

NEIHARDT, JOHN G. *Black Elk Speaks: Being the Life Story of a Holy Man of the Ogalala [Oglala] Sioux*. New York, 1932. (Paperback edn., Lincoln, Nebraska, 1961.)

NEUMANN, ERICH. *Amor and Psyche: The Psychic Development of the Feminine. A Commentary upon the Tale by Apuleius*. Tr. by Ralph Manheim. New York (Bollingen Series XLVIII) and London, 1955. (Paperback edn., Princeton, 1971.)

——. *The Great Mother: An Analysis of the Archetype*. Tr. by Ralph Manheim. New York (Bollingen Series XLVII) and London, 1955. (Paperback edn., Princeton, 1972.)

——. *The Origins and History of Consciousness*. Tr. by R. F. C. Hull. With a Foreword by C. G. Jung. New York (Bollingen Series XLII) and London, 1954. (Paperback edn., Princeton, 1970.)

OTTO, RUDOLF. *The Idea of the Holy*. Tr. by John W. Harvey. London and New York, 1928; rev. edn., 1936.

PLATO. *The Collected Dialogues*. Ed. by Edith Hamilton and Huntington Cairns; tr. by various hands. New York (Bollingen Series LXXI), 1961. (*Protagoras*, tr. by W. K. C. Guthrie.)

RADIN, PAUL. *The Trickster: A Study in American Indian Mythology*. With commentaries by C. G. Jung and Karl Kerényi. New York and London, 1956.

READ, JOHN. *Prelude to Chemistry: An Outline of Alchemy, Its History and Relationships*. London and New York, 1937.

RENAULT, MARY. *The King Must Die*. London and New York, 1958.

Rituale Romanum. Editio typica. Vatican City (Typis Polyglottis Vaticanis), 1952. ("Ritus exorcizandi obsessos a daemonio," pp. 843-73).

STEVENSON, ROBERT LOUIS. *The Strange Case of Dr Jekyll and Mr Hyde*. London, 1886.

TENNYSON, ALFRED, LORD. *Poetical Works, Including the Plays*. London, New York, and Toronto, 1953.

LIST OF WORKS CITED

TERTULLIAN. *Apologeticus.* In: JACQUES-PAUL MIGNE, *Patrologia Latina,* vol. I, cols. 257-536.

THOMAS A KEMPIS. *The Imitation of Christ.* Tr. by Leo Sherley-Price. (Penguin Classics.) Harmondsworth, Middlesex, 1952.

TRISMOSIN, SOLOMON. *Splendor solis: Alchemical treatises.* Reproduced from the MS dated 1582 in the British Museum. With an introduction by J. K. London, 1920.

UEXKÜLL, JACOB J. VON. *Theoretical Biology.* Tr. by D. L. Mackinnon. New York and London, 1926.

VALE, EUGENE. *The Thirteenth Apostle.* New York, 1959; London, 1960.

WAITE, ARTHUR EDWARD. *The Holy Kabbalah.* New York and London, 1929.

WEBB, MARY. *Precious Bane.* London, 1924.

WILDER, THORNTON NIVEN. *Our Town.* New York, 1938.

WOUK, HERMAN. *The Caine Mutiny.* New York and London, 1951.

ZIMMER, HEINRICH. *Myths and Symbols in Indian Art and Civilization.* Ed. by Joseph Campbell. New York (Bollingen Series VI) and London, 1946. (Paperback edn., Princeton, 1972.)

INDEX

* The Plates referred to in this index are to be found in the Appendix, following page 218.

231

man: dignity of, 201; evolution of, 204

mana, 38, 39, 43, 180, 181, 183, 186, 191

mandala, 129, 175

marriage: arranged, 122; broadening effect of, 42; causes of breakdown, 120 ff.; Hindu, 114; perfect, 114; wife's role in, 124

marriage partner, choice of, 63

marriage service, 114

Mary (Mother of Jesus), 147; *see also* Madonna; Guadalupe, Virgin of

mascot, 183

masturbation, 128

matriarchy, 149, 151

Matthew, Gospel of, 205 n.

Mead, G. R. S., 142 n., 148 n., 175 n.

meaning, 133 f.

mediocrity, expectation of, 54

medium, woman, 112

menstruation, and moods, 159

Meru, Mount, 200, 201

Messiah, 154

Mexico, 186

microscope, 19

misunderstanding, 20

mob, 48, 153

monkey-play, 66

moods, 110, 126

Moon Mother, 114

morality, changing conception, 202

moral laws, 33

Moses, 147, 182

mother: actual and archetypal, 105; archetypal projection of, 68; archetype, 105, 137, 138, 143 ff.; child's relation to, 49 f.; complex, 143 f.; experience with, 104; gaining freedom from, 156; myth of, 164; resistance against, 157 f.; revolt against rule of, 147; search for replica of, 104 f.; separation from, 141

mother-consciousness, separation from, 54

Mother Goddess, 149

mother-imago, 123

mother-love, 144

mother-unconscious, 58

mountain, archetypal form, 170

mouth, functions of, 9

mulungu, 180, 181

Musmanno, Michael A., 93

Myers, F. W. H., 159

myness, sense of, 182

mysteries, 4; women's, 107

mystics, women, 112

myth(s), 136, 163 f.; American Indian, 142; archetypes and, 51, 131; Babylonian, 188, 193; basic, of individual, 164; Celtic, 142; Chinese, of Great Mother, 113 f.; early, and development of consciousness, 189; Hindu, of Golden Garment, 200 f.; mother archetype in, 105; *see also* Creation myth

mythologems, 131 f., 137, 172, 187, 189, 211

mythology, 137; personification in, 9

Nakedness, 96, 191

Nature, relation with, 40

Navajo, 99

Nazi movement, 132

negative factors: expressed in group, 48; within family, 52

Negroes, American, 142

Neihardt, J. G., 142 n.

Nemi, King of, 155

Neumann, Erich, 63 n., 64 & n., 138 n., 146 n., 148, 161

neurosis, 110, 169; and amulets, 181; cause of, 32 f., 59, 78; danger of, 86

New Testament, 203

Nicodemus, 212

nightmares, 58

night sea journey, 133

night terrors, 50

"not-I," *see* unconscious, collective

novels, 52, 118

numinosity/*numinosa*, 4, 38, 43, 175, 179, 202, 210; experienced psychologically, 187; expression of,

42; of primitives, 181; and shadow, 73 ff.; in visions and dreams, 185

promiscuity, 66

prophets, 186, 191

Protestantism, and "idols," 206

Psyche, *see* Amor and Psyche

psyche: personal parts of, 73, *Pls. I-VI*; separation of conscious and unconscious, 130; "should-be" contents of, 42

psychoid, 209

psychology: depth, 53, 204; as living myth, 139; and religion, relation, 206; statistical, 26

psychosis, danger of, 86

puberty, 15, 64, 147, 163; in girl, 159

Puech, Henri-Charles, 209 n.

puer aeternus, 145, 146

purgatory, 205

Puritan standpoint, 5

Pygmalion, 115

Quispel, Gilles, 209 n.

Rabbit, 143; *see also* Brer Rabbit

Radin, Paul, 10 n.

rays, extraterrestrial, 77

Read, John, 174 n.

reality: external, "not so external," 43; metaphysical, 177 ff.; outer, *Pl. II*; subjective experience of, 17 f.; Transcendent, 209

rebirth, symbol of, 212

recalling past experience, 35

receptors, afferent and efferent, 133

regression, 11

relatedness, 103, 108

relations/relationship: human, problems of, 21; parent/child, 53; personal, importance to women, 66

relics, of saints, 43, 183

religion: evolution in, 203 f.; primitive, 43; and psychology, relation, 206

religious experience, 28, 33, 94, 134, 179; in holy men, 194

religious function, in unconscious, 178

Renault, Mary, 155 n.

repression, 49, 69, 73, 74, 100, 169

resentment, 8 f., 110 f., 119

responsibility, 211; growth of, 82; personal, 32, 201

right, being always, 86

rites, burial, 44

ritual, religious, 5

Rituale Romanum, 172 n.

river, as archetypal form, 170

Rodin, Auguste, 112

Roman Catholic Church, 172, 205

Romans, Epistle to, 33

Romulus and Remus, 146

rose, celestial, 175, 186

rumors, projections as, 77

Sabbath, sexual union and, 114

sacrilege, 197

Sadducees, 205

sadism/masochism, 53

saints, 112, 186, 194

sanctions: group, 49; moral, 41

Saracens, 183

Satan, 192, 193, 217

savior, 180; longing for, 154; myth of, 164; suffering, 109

school curriculum, and archetypes, 140, 195

second half of life, 69

secretaries, women, 110 f.

secret wisdom, 4

seedlings, 42

Sekhmet, 170

Self, *Pls. I-VI*; appearance of, 216; elements in, 5; experience of, 70; giving up of, 214; as image of Christ, 203; Jung's conception of, 69, 129, 198; loss of, 94; objects as extensions of, 71; recognition of, 70; restoration of, 215

self-absorption, 30, 34